Catholics and American Politics

Catholics and American Politics

Mary T. Hanna

Harvard University Press
Cambridge, Massachusetts
London, England
1979

Publication of this book has been aided by a grant from the
Andrew W. Mellon Foundation

Library of Congress Cataloging in Publication Data

Hanna, Mary T   1935-
  Catholics and American Politics.

  Bibliography: p.
  Includes index.
    1. Catholics — United States — Political activity.
  2. United States — Politics and government — 1945-
  3. Christianity and politics.   I.   Title.
E184.C3H36   322'.1'0973   79-11035
ISBN 0-674-10325-4

To my parents,
Genevieve and James Colacecchi,
with great love

Acknowledgments

At the time I chose to write about religion and ethnicity, the subjects were rather unusual ones to discuss in the field of American politics. I owe my continuing interest in these topics to the influence of a number of people, to whom I am grateful.

My Polish-American mother and Italian-American father first stimulated my curiosity about ethnicity, Catholicism, and politics. Later, at the nerve center of the Foreign Press Association in Rome during the planning and first year of the Ecumenical Council, I had the opportunity to observe at close hand the Council debates and became aware of the impact a socially and politically motivated Church could have on societies and political systems.

I was very fortunate to work with Monsignor Robert J. Fox, director of Full Circle, a community action program in New York City, from 1965 to 1970. That experience also made me think about the ways in which religion could affect political and social action.

The religious and political leaders who gave so much time to me in interviews for this book deserve my deep appreciation. There is an old saying that two things one should never discuss are religion and politics. I found instead that most people love to talk about both. Certainly my interviewees did, for they discussed the subjects with insight and concern.

Professor David Danelski and Arch Dotson of Cornell University, who have been my friends since I first went to Cornell in 1970, encouraged my return to the university for the Ph.D. degree and advised me on the research and writing of this book. Professor Norman Uphoff of Cornell made many valuable suggestions. My colleagues at the State University of New York at

Binghamton were always helpful, particularly Professors Richard Hofferbert and Richard Rehberg, who advised on survey research uses, and Professor Dennis Thompson, who shares my fascination with ethnicity, religion, and politics.

Thanks are also due to the people at the Center for Social Analysis at the State University of New York at Binghamton, especially Gary Klass, Corwin Yulinsky, and Mary Conklin, who assisted with the computer analyses. I am grateful, too, to Arline Blaker, who expertly typed the manuscript.

Finally, I cannot imagine how anyone who isn't married ever completes a book. There are times of great excitement and joy but also periods of depression and despair. My husband, Parker D. Hanna, Jr., shared all of these moments with me and gave me the benefit of his years of experience as a writer and editor.

M. T. H.

Contents

1

Introduction

MAHATMA GANDHI reportedly once said that if you believe religion has nothing to do with politics, you don't understand religion. Yet surprisingly little has been written about the relationship between religion and politics in America.[1] Scholars and writers may be inhibited by the Constitutional doctrine of church-state separation, the supposed "wall" between religion and politics, or the melting-pot concept, which makes it somehow unpatriotic to emphasize differences in religion, race, and national origin.

Religion and religious identity, however, have always been important to Americans. One of the earliest and best-known commentators on the United States made religious feeling a focal point of his book *Democracy in America*. "On my arrival in America," de Tocqueville wrote, "the religious aspect of the country was the first thing that struck my attention; and the longer I stayed there, the more I perceived the great political consequences resulting from this new state of things."[2] Americans still tend overwhelmingly to identify themselves by religious group. In a national survey conducted in 1973, only 6.4 percent of Americans said they belonged to no religious faith.[3] Most Americans also remain within the faith of their childhood and marry people of the same faith.

Some scholars and theologians have questioned the depth of American religious commitment. Will Herberg, like the sociologist Robert Bellah, insisted that American Jews, Catholics, and Protestants actually were displacing the traditional, conflict-producing beliefs and rituals of their faiths with a kind of "civil religion," a bland combination of mutual tolerance and mild ethical

1

standards designed more to promote good citizenship and American nationalism than the teachings and spirit of Moses, St. Thomas Aquinas, and Calvin.[4] But other analysts and commentators have insisted that important differences and traditions based on both religious belief systems and religious community norms have continued among adherents.[5]

More than systems of beliefs regarding the Divine, religion also involves those aspects of life closest and usually dearest to everyone: one's childhood and family, particular ways of celebrating holidays, births, and marriages, ways of mourning death, one's roots, traditions, and community. Richard White argues that religion is a unique group phenomenon because the religiosity of an individual is not so much based on personal belief as on a whole system of communal values and attitudes, secular and sacred, affecting an individual to the extent that he feels himself part of the group and is subject to its socialization and sanction patterns.[6] Describing this process explicitly in regard to Catholics, Michael Novak writes, "To be a Catholic is not so much to belong to an organization as to belong to a people. It is, willy-nilly, even without having chosen it, to have a differentiated point of view and sensibility, to have participated in a certain historical way of life, to have become a different sort of human being . . . Catholics *do* tend to differ [from other people] in their sense of ultimate reality, in their version of realism, in their particular passion for justice, in their sense of the meaning of family and children, in facing death, in their approach to education, to suffering and to personal relations."[7]

The importance of religion as a group phenomenon with possible implications for political life and activity is enhanced today by the astonishing growth of ethnicity and ethnic politics. Defining ethnicity as the condition of belonging to an ethnic group or having a sense of ethnic pride, Moynihan and Glazer argue that the group can be based on race, religion, language, or national origin. Further, they insist that "ethnic identity *has* become more salient, ethnic self-assertion stronger, ethnic conflict more marked everywhere in the last twenty years."[8] They suggest that a major reason for the rise in ethnicity is that ethnic groups to a great extent are now behaving as political interest groups. A circular pattern emerges. As ethnic groups prove influential in achieving political goals, their perception of the political benefit to be gained from increased ethnic identity and organization leads to intensified development of their identity, cohesiveness, and political activity.

Moynihan and Glazer suggest a number of reasons for the development of ethnically based political interest groups. They believe that identification with a religious, racial, or other ethnic group is easier and more satisfying to people, giving them a sense of belonging, than is identification with the more general and anonymous concept of class, for example. Large, centralized welfare states—postwar phenomena in much of the world—find it simpler and more rewarding politically to distribute benefits to smaller, more cohesive ethnic groups that are unified enough to recognize and be grateful for them than to award perhaps unperceived benefits to larger, more amorphous groups of citizens. But ethnic groups see in political activity and organization more than the chance to gain economic or social benefits: they see a chance to alter the norms of society. Every society establishes norms selected from a universe of possible values. Inequalities arise, among groups as well as individuals, from differential success in meeting these norms. The cry of black and Irish and Jewish pride and power is, in a sense, an attempt, organized around ethnicity, to affect the group's success in society by altering the society's norms, or at least by obtaining recognition of the legitimacy of one's own group's norm system. Finally, the rise of ethnicity has occurred because ethnic identification transcends political and economic interests. While striving to obtain economic and political goals, ethnic groups can still claim to be more than mere interest groups, and so gain a great emotional boon.[9] Moynihan's and Glazer's thesis is an intriguing one which would seem to have implications for a study of religion and politics in America today, or indeed for any ethnically based group study.

The classic study of American group politics is David Truman's *Governmental Process.* Except in regard to the tangential relations of some Protestant churches with the Anti-Saloon League, he himself never considers churches as political interest groups or religion as the basis for interest group activity. However, he establishes a number of criteria by which the existence and probable success of a political interest group may be judged.[10] In this book, I offer an examination of American Catholics in terms of the thesis suggested by Moynihan and Glazer—that is, as an ethnically based interest group—and use in my analysis of Catholics and politics the criteria Truman ascribes for political interest groups in general.

No conclusions drawn from a study of American Catholics could, of course, be considered automatically valid for all other ethnic groups, nor even for the effects that religion in general, or any other religion in particular, may have on American politics. However, I suspect that some of the internal problems Catholics must overcome in order to act effectively in the political arena, such as the diversity of the group caused by differences of class and national origin, may be true of other ethnic groups as well. I am reminded immediately of the probable differences between black Muslims, black (often middle-class) Catholics, and black Protestant ministers and their followers who spearheaded the civil rights demonstrations of the 1960s. And I suspect that some of the group cohesiveness shown by Catholics, such as their tendency to maintain their own communities and neighborhoods in urban centers and to recreate them in the suburbs, may also be shared by other ethnic groups. While what I say here about Catholics cannot be conclusive for other groups, it may be suggestive, and this could be important at a time when, as Geno Baroni writes, "we are rediscovering the pluralistic character of America."[11]

In many ways one would expect Catholics to be in a better position to engage in political activities and exert political influence than many other ethnic groups. Since World War II they have achieved rather significant upward economic and educational mobility. They combine this advance with a fairly well-developed sense of group consciousness. If they have declined somewhat in church attendance, by this and other measures they still show marked loyalty to their institutional Church and attachment to their religion.

Catholics form a fourth of the total population of the United States. As the historian David O'Brien points out, within the last decade "American Catholics have 'come of age' in their society; they are no longer a minority in an alien country and they know it."[12] At the same time, the Ecumenical Council (1962-1965) promulgated documents specifically calling for involvement by Catholics in political and social issues. The participation of Catholics in civil rights actions, Chicano labor struggles, and the Vietnam antiwar movement would seem to show that Catholics in

America have been responding to what one Catholic leader called "the Council's license to act."[13] Catholic representation in Congress and among presidential candidates has been growing steadily over the last twenty years. During the Ninety-third Congress, in session during the period of this study, Catholics formed nearly 25 percent of the House of Representatives and 14 percent of the Senate.[14] The names of Catholic political leaders alone recall much of the history and many of the issues of the last decade: the Kennedy brothers, Eugene McCarthy, Mike Mansfield, Edmund Muskie, Sargent Shriver, Thomas Eagleton, John Tunney, James Buckley, Robert Drinan, Thomas (Tip) O'Neill, and Peter Rodino.

Further, Catholics have provided much of the intellectual and organizational leadership for the rise of ethnic consciousness and ethnic group association in America in the last decade. Catholics Daniel Moynihan, Andrew Greeley, and Michael Novak have written a number of the major books and articles that substantiate the continued pluralistic character of America and call for respect for ethnic differences and for group organization around them.[15] Two national associations working with largely Catholic groups in more than twenty cities for community action and political power goals were organized and are led by Catholics: the National Center for Urban Ethnic Affairs, led by Monsignor Geno Baroni and begun with the encouragement of the National Conference of Catholic Bishops, and EMPAC (Ethnic Millions Political Action Committee), organized by Michael Novak.

Only philosophers and theologians tend to define religion solely in terms of the personal and poetic relationships between the individual and the Divine. Alfred North Whitehead called it "what the individual does with his own solitariness."[16] The radical priest Ivan Illich speaks of religion as "the surprise in the net, the pearl."[17] Most scholars, like White and Novak, define religion in regard to both the individual and the religious organization or institution or group of adherents to which he belongs. Will Herberg in *Protestant—Catholic—Jew* defined religion as "the divine-human encounter," but also "part of the social and cultural situation."[18] Gerhard Lenski described his book as a study of the effect of religious commitment on daily life, defining religious commitment in great part as the commitment of individuals to a socioreligious group — as an active member of a formal church structure or as part of a communal network of individuals, families, friends, and neighbors interacting with others belonging to the same religious faith.[19]

In this examination of the Catholic world, I define Catholicism in ways closely approximating these definitions, using religion to describe a group phenomenon. Thus, Catholics are regarded as members of a particular religious group with a well-developed value system and a strong institutional and communal structure. I shall discuss three sectors of that group: the Catholic people as a whole, their institutional Church leaders, and their political leaders — Catholic congressmen and senators — and the interrelations among them. In discussing Catholic value systems, I shall examine beliefs derived from theology, but also attitudes with social and political import, including new emphases derived from recent Church reforms as well as common American Catholic cultural and historical experiences such as immigration and poverty. The study thus reflects Richard White's belief that "any given religious groups are characterized by group-specific norms; these norms constitute the 'religious factor' regardless of whether they have been logically derived from theology or picked up somewhere on the Italian countryside."[20]

Because I am examining the Catholic Church's role as a political interest group attempting to achieve its goals in or through political activities and structures, it is important to clarify what I mean by the term "politics." My own research on ethnic politics and my analysis of the research of other scholars lead me to the conclusion that religious, racial, and other ethnic groups hold concepts of politics that somewhat expand the common social science definition of politics as power or influence.[21] Ethnic groups certainly understand politics as the process of deciding who gets what, when, and how, in Harold Lasswell's phrase, or as influence and bargaining, as Robert Dahl maintains, but they understand both benefits and power in specific and enhanced terms.[22] Ethnic groups see politics as a means to extract economic, social, political, and cultural benefits and to achieve recognition of the legitimacy of their own value systems as well as (and sometimes rather than) those held by the general society. They add to this a sense that, to consolidate the achievement of material benefits and norm recognition, they must gain influence in, if not overturn, the large institutions dominating American society — financial institutions, industry, the government, the military, and so on. Therefore, politics is defined here as attitudes and activities designed to influence the acquisition of particular benefits, the acceptance of particular norm systems, and the achievement of decisive power in or over great national institutions.

In summary, then, in this study I shall explore the extent to which Catholics function as a political interest group, their goals and methods when so acting, and the political influence that Catholic interest group activities seem to have: the benefits they obtain, the norms they affect, and the institutions of society they challenge. In particular, I shall discuss some of the problems Catholics face in functioning successfully as an ethnically based political interest group, in the hope that this may be suggestive for an understanding of ethnic politics in general and for the implications such ethnic interest group activity may have for the future of American society and its political system.

My study begins with an exploration of the leadership of the institutional Catholic Church, concentrating on the changes that have occurred in the American Catholic Church since the Ecumenical Council and their possible political import and on Church leaders and organizations specifically concerned with social and political issues. I deal next with Catholic political leaders, United States congressmen and senators, in the belief that they can be informative about religious influence on the working of the congressional and electoral systems. They, as Catholics and as political power holders, provide a test of the extent to which Catholic values and Catholic interest group activities affect the conduct of political affairs. Material on the Church and political leadership is based on a series of interviews conducted in 1973-74.

The fourth chapter explores the American Catholic people in general, especially their status in the country and their attitudes on political and social issues. This exploration is based primarily on an analysis of a series of national surveys conducted by the National Opinion Research Center of the University of Chicago from 1972 through 1975. I also use information derived from interviews conducted with Catholic community leaders. These are leaders of what has been called the white Catholic working-class movement or the white Catholic "ethnic" movement, various kinds of neighborhood and community associations grounded partly in the Catholic religion but largely in national origin

(Irish-, Italian-, Polish-American Catholics). I was only able to interview nine of these leaders, so dispersed are they around the country—that is, about half the leaders generally regarded as major spokesmen for the movement. The number is too small for the kind of detailed analysis done of Church and political leaders. These community interviews are referred to when appropriate, however, because they illuminate statistical data and because they are the closest I could come to the opinions and reactions of the average Catholic.

In the fifth chapter I examine an issue of great religious and political relevance—abortion. My objective is to use abortion as a case study to determine in concrete terms Catholic group cohesion, interest group tactics, their success with Catholic and non-Catholic lawmakers, and the influence on the Catholic lawmakers of their own Catholic value systems and Catholic interest group activity.

Ethnic politics has come to play an increasingly important role in the American political system. My study of the Catholic world and its political activity indicates that this will probably continue to be true, at least for some time. The growth in importance of ethnic politics may mean an increase in conflict for our society, but there are also strong factors that seem to modify the conflict and make ethnic politics an ultimately healthy development for our political and social systems.

Chapter 4, a discussion of the socioeconomic circumstances and political and social attitudes of the American Catholic people, is based on an analysis of national survey data. I used a composite sample from the General Social Surveys conducted by the National Opinion Research Center of the University of Chicago in the years 1972 through 1975. That is, the surveys for those four years were combined to form a single data collection large enough to permit significant comparisons when respondents were divided into racial and religious groups.[23] The combined surveys also provide a clear picture of subgroups such as white and non-white Catholics, allowing a comparison of the socioeconomic status and political and social attitudes of the Catholic people in the 1970s with other American ethnic groups and with their own leadership.

To study Catholic congressional and Church leadership (chapters 2 and 3) and local community leadership, I adopted interview techniques initiated in the social sciences mainly by Lewis Dexter and widely utilized for at least the last twenty years. Dexter calls this particular method "elite" interviewing, to describe the technique used and not the kind of persons interviewed. Rather than the mass survey's prearranged, standardized questions asked of everyone in the same way, for example, interviewees under the "elite" method are encouraged to explore in long, unstructured conversations a subject in which, for one reason or another, they are particularly knowledgeable.[24] Dexter used the method with congressmen and businessmen, but Robert Lane used it with ordinary workingmen in his book on working-class ideology.[25] The technique gives people who are experts in a particular area great freedom to explore, explain, and expand and thus essentially to determine definitions and structure because their very choices give insight into the problems being studied.

My major reason for choosing this interviewing method was that the subjects I wanted to cover — religion and what it means to people, value systems and their derivation and practical effect, patterns of internal institutional influence, patterns of religious influence in and on the Congress, and so on — seemed difficult to explore except through long, fairly unstructured conversations. I was also influenced in the decision by the fact that none of the few studies of religion and politics conducted by political scientists thus far has used the elite interview method. Catholic studies particularly all rely on documentation and they tend to examine almost exclusively the statements and actions of the Church hierarchy. Use of elite interviewing methods allowed me to explore what many churchmen and scholars regard as the new postconciliar heterogeneity in Church leadership and to trace patterns of influence within the Church.

Selection of Church interviewees was done through various means. The first was my own knowledge of the Church. From long experience I was acquainted with its organizational makeup, the various philosophical divisions within it, and most of the people with the reputation of being leaders. I also paid close attention to the general and Catholic media and to the work of scholars David O'Brien and Cushing Strout, whose recent books have analyzed the heterogeneity appearing in the American Catholic world since the Ecumenical Council. In addition to the bishops,

for example, O'Brien describes Church intellectual leaders, journalists and editors, and leaders of conservative and radical movements as being politically influential, and Strout makes many of
the same divisions.[26] Leaders of these groups were all included
among Church interviewees. Because political interest group
activity implies a conscious effort to work in or through politics,
Church interviewees were chosen from among those people who
held formal or informal Church positions or were leaders of
movements with social and political impact.

In the selection of political interviewees, I used two bases for
decision. First, most Catholics in what were generally considered
the leadership positions of the Ninety-third Congress were interviewed, that is, the party leaders, the committee chairmen, and
those senators, often presidential candidates or aspirants, who
acted as spokesmen on national issues, thus assuming a role that
transcends the Senate. Presumably these leaders exercised the
particular power inherent in their positions, so it seemed especially critical to determine religious influences on them. Second,
I sought to examine the views and experiences of rank-and-file
Catholic politicians in the Congress. These political interviewees
were chosen by random sample, with controls to ensure that interviewees were representative of Catholic congressmen as a whole
with regard to party affiliation, ideological affinities, age, percentages of senior and junior members, Catholic state delegation
strength, and national origin (Irish, Italian, Mexican, and so on).
Altogether, detailed interviews were conducted with half the
Catholic members of the Senate and a fifth of those in the House.

Interviews with the Church leadership were surprisingly easy to
obtain. I believe this was in part because church leaders are one
of the last prestigious groups of Americans still unaccustomed to
being interviewed by scholars. They seemed intrigued by the idea
and, almost without exception, cooperated willingly. Political
interviews required more effort, mainly because by chance I did
most political interviewing during what turned out to be the year
of Watergate, and many of the people I wanted to see—and did
see eventually—were forced to postpone appointments. The interviews were exploratory and instructive, as Dexter says elite
interviews should be. They also were often exhilarating, as anyone attempting this technique has surely discovered.

2

The Leadership
of the Catholic Church

"THE CHURCH IS LIKE a barge," explained the editor of a Catholic magazine. "It seems to move so slowly but somehow it always gets there and always keeps moving. In the last ten years alone, this barge which seems to have moved so slowly has covered so much ground! It's unbelievable. The change has been immense."[1] Interviews with leaders of the American Catholic Church demonstrated near universal agreement with this description. Change, the leaders said, has been evident in the institutional structure and political and social positions as well as the activities of the Church.

Twenty-two Catholic Church leaders were interviewed: thirteen from the clergy and nine from the laity, fifteen men and seven women. All of them had attended Catholic institutions of higher learning, although three had also done graduate work at secular universities. More than two-thirds were Irish in descent, illustrating the traditional strength of the Irish in the American Church leadership, which only very recently has begun somewhat to recede.[2] The youngest person interviewed was twenty-five, the oldest was sixty-three, but both of these were extremes: more than two-thirds were between forty and sixty, with eleven in their forties and only four in their fifties.

Interviewees were selected because of the offices they held or because of their being generally accepted as leaders of and spokesmen for the Church or some sector of it. Included were bishops and representative leaders of such institutional Church organizations as the United States Catholic Conference (USCC), the national research, education, coordination, and lobbying arm of the American Catholic Church; its New York State equiv-

11

alent, the New York Catholic Conference; the National Council of the Catholic Laity, which coordinates activities of the Catholic men's and women's organizations present in nearly every parish; and the National Conference of Catholic Charities, the principal social work agency of the Church.[3]

Following Vatican Council reforms, nuns, priests and brothers with similar interests and attitudes toward Church reform and social concerns organized a number of coalitions to pursue their religious and social aims, and I interviewed leaders of these coalitions. Also interviewed were leaders of organizations which, although not formally under the direction and control of the hierarchy, were and are entirely or largely Catholic in orientation and personnel: the editors of the major Catholic magazines; anti-abortion organization leaders; and spokesmen for the radical or prophetic wing of the Church as well as the conservative Catholic movement. The prophetic wing of the Church developed mainly in the late 1960s. Insisting on a particular interpretation of what it means to be Christ-like, its members have tried to challenge both the Church and the government to move toward more socially concerned programs. The conservative Catholic movement is a loose alliance of Catholics who oppose many Vatican Council reforms, especially those they believe have led to a breakdown of traditional Church beliefs and authority; they are generally also conservative in political ideology.[4]

The majority of Church leaders interviewed probably can best be defined as political liberals. They supported a range of measures intended to ameliorate unjust and discriminatory conditions in the country. Theologically, they supported Council reforms and often wanted further reforms, especially those opening up the Church's decision-making processes. Five, including one bishop, were politically radical, people desiring major changes in American institutions, not merely ameliorative programs. Two led movements or organizations that were both theologically and politically conservative, and two more, who held official Church positions, were basically conservative politically. These labels, though, are in many ways misleading: some radicals refrained from certain political actions, despite their convictions, in order to maintain their ties to the Church, and the most extreme of the conservatives denounced the search and destroy missions in Vietnam as "immoral."

Political Participation

Although I selected interviewees not because of personal characteristics but because of the offices they held in formal or informal Church organizations, they revealed a surprisingly similar concern for political and social issues and a widespread participation in activities related to these concerns. Two-thirds of all Church leaders interviewed devoted much of their conversation to what they called "social justice" issues — poverty, war, the plight of minorities, migrant labor, health, housing, welfare and prison reform, and general institutional change, topics they usually introduced spontaneously. Fourteen of them were directly involved in some way with activities that effect social change.

This new activism contrasts strongly with earlier accounts of Church political and social attitudes and activities. David O'Brien, for example, concluded his study of Church social policy during the New Deal era by describing the Church leadership then as "still quite narrow in social outlook," and the efforts of some Catholics to change this as "novelties."[5] Dorothy Dohen, in her 1968 study of the American Catholic Church and nationalism, insisted that throughout most of its history the American Catholic Church has been acquiescent to the status quo.[6]

Most striking is the way in which present-day Catholic Church leaders have participated in direct, personal ways, rather than as official spokesmen for the Church or Catholic groups, in the major political and social struggles of the 1960s and 1970s — civil rights, the war on poverty, and the peace movement. One, a lobbyist particularly interested in prison reform, was also an associate of the Berrigan brothers, helped raise money for their defense, and arranged meetings in his home when government pressure against the Berrigans was most intense, where they and their associates could gather for discussion and planning. Another, an adviser to Cesar Chavez and his Farm Workers Union, had gone into the California fields to investigate Teamster claims that migrant workers had willingly signed with their union. A national leader of the Campaign for Human Development, the Catholic Church's version of the antipoverty program, was also active in Sisters Network, a religious group that lobbies Congress on issues and teaches nuns the tactics of lobbying. Two had been leaders of the community action program in New York City — one partly as a result of participating in the Selma March organized by Martin Luther King. They had worked on the streets organizing block associations and had tried to act as liaison between the poor, the police, and the city during riots in East Harlem and on the Lower East Side.

A bishop had led the boycott against the Farah Company in his diocese, a nationwide boycott organized mainly by the Church at the request of the bishop of El Paso to help get union representation for poor Mexican-Americans working for the clothing company in Texas. "We went through a five-month process of investigation," he said. "We investigated Farah and the unions and the retail outlets. Then we stood up for the workers. I talked to the President of X department store chain. I even got him to read the social encyclicals."[7]

Another bishop, in describing the motives behind his trip to South Vietnam and his efforts to expose the "tiger cages" housing political prisoners there, displayed the mixture of spiritual and political aims which lay behind all of these personal excursions into political concerns: "I thought of it as a religious activity, but one with hopefully political repercussions. I hoped it would do a number of things. First, to bring hope and consolation to people who were suffering, especially suffering injustice and oppression. And, besides, I thought of it as an action on behalf of justice, a part of the preaching of the Gospel. And third, I hoped it would have an effect on political institutions. I was definitely hoping for that, that it would help change political institutions — the Congress, the State Department."[8]

Certainly it seems significant that a large number of the Church leaders interviewed had at some point left their offices and participated directly in the major social and political struggles of the last decade. Perhaps even more important is the way in which the organizations they led illustrate changes in Church concern for those struggles. One interviewee spoke at length of the tie between the recent increase in new and renewed Church organizations and the development of Church political interest:

Important here is the creation of Church and Church-related organizations around these social justice issues. There are a whole series of new organizations now working to implement these issues. The Sisters Network is just one example. It's active now, it's becoming known, it's effective. Then, too, Catholic Charities has expanded lately into whole new areas. There are the Jesuit Office for the Social Ministry, Catholics Concerned for the Urban Ministry, the National Council of American Nuns, Baroni's organization, the National Federation of Priests' Councils, the Conference of Major Superiors of Men.[9] Not all of these are new, but all have greatly expanded their social concerns and some have been created lately for that sole purpose, as Network was. These new organizations and the expansion into social concern of the old ones is bound to have an effect because of their lobbying and educational aspects.[10]

The positions held by interviewees reflect this expansion of socially-interested organizations. Ten of the twenty-two Church leaders headed organizations that did not exist fifteen years ago. Three of these were antiabortion or antiabortion-related organizations. One was a newly created pastoral research post with both religious and social aims. (The interviewee here was charged, for example, with training and evaluating clergy engaged in ghetto organization work). Six were designed to facilitate social action, five of them with the poor and one with the white urban working class. In addition to these ten people, three others were in organizations that had long histories but were in the process of reevaluation and renewal. The evaluation report on the National Conference of Catholic Charities, for example, looked "at the social problems and conditions facing our country, to explore the theological basis of Catholic Charities, particularly in the aftermath of Vatican II and, in the light of these elements, to examine the Goals, Roles, Structure, staffing and financing of the Conference."[11] Finally, four were officials with the United States Catholic Conference, the largest and most influential of all national Catholic organizations, with the single exception perhaps of the National Conference of Catholic Bishops. One USCC official showed me four closely-typed pages listing dozens of political issues on which the organization had written to or testified on before Congress in the past three years, to demonstrate to me the change and expansion in USCC political concerns.

Altogether, then, seventeen of the twenty-two Church leaders interviewed represented new or renewed and reformed Catholic organizations whose original organization or renewal was largely undertaken to enable them to participate more efficiently and fully in political and social concerns.

Attitudes toward Changes in Church Concerns

Considering the degree of their participation in social and political activities, both personally and through their organizations,
it is not surprising that most of these interviewees demonstrated a
strong belief that Church concerns in these areas had changed
and expanded greatly in the past fifteen years. Only three did not
assert strong conviction that this change and expansion had occurred. Two of these were antiabortion leaders who talked almost
exclusively of this one issue. While not denying expansion of
Church concerns, they failed to address the question in any
lengthy or determined fashion. The third person's discussion was
too abstract and conflicting to draw a firm conclusion from it
alone, although he was engaged in three separate Church-con-
nected activities with social and political import. The other nineteen displayed a firm conviction in their interviews that the
Church had moved into social and political activity in a new and
greater way than was its custom a decade ago. "We realize," said
one, using the experience of American nuns as an example, "that
people who are Church people have a right, a duty, to be politically sensitive . . . We have made statements on Rhodesia . . . We
stood with the farmworkers to the point of going to jail with
them. This social sensitivity is the best thing that ever happened
to us."[12]

One leader emphasized the fact, as did many of his confreres,
that since the Ecumenical Council, previously politically inactive
Catholics and Catholic groups had been drawn into participation. "I think one of the main changes has been that social activism is no longer looked upon as the duty of the few, the specialists
in that area."[13]

Another echoed a theme common in many interviews: the
change in the institutional Church's way of perceiving issues and
solutions today. "In the past the Church was good at meeting
immediate needs—through Catholic Charities, through the St.
Vincent de Paul organizations. But now in the teachings of the
Church there is much more emphasis on getting at the causes of
injustice. The Synod Document of 1971, for example, says that
action on behalf of justice and participation in the work of the
world is a constitutive element in the preaching of the Gospel.[14]
Otherwise we are not preaching the Gospel. The document also

specifically declared the idea of social sin. 'People being kept poor,' it said, 'because of the system is a social sin.' "[15]

Not only did Church leaders believe Church concerns had changed and expanded; they also viewed this change as beneficial for the Church and the country and as closely related to, even obligatory under, Church doctrine. Only three of them, while acknowledging the changes, demurred from this, and one of these disagreed only in part. He indicated that the change was at least partly good and that the changes did stem from the Vatican Council and papal documents, but he was greatly concerned over the divisions he believed these changed political stances and activities were causing within the Church and its adherents as a whole. The two others questioned the extent to which Church political and social participation was truly a "Catholic" response.[16] "The right wing of the Church is growing," said the editor of a conservative Catholic magazine, "because the attempt to synthesize Catholicism and liberalism . . . is a failure. It can't be done. In trying to organically combine Catholicism and liberalism, synthesizing them, Catholicism disappears completely and liberalism takes over." Later, he added, "During the decade of the 1960s Catholicism disappears as a political influence. We saw the disappearance of Catholic intellectualism, of Catholicism as a controlling set of norms, in favor of the liberal agenda. What was not done by the Vatican Council in getting rid of Catholic intellectualism is done by *Humanae Vitae*."[17]

The other interviewee, a priest, in part echoed his argument. In talking about Catholic involvement in community organization work in the 1960s, he said, "The people doing the organizing had values and they thought that by organizing they could impart those values to the poor they were organizing, but they didn't build the values into the process and they found they didn't therefore impart the values."[18] He went on to say that he believed new beginnings were now being made in which values are part of the process.

The argument of the conservative editor and its echoes are important in indicating a liberal-conservative division which many feel has developed in the American Catholic world. Significantly, the conservative point of view appears only to a very limited extent in the interviews with Church leadership. Only two interviewees made it the major thrust of their argument on changing

Church concerns. Sixteen of the nineteen interviewees, asserting greatly changed and expanded Church interest and participation in politics, took the contrary position: they viewed political and social participation as the direct, even obligatory, outcome of Catholic principles. In seven interviews this conviction was implicit, in nine, explicit. Generally, in my interviews where there was no explicit, word-for-word discussion of this topic, the conviction was still clear from the thrust of the entire interview and its tone. These interviews were marked by long, happy recitals of the Church's and the individual's own involvement in social and political concerns, coupled with statements of obvious, deep religious faith and commitment. In most cases these same seven interviewees at one time or another had also given public speeches or published articles or interviews in which they had made the explicit connection between social and political concern and action and Catholic principles. In the other nine interviews the connection between religion and social action was directly and lengthily argued. One woman prefaced her entire discussion of religion and politics by saying, "The basic teaching of the Church concerns the implementation of social justice."[19] A Catholic lobbyist, admitting love for his job, added, "I like being in politics. To me it's one of the best ways of fulfilling Christian witness."[20]

Interviewees constantly referred to the teachings of the Gospel, of Christ, of the popes, bishops, and the Vatican Council to explain the connection between Catholic principles and the Church's and their own social and political concerns. Said one, "The Gospel in its nature is social Gospel."[21] "The motivation [for social action]—and the despair—is there, channels for the popes' social doctrines," a nun declared. "The whole idea of social sin is being emphasized now in the Church. Personal sin was emphasized before—don't eat meat on Friday, go to Mass. Religion was a personal relationship between you and God. Now we have the social responsibility idea. If we keep people poor, [we] are guilty."[22] Stressing a theme common in other interviews, a bishop explained, "In the teachings of the Church now there are these kinds of documents, foundation stones for action. We have the Vatican Council documents, John's encyclicals, Paul's Eightieth Year Letter. These are fundamental documents which give Church people platforms from which to act, licenses."[23]

Reasons behind Changes in Church Concerns

The same binding of social and political concerns with Catholic values and teachings is again evident when the leaders' explanations for the expansion of Church concerns in the last decade are examined. Eight of the twenty-two did not discuss the subject directly: in five of these cases, interviewees simply happily discussed their own and the Church's expanded activism without speculating as to why it occurred; one of the remaining three was concerned almost exclusively with the abortion issue, one believed the Church was only slowly moving away from its "immigrant mentality" in regard to political action, and the third viewed the movement of the 1960s wholly in terms of individual Catholics rising economically and politically without Church impetus or profit.

Fourteen, however, did give reasons for the change. Twelve of them cited the Vatican Council, eight describing it as the chief catalyst for change and four listing it among other catalysts.[24] Again and again in the interviews Church leaders spontaneously returned to the Council as a touchstone, a unique and magnificent event in Church history and in their own personal lives.

The Council is credited with three general results, all viewed as greatly affecting Church participation in social and political concerns. First, it was seen as having helped break down psychological and physical barriers between the Church and the "world." One of the main effects of the Council, said a priest, was "the contact made between Church and world. The Council showed that the division wasn't airtight. It provided a new definition of what it means to be Church."[25] "Attitudes supposedly missing in the Church," a bishop said, "were filled in by the Second Vatican Council . . . . The Communists, you know, some of them anyway, have charged religion with sealing people off from the world, of being the opium of the people. The Second Vatican Council stressed the great obligation we have to address ourselves to the needs of the world."[26]

Second, the Council was seen as energizing many different kinds of people to become active in the Church and with the Church's concern now for the world and its problems, thus leading indirectly to the blossoming of new Church organizations fac-

ilitating political and social participation. A USCC official centered his interview around this theme. "There is a tendency now
to see the whole Church working for social concerns. Before the
Council there was no national organization of priests and nuns,
for example. They are organized now. There is a social activity
chairman for each priests' senate. Various nuns and nuns' groups
are also involved. More people are involved."[27] Many leaders explained their own group's social concerns by referring to the effects of the Council. "Vatican II gave a kind of license . . . for lay
people to be active";[28] "the people involved here at the USCC now
have been shaped by Vatican II and they aren't satisfied to address themselves to the same old questions."[29] "I don't think we
can measure what took place as a result of the Council. Vatican
II hit religious women as it did no other group. Once the documents encouraged a reexamination of our lives, freeing us, opening our eyes, there was a real blossoming, a real development of
religious women."[30]

Third, and most cited, was the effect of what interviewees
termed "the documents": John's encyclicals preceding the Council, the decisions passed by the Council and signed by Pope John
and Pope Paul, and the encyclicals and bishops' letters furthering
reform after the Council ended. The documents were viewed as
both licenses and blueprints for action. According to one bishop,

> Twenty or thirty years ago the Catholic people had no concept of
> acting on issues like welfare rights, war action. It just wasn't the
> kind of thing they did. There wasn't a teaching foundation for it,
> either. Of course there were some documents. Some of the docu-
> ments I cited earlier built on them, the Eightieth Year Letter built
> on *Quadragessimo Anno*, for example. There was the American
> bishops' document on race in 1948. But these earlier documents
> were much more philosophical, theological letters; they were not
> designed for taking action for change, which rather was an out-
> growth of Vatican II and Pope John. John's encyclicals were the
> real turning point for Catholic documents. John's encyclicals were
> so different from the statements of Pope Pius. And Paul's encycli-
> cal, *Populorum Progressio*, carries on. It is one of the strongest
> statements of social doctrine. It does ask immediate help for the
> poor, raising funds, and so forth, but it also wants to set up justice
> and peace commissions, which are not yet entirely implemented.[31]

"We had documents before," agreed a USCC official, "but
they implied that experts do something about these problems.

The Council addressed itself to everyone, the whole Church. It opened doors for normal Christians to become involve . . . Take, for example, the priests' council's doctrine on justice of a few years ago. It said social justice involved the participation of all the faithful."[32]

In addition to the impact of the Council and its reforms, the other critical factor cited for increasing Church concerns was American social and political change. Six people cited this factor, four describing it as the major factor. Only one meant by this the effects of internal dissent and rioting during the 1960s. Five spoke of American social and political change in terms of the social and economic rise of American Catholics and subsequent conferral of status on them by the rest of the country. A monsignor said,

> Yes, there has been change, partly for historical reasons because conditions have changed. Statehouse and Congressional politics always used to be WASP precincts. Catholics were in the local machines. When we were in the ghetto that was what could produce what our people needed. Interests were more readily obtained at the local level. Then, too, the relationship then of the clergy to the local politician was the real relationship rather than the relationship of bishops to national leaders. Partly, too, the Church was not prepared to act in the American political situation. In Europe politics had been a sort of gentlemen's club, with the Church involved in gentlemanly arrangements with various monarchs. A democracy requires different methods which we had to learn.
>
> Then there were other historical changes. Catholic social teachings had their beginnings in the labor movement. Catholics first worked with labor-management relations. These drained off the energies of the Church for political activity for a long time. The opening up came when we began to realize that we couldn't solve the problems of modern society in just a labor-management context.[33]

"Thirty years ago [political action by Catholics] couldn't have happened," a Catholic layman argued. "Polarization was still too high. This was still then basically a Protestant country. It could have been seen as too threatening. The confusion that could have been caused by mixing religion and politics would have been profound."[34]

Another lay leader made the same point, although in somewhat different terms. "The laity is more educated now. We have gotten more involved, in general and in the community. We are part of the community now. The laity is speaking about conditions now, urging Church involvement. As individuals, Catholics are definitely increasing their influence on the local level in civic and social affairs . . . The American Catholic is secure now, feels secure about saying what he thinks."[35]

Finally, while they also cited the Council and historical changes as factors, three of the interviewees viewed the growth of concern as quite natural, as the culmination of a steady, historical evolution in American society and in the Church. It was simply, in their opinion, part of a continuum of development, not something triggered by any one factor, but rather something bound to occur.

"You can't condense, I don't think," said one, "the elements that produced the change. It wasn't just John or Vatican II. Through the years there had been a gradual opening to the community, not just the Catholic community, but to the problems of the total community." Reflecting on the 1960s, this man, leader of an organization long active socially, added somewhat wryly, "All of a sudden lots of people got religion on welfare."[36] A comprehensive examination shows that the great majority of his confreres in the leadership who agree the Church did get religion on welfare in the last fifteen years specifically date its conversion from the impact of Council reforms on a changing America.

Evaluations of the Church's Political Influence

By 1973 the worst nightmares of the Know-Nothings, the Ku Klux Klan, and the other old anti-Catholic groups seemed to have come true. Catholics formed the largest single religious body in America. Their leadership, at least, was not only speaking on and participating in social and political concerns, but it was justifying activism by recourse to Catholic teachings and values. Had this led, as would seem likely, to an increase in political influence on the part of the Church? Rather curiously, in light of leadership agreement that concern and participation had increased, it is on this question of political influence that the widespread unanimity of opinion we have seen thus far among Church leaders breaks down.

No interviewee spontaneously introduced this subject; each

time, I had to ask the question. A few people seemed to regard it as unimportant: one must do what is right without worrying about the consequences. The question clearly intrigued some others; most answered it thoughtfully, analyzing and assessing pluses and minuses. But no clear-cut, widely shared assessment emerged.

Six interviewees, five of them closely involved in political concerns, never answered the question at all. Three of them were leaders of the antiabortion movement, one was a lobbyist, and one was a member of an ad hoc Catholic group that met periodically to draft bills and pass them to friendly state legislators for introduction. They concentrated on their own particular spheres of activity and influence and did not stray into the larger concern of general Church influence. Five others answered that they simply did not know, that they could not judge whether the Church had gained or lost influence in the postconciliar period.

Three interviewees felt that the Church had definitely *lost* influence in the past decade, and an equal number were just as certain that it had gained. Five others believed that the Catholic Church had gained influence if careful definitions are given for what constitutes the Church and what kind of influence is meant. At least to the extent of a plurality, then, Church leaders did believe the Church had gained some influence in some areas.

Two of the three who felt the Church had lost influence based their assessment, once again, on their belief that some Catholics, including some Catholic leaders, might be more active politically and socially but that they were acting on a "liberal" and not a "Catholic" agenda; they believed that the Church, as a Church, had declined in influence. The third, who works in New York City, based his statement entirely on a comparison between the political aptitudes and "clout" of the late Cardinal Spellman and the present New York cardinal, Terence Cooke. Cooke "is not a political man; he doesn't think in political terms . . . The way it is now the politicians can ignore Catholics because they know the archbishop couldn't deliver any votes . . . The Catholic ethnic structures are being verbally mugged by the politicians."[37] This man, however, did think that there were signs that the Church in New York was beginning to "remobilize politically," pointing, as an example, to the political education committees Bishop Francis Mugavero was then organizing in his Brooklyn diocese. He added that if the Church did remobilize politically, it could be very powerful in New York.

The three who were outrightly and unqualifiedly in agreement that the political influence of the Church had increased based their arguments on the impact of greater participation in political and social concerns by Catholic groups and the Catholic leadership in the last decade. "The whole business now is involving more Catholics," said one, "involving more understanding of politics. This can be a stronger political influence than any one-to-one situation of the bishop or a group of bishops relating to a congressman, the President, or the mayor."[38]

The person quoted above and the priest critical of Cardinal Cooke each stressed specific factors in assessing political influence which the five interviewees who gave qualified agreement that influence had increased would insist could not be separated. These five leaders gave essentially the same answer: Influence depends on how you measure it; if you talk of the institutional Church (essentially, in their meaning, the hierarchy) and institutional issues, such as parochial school aid and abortion, influence has lessened. If you talk of more than the hierarchy—the American Catholic world in general—influence has greatly increased.

"It depends on what you mean by religion," said one. "If you mean the institutional Church . . . I would say no. The politicians don't listen to the Church. The Church doesn't have any real power in politics. Oh, sure, some people mention Cardinal Cooke's personal friendship with Nixon, whatever that means. But the Church doesn't have any real power. But if by religion you mean morality, moral values, yes. We are raising up some great laymen."[39]

"The influence of the institutional Church, I believe," said a Catholic magazine editor, "is greater than ever, depending on how you define influence. If you mean pressure politics, influence is probably less because the Church is no longer monolithic. It can't 'send out the word,' so to speak, can't mobilize people as before. But I think that's good, for often before it mobilized for petty purposes which in the long run were counterproductive . . . If by influence you mean influence in greater, subtler ways, though, as referents, seeders, infiltrators, catalyzers of ideas, the Church's influence is much greater and this is in part because it is not monolithic, it sees differences between Catholic groups and spokesmen, and these very differences, the heterogeneity, the growth this means, mean the Church has greater influence."[40]

A lobbyist emphasized virtually the same points: "Years past, we were much more influential, I think, in limited areas, institutional areas for the most part. If the Church wanted something done in an institutional area, wanted a Catholic appointed as ambassador or a Supreme Court justice, for example, it probably would have found it easier to have influence. Maybe it's because of the style in which things were done years ago, the more informal basis. Authority meant more then. Spellman could make a call to an influential person in the government and get something done. I think there's been a change in the dimension of our clout in certain areas, like those I've mentioned. On the other hand, the Church is now seeing whole new areas opening up where its influence is being felt, especially in social justice areas."[41]

Finally, of the five interviewees who confessed they just did not know whether the Church's political influence was growing, two bishops said that it depended on the circumstances, that the Church could exert influence when it took the care to organize. "Bishops and priests can't deliver the vote the way some say they could before. You have to make an effort now to convince Catholics, especially if you are talking about legislation . . . It's not like the old days when you told people how to vote. I think it's a good thing because if we make the effort, the possibility is there of moving Catholics. This shows there is a Catholic vote and some politicians realize they have to pay attention to it."[42]

Three other leaders insisted political influence could not be measured in general, although two of them did cite a particular issue in which they believe Church influence was felt. "I don't know how effective the Church has been in politics," remarked one. "I don't think it can be measured. Certainly sensitivity and responsibility for political matters has increased in the Church and this is important. I believe the peace movement — and we were one segment of the peace movement — forced Nixon to end the war. We influenced the bringing about of the end of the war. I feel quite certain of that."[43]

Another interviewee in this don't-know category, one of the oldest and most politically experienced of the leaders interviewed, gave what was probably the most pessimistic opinion of all.

I'm not sure we ever had much influence. We are one voice among many. The only time our influence was measurable was perhaps in the 1964 Civil Rights law. Maybe we've been indirectly influential at other times, but only in 1964 was it measurable and that was an unusual situation because of the issues and because the churches were united and because the time was right. We have a government affairs office [at the USCC] but I don't think they would claim a significant effect on legislation.[44] In areas of traditional Catholic interest — like school aid and abortion — the Courts have boxed us in so Congress can't really be affected and, of course, the Courts can't be reached.

Catholics are in ample proportion in the Congress but I don't know the extent to which Catholic values affect congressmen . . . I suspect congressmen balance their values and decide issues on all kinds of bases . . . I myself haven't been on the Hill more than ten times in the last twenty years. I have testified on different issues but, for example, I would be one out of fifty witnesses on a farm labor bill.[45]

In trying to draw some conclusions about the Catholic leadership's assessment of political influence, probably the best that can be done is to say that the majority believed the answer was not yet clear. The majority also believed, however, that the Church has had some influence in at least some ways, on at least some issues, primarily civil rights and the Vietnam war. They also believed that it can be influential if it takes time to educate and organize its adherents on issues. Finally, the majority seemed to believe that the very fact that more Catholics have been drawn into political concerns and that Church leadership is assuming responsibility in areas, especially social justice areas, where it was viewed as inactive previously must in the long run be significant.

One interviewee perhaps best summed up much leadership opinion when in answer to the question she said, "The baby was just born. We have to nurture it."[46]

Church Organizations

It is possible to question the extent to which Church leaders, deeply committed as they are to today's mission of political and social action, may be inclined by their own personal involvement to exaggerate the kind and degree of change the Church has undergone. Documentation, however, appears to confirm the interviewees' feeling that the American Catholic Church has indeed moved to a far more active posture in regard to political issues.

A good place to begin examination of this confirming documentation is the United States Catholic Conference, which has been called the "national-level action arm of the Catholic Church in the United States."[47] It traces its origins to a national organization developed by the bishops to minister to servicemen during World War I. After the war the organization was continued but redirected so that it would fill the vital and heretofore absent role of a central bureaucracy for the American Catholic Church. The organization was known as the National Catholic Welfare Conference until 1966 when its name was changed to the United States Catholic Conference.

Specifically, the USCC was charged with carrying out the policies set at the bishops' annual meetings, serving as a research center and clearinghouse of information for the bishops and their dioceses and local organizations, coordinating Catholic efforts in fields such as education and relief, and representing, when requested, the hierarchy's views on national issues affecting the Church. The Conference was and is a voluntary association to which each bishop adheres through choice. It had and has no ecclesiastical jurisdiction or compulsory authority.

However, as the central bureaucracy of the Church in America, the USCC and its predecessor exercised and continues to exercise enormous influence. As David O'Brien commented, regarding the work of the NCWC in the 1930s, "while the actions of the departmental staffs could not bind bishops, religious orders or Catholic agencies, the leaders of the NCWC were left relatively free to work for the spread and adoption of positions they supported, and the prestige of their posts gave their work a sanction that was often invaluable."[48] Luke Ebersole, in his 1951 study, *Church Lobbying in the Nation's Capital*, indicated the importance of the then NCWC by devoting two-thirds of his chapter on Catholic lobbying to the activities of this one organization.[49]

Ebersole's is the only detailed, scholarly study of church lobbying. A comparison between his description of NCWC goals, organization, and activities as they existed in the late 1940s and early 1950s with those of the present-day USCC provides significant substantiation of the change in the Church's attitude toward and participation in political and social concerns.

The NCWC, like its successor, was divided into a number of departments, each with its own sphere of responsibility. Ebersole, who used materials furnished by the NCWC to describe its goals as they were defined in the late forties and early fifties, revealed an organization whose educational and lobbying activities were overwhelmingly defensive in nature. The goals of departments in regard to political action were to protect against legislative and administrative decisions adversely affecting Catholic interests and to gain a share of the national, state and local funding available. For example, concerning the NCWC News Service:

> [A Catholic] is interested in a wide variety of legislative measures . . . These may relate to taxation, to education, to a wide variety of social nostrums which, upon investigation, are found to harbor — and maybe with some deliberation — the most devastating threats to the temporal welfare institutions and the eternal welfare of individuals.

Concerning the education department:

> It has been the duty of the Department of Education to scrutinize prepared legislation for the protection of the rights of private and non-public schools and to discourage the enactment of discriminatory legislation.

Concerning the legal department:

> But for this interchange of information between the Legal Department and the Government many of the regulatory and congressional enactments would fall short of their purpose of properly integrating the private institutional system into our community life.[50]

Current USCC brochures detailing the goals of its departments and divisions show the defensiveness displaced and, instead, an emphasis on working with both Catholic and non-Catholic public and private organizations and on working toward social concerns transcending merely institutional interests. Institutional interests are still a USCC responsibility, but these, too, are now viewed in cooperative terms, and services are stressed as being provided for all people. The armed-camp mentality is no longer apparent even in institutional matters.[51] Further, the postconciliar reorganization which saw the name change from the National Catholic Welfare Conference to the United States Catholic Conference also involved the creation of new departments, or the addition of new divisions to older departments, which were specifically designed to facilitate Church activity in the area of general social and political concerns, not of institutional interests.

Among these new departments and divisions are, for example, the Campaign for Human Development, an antipoverty program that funds community action organizations without regard for race or creed; the International Affairs Department, which is concerned with the social and economic development of Third World nations; the Division of Peace and Justice, called for by Pope Paul to work for peace, economic development, and social justice; and a renewed and reformed Department of Social Development, to work for the elimination of poverty and discrimination in this country.[52] The language used to describe the goals of the new or reformed departments and divisions is strikingly at variance with the defensive tone used to delineate the goals of the NCWC departments. The following quotations from a current USCC brochure are typical.

> The U.S.C.C. Department of Health Affairs represents the Catholic bishops . . . in meeting the needs of all men.
>
> The Division of Migration and Refugee Services works on an "open door" policy in its assistance to the migrant with no regard paid to race, religion or national origin.
>
> The Campaign for Human Development . . . seeks to inform people about the facts of poverty in this country . . . It also raises seed money to fund projects—not necessarily under church sponsorship—intended to help attack the root causes of poverty in America.[53]

Significant change can be seen also in the lobbying done by the Church in the late 1940s compared to this activity today. Specifically examining the Catholic Church's efforts to promote what he termed "the interests of the citizenry apart from benefits to the churches," Ebersole pointed out that from 1945 to 1949 Catholic organizations or individual leaders presented written or oral testimony before congressional committees on twelve issues of this type: fair employment practice, fair labor standards, health insurance, housing, social security, displaced persons, the European Recovery Program, federal aid to education, child research, compulsory military training, subversive activities, and the North Atlantic treaty.[54] In striking contrast to the activism of Church

leaders which was emphasized in the interviews, political participation in this earlier period seems to have been much more limited. In more than a third of all cases in which Catholic leaders
testified before Congress between 1945 and 1949, a single individual, Monsignor John O'Grady of the National Conference of
Catholic Charities (seven times out of twenty), is listed as the testi-
fier.

In contrast, in just the two-year period of 1972 and 1973 the
USCC was involved in lobbying Congress on several institutional
issues but also on more than twenty-five public interest issues.
The institutional issues included social security for clergy, tax
credits for parents of private school students, and abortion. Public interest issues involved a wide range of domestic and international concerns, most of which can be described under the social
justice rubric. These included welfare reform, aid for illegal
aliens, regional development in the United States, mass transportation, unionization and other benefits for farm workers,
subsidized housing, child welfare in Vietnam, foreign aid, immigration, international protection of human rights (especially
investigation of political imprisonment and torture in Brazil),
prescription drug prices, United States adherence to the United
Nations boycott of Rhodesian chrome, restoration of United
States funds to the International Development Agency, and
amnesty for war resisters and deserters.

Rather than the limited participation Ebersole described in the
early postwar period, concern is now shown for a greater range
and number of political and social issues and for large-scale participation in this kind of political activity. As the USCC lobbyist
explained, to give an issue seen as particularly important for spiritual and social reasons "more clout," bishops and cardinals are
being persuaded to an increasing extent to appear before Congress. In the 1972-73 period, for example, Bishop John Dougherty
appeared before the Senate Subcommittee on Anti-Trust and
Monopoly to urge economic development of the Third World
and restrictions on the power of multinational corporations;
Archbishop Joseph Bernardin urged economic sanctions against
Rhodesia in an effort to change its racial policies; and John Cardinal Dearden spoke before the House Foreign Affairs Committee
urging the strengthening of the United Nations in the field of
human rights and condemning South African apartheid, torture

in Brazil, and increasingly brutal warfare, especially in the Indo-china conflict.

On other issues, the USCC has relied recently on Church experts, encouraging leaders with particular knowledge and experience in a field to testify before Congress. Thus, during the 1972-73 period, the Reverend J. Bryan Hehir, Director of the USCC Division of Justice and Peace, urged Congress to give amnesty to Vietnam deserters and resisters, and John Cosgrove, Director of the Division of Urban Affairs, outlined a plan for more equitable regional planning and development before the House's Public Works Committee.

A lobbyist for the USCC stressed this change in the Church's attitude toward political and social issues by making the point that not only is the Conference "addressing itself to many more issues, seriously, than it was ten or twelve years ago," but it is trying to apply real resources to lobbying, it is convincing bishops to appear before Congress to lend their prestige to Church positions, it is asking state counterparts to the USCC, such as the New York State Catholic Conference, to stir up their own constituencies to contact senators and congressmen, and it is trying to educate the general Catholic population on issues so that they will lobby their political leaders.[55]

The lobbying practices of the USCC, supported by the National Conference of Catholic Bishops, illustrate a reorientation and revitalization of Church leadership which both called forth and is called forth by the postconciliar concerns with the world and its social problems. Concern for social problems helped to stimulate a new kind of leadership and new concepts of leadership. These, in turn, are affecting the development of Church concern over issues and the positions, often in striking variance with the past.

Church Leadership Structure

Earlier studies have viewed the leadership of the American Catholic Church throughout most of its history almost exclusively in terms of the hierarchy—the bishops—and leadership structure and authority were portrayed as having a rigidly vertical pattern, with all real power concentrated in their hands. Ebersole quoted an NCWC publication as proclaiming, "The soul of the NCWC is the bishops; apart from them it has no existence."[56] Dorothy

Dohen conducted her analysis of American Catholicism and nationalism solely through a study of the writings and speeches of the bishops of the United States, justifying the practice with a quotation from Guenter Lewy: "According to Catholic teaching, of course, the Church is a *corpus Christi mysticum* and includes more than the hierarchy and clerics. But policy and pastoral pronouncements are made by bishops, not laymen."[57]

My institutional interviews indicate that Church leadership is now considered, even by the bishops themselves, to be far broader than the hierarchy and to be collegial rather than hierarchical in nature. "Interview bishops to find out what bishops are like," a Church leader advised me. "But don't think that's where the power is . . . Remember St. Paul's definition of a bishop? A family man who doesn't drink, who is kind, gentle, amiable.[58] This is what bishops have always been: men of good appearance, kind, ceremonial figures who will give stability . . . Bishops really aren't leaders in a dynamic sense. The ideas don't come from them . . . Influence and power lie with the professionals who aid them."[59]

This priest struck what was to emerge as a common theme in interviews with the Church leadership: the shared nature of power in the Church today. The Church probably was never the monolith scholars and popular writers described. Indeed, four interviewees specifically rejected this idea. "I don't see it as a block of ice," one woman rather angrily declared. Yet the word "monolith" to describe the earlier Church was spontaneously introduced into discussion by two of the first Church leaders interviewed. Also, others implied acceptance of the monolith idea in their comparisons and descriptions of the changes they believed had taken place: the widespread emphasis in the interviews, for example, on the increased numbers of Church people and organizations taking positions now on political and social issues.

Bishops may still make the Church's official pronouncements but, as one bishop said, "when we speak now in a common voice, it's after we've consulted with all kinds of people."[60] Another bishop described the change with both humor and poignancy by quoting his predecessor, now retired: "Bishop *X* now says that he was bishop in a golden age and that he got out just in time. There was an aura of dignity around bishops before. They worked with a few Chancery officials. They went to a few dinners. Now you must get right out of the Chancery; you must do a lot of listening.

There's co-responsibility now. You must be more open. It keeps you humble and many of those who are critical really have a lot to say. You've got to do a lot more listening than talking."[61] Even the USCC describes itself now as "an agency through which the bishops collaborate with other members of the Church—priests, religious and laymen."[62]

Interviewees tended to date the change in the Church's concept of leadership from the Ecumenical Council; one woman, for example, insisted that one of the most important results of the Council was the fact that it "began a dialog on co-responsibility."[63] The picture that emerges both from interviews and from documentation is one of an organization in flux, an organization in which planning, persuasion, decision making, decision pronouncement, and decision implementation are widely shared, with players often both sharing in and, to a certain extent, exchanging roles. Two factors seem responsible for this leadership change. The first is the Council with its emphasis on the Church's obligation to concern itself with the problems of the modern world and on the Church as a collegial body in which all Catholics have a voice and a role to play. A USCC official perhaps summarized this Council influence best: "Since the Council the idea has developed that it shouldn't be just a few working for social concerns. There is a tendency now to see the whole Church working for social concerns."[64]

The second factor seems to have been the general rise in educational and professional levels among Catholics and the emergence of a new vocal leadership. This new leadership group has been unwilling simply to listen to the bishops but rather insists on its own right, even responsibility, to influence Church positions and activities on issues of Christian political concern. Church liberals and conservatives, in the theological and political senses, have both insisted upon much more active roles in the decision-making process. However, the recently emerged broad professional stratum in the Church has largely tended to be liberal. A lobbyist explained the effect of this new educated leadership in an example from his own organization, "The USCC in the last few years has many more professional lay people to work for it. This wasn't true earlier and it means it has added a degree of professionalism that wasn't here before in the same way . . . The USCC is bigger and more professional and the people coming to work here feel a responsibility for the implementation of Vatican II and the social teachings of the Church."[65]

This emphasis on personal involvement and professional and educational achievement can be seen in the records of my institutional interviewees, many of whom participated in the civil rights, antipoverty, and antiwar struggles of the 1960s and 1970s. All twenty-two institutional interviewees were college graduates and twelve had also done some postgraduate study. In two cases— both bishops—this postgraduate work was theological: one bishop is a doctor of canon law and the second had done advanced study at the Pontifical University in Rome. But ten interviewees did postgraduate work in secular professional fields: two were lawyers, two had Ph.D.s, one held a master's degree in social work, and two held Master of Arts degrees. Three others began graduate studies without continuing on to the degree. All the interviewees were professional people. Three had taught at the university level and two at the secondary school level, two held research posts, and four had been professional social workers at some stage in their lives. Seven had been or were professional columnists, writers, or editors, and one was a television and film specialist. Two had served on presidential commissions.

James Hitchcock, in his book *The Decline and Fall of Radical Catholicism*, insisted that Church social policy in America in the postconciliar period has been essentially determined by two groups, the experts and the prophets.[66] To a large extent this seems true and illustrates the new decision-making structure and process which has evolved in the Church. I have examined the combination of personal involvement and professional achievements in Church officials who might be termed the "experts," but to name and describe the "prophets" is more difficult, even though their role has probably commanded more public attention in recent years than that of any other sector of the Church.

Most observers agree that throughout its history the American Catholic Church has been supportive of the nation and of American societal values generally.[67] The prophetic element is new to it. Prior to the last decade and a half, perhaps only Dorothy Day and her associates, among Catholics, could with any justification be said to have belonged to the prophetic church. In the 1960s, however, a segment of the Catholic world began to assume the prophetic stance, the role of challengers, denouncers, and guides to both the state and the institutional Church. Like the Hebrew prophets of old, they were willing to become "outsiders" and, in many cases, to suffer abuse and imprisonment. Rather than work in conventional ways within the political system, they were willing to adopt unconventional political behavior, passive resistance, and civil disobedience. Yet they were different from many other radical leaders and groups of the 1960s because they based their criticisms of society on Christian, often specifically Catholic, principles, and acted out of what they believed to be traditional Judeo-Christian witness, challenging Mother Church while still insisting they were part of her—the truest part, some said.[68] Many of them are well-known to the country in general—Dorothy Day, the Berrigan brothers, Father James Groppi, and Cesar Chavez. Others are less well-known but are often tied in a kind of radical fellowship with these leaders, acting out of the same principles and in many of the same ways.

Although the prophets see themselves as challengers of both state and Church, they have probably been able to exert influence over Church policy and activity in political and social concerns because of the extent to which they have remained part of the Church. Dorothy Day demonstrated personal piety and orthodox devotion in the "credo" she included in *Meditations*.[69] James Hitchcock described Father Daniel Berrigan as "a true contemplative [who] reads Scripture and St. John of the Cross to sustain himself."[70] The prophetic element is not apart from but inextricably intertwined with the experts and the hierarchy itself and thus exerts influence on the institutional Church. This was particularly true in the late 1960s and early 1970s during the antipoverty and antiwar struggles, but the intertwining and the influence can still be seen today, both in the continued activity of some of the prophets and in that of other Church leaders they have inspired.

This close intertwining and collaboration can be demonstrated in a number of ways. Three interviewees holding important official positions were also involved with the Chavez movement. Three had been involved with the Berrigan movement. One interviewee, regarded widely as a leader in the prophetic Church, listed two bishops who, in his opinion, belong to the prophetic element; he had spent two years as an invited organizational "outsider" to help in the reevaluation and reform of an old, traditional Church organization.

This sense of mutual need and collaboration is manifested in interviews with members of both the prophetic and the expert sectors of the Church. A prophet, asked why he had chosen to remain in the Church, answered, "Christianity is part of the Church. It is embedded in the Church. It is part of our history. It is part of our insights. The Church is so heterogeneous. It still has so much to offer, and then we still believe we may affect it."[71] An expert commenting on the role of the prophets, said, "I see the prophets as important, as having enormous political influence, but I believe they need the institutional Church as much as the institutional Church needs them. [St.] Paul can speak on the street corners — dynamic, flamboyant, irritating, perhaps, a lot of people. Then he moves on to the next place and the bishops, the institutional Church, come in and perform the mop-up operation. They give stability to what the prophets started, give it structure, organization, make it endure. Sure the prophets are tied to the Church by common feeling, history, faith, beliefs, and traditions, but also because they need the Church."[72]

The Problem of Pluralism

There is a tendency to view the earlier Church as monolithic, moving as one body when ordered by the bishops.[73] There is also a greater, sometimes clamorous participation now in Church activities brought on by the better education, greater self-confidence, and therefore greater assertiveness of its hundreds of clerical and lay directors and activists. Both factors tend to project to many Americans an image of the Church today as internally divided, or at least as a pluralistic body. Interviews certainly portray this pluralism in part. Witness the small minority of Church leaders who criticized Church activism, to a greater or lesser degree, because they felt Catholicism was being confused with liberalism, to the detriment of the Church's integrity as an institution and as a value system. Or, from another direction, the liberals who criticized the institutional Church, particularly the hierarchy, for its behavior during the Vietnam war. Even a bishop criticized his colleagues for failure to stand by Catholic teachings on the moral imperative of individual conscience, even against state authority.

To some extent the impressions of internal division seem based on observable fact, although they may result, in part, from a failure to judge the Church by the same standards we judge our heterogeneous country which we regard as basically united if pluralistic.

Particularly at the end of the 1960s and early 1970s the Church, like the country, was divided by the Vietnam war, with radical Catholic activists such as the Berrigan brothers denouncing Church and state. The sense of conflict within the Church was intensified by internal reforms and new attitudes sparked by the Vatican Council and not yet digested. By the mid-1970s the worst of these divisions seem over. A number of the most extreme Church radicals, such as Philip Berrigan and James Groppi, are no longer very active either in politics or in Church affairs, although their influence is still felt, particularly through the people in the Church whom they have inspired. With the Vietnam war ended, the Church, like the country, has been relieved of a painful source of division. The overwhelming majority of Catholics have come to accept liturgical reforms. And abortion has become an important issue that seems to have brought dissident sections of the Church together.[74]

Pluralism, which history demonstrates was always present in the American Catholic Church, is now an open, avowed phenomenon. What may be new is the fact that criticism and insistence upon participation in decision making now have a legitimacy within the Catholic world and especially within the leadership of the Church not previously accorded them. The bishops I interviewed were witnesses to this. What may also be new is the fact that, in the development of collegial leadership and the interplay of hierarchy, expert, and prophet, structures and processes have been established to permit both participation in and eventual compromise or resolution of issues.

The operation of this structure, the intertwining of the new prophetic and expert elements and the effect they have had in moving the institutional Church toward greater and generally more liberal political participation, can be clearly seen in the Church's response to two vital political and social issues: labor relations, especially those concerning the Catholic Mexican-American minority, and war and peace.[75]

Given the working-class makeup of the Catholic people during much of their history, the Catholic Church generally has been regarded as more supportive of labor than the Protestant churches have been. David O'Brien's history of the Church in the 1930s is largely concerned with the efforts of some Church leaders to further the cause of unionization and the rights of labor. The Church's earlier efforts in this area were admittedly uneven but often very strong. Yet O'Brien noted that the Church hierarchy in these earlier, preconciliar days was so deeply concerned about Catholic acceptability and respectability in the United States that most Catholic leaders enthusiastically supported American wars and championed the basic tenets of business culture. Dorothy Dohen made much the same point when she discussed the seeming acquiescence of the American Catholic prelates to the status quo of capitalistic industrialism.

By the early 1970s, however, the institutional Church had come to forsake some of these more cautious positions. In authoritative statements, the National Conference of Catholic Bishops voted to support the produce boycotts called by Cesar Chavez and the Farah boycott and to condemn the Vietnam war—actions which have received relatively little examination in secular or scholarly publications but which represent changes in long-time Church policy on crucial issues.

The diocese in which Cesar Chavez began organizing in the middle 1960s was at first hopelessly torn between Catholic growers and the Catholic farmworkers. However, support within the Church for Chavez slowly began to grow. The development of that support illustrates the intertwining of prophetic, expert, and hierarchic elements in Church decision making in regard to political and social issues. Chavez has had many critics, some of whom have deprecated his piety and questioned his goals, but he was and is widely regarded by most Catholic leaders as a part of the prophetic element in the Church. One interviewee said that to think of Chavez as only another labor union leader is completely to misread the man. "All of his thought, his work, spring from deeply Christian motivation. He looks at things from a Christian way. He is about changing values and ways of life."[76] A bishop also expressed this view of Chavez as a challenger of society in the prophetic manner saying, "He's working to change the whole setup."[77] Almost from the beginning of his attempt to organize California's Mexican-American migrants, Chavez attracted young Catholics, clerical and lay, who had been stirred by the Council's call for involvement with the poor and their problems and saw his movement as an implementation of this.[78]

Many Catholics, acknowledged to be part of the prophetic Church—particularly Dorothy Day and the Berrigan brothers—aligned themselves with Chavez. He preached nonviolence and a community of believers. In his struggle to aid the migrants and the poor and his challenge to growers and the economic system, he was closely linked to profoundly Christian religious convictions. In order to achieve his aims, he was prepared to adopt unconventional political techniques—what he called "creative nonviolence," marches of a half-political, half-religious nature, peaceful demonstrations, boycotts, and fasts. Slowly, what was seen by many Catholics as the deeply spiritual, Christian thought and behavior of the man and his movement proved a challenge and an attraction to larger and larger sections of a Church reacting to the spiritual and social impact of the Vatican Council reforms and the political and social reforming spirit of America in the 1960s and early 1970s.

The experts of the Church as epitomized, for example, in its national bureaucracy, the USCC, began to aid Chavez as well. Monsignor George Higgins, a long-time labor specialist and Director of Research for the USCC, became one of Chavez's chief advisers. The Committee on Social Development and World Peace of the USCC, after a field study of the situation in 1973, denounced the "sweetheart" contracts being signed by growers and the Teamsters Union to the destruction of Chavez's Farm Workers Union; the committee urged free and secret elections by the migrants and endorsed the boycotts called by Chavez. The Catholic churches in Delano, the center of Chavez's organizing attempts, had already spoken out in 1968 in support of his programs. Early in 1973, under the threat of possible Teamster-growers' destruction of the Chavez movement, the bishops of California issued a joint statement also denouncing the sweetheart contracts and calling the right of farmworkers to organize and join a legitimate organization of their own choosing "the dominant moral issue in this dispute."[79]

When the bishops of the United States met for their annual assembly in November 1973, they had been prepared for a major break in traditional Church support for the "capitalist status quo." Not only had Chavez's deep religiosity stirred them, but the support he had gathered from the prophetic element challenged them and the facts on the dispute gathered in its usual, careful way by the USCC impressed them. Moreover, their own recent actions in regard to the Farah boycott had predisposed them to support the boycott weapon. The boycott of Farah clothing, in an effort to secure for workers the right to a union of their choice, had been spearheaded by one of their own colleagues.

In an unprecedented action by an American bishop, Bishop Sidney Metzger of El Paso in February 1973 had send a letter to each of the bishops in the United States outlining the struggles of the Mexican-American workers in his area against the local Farah plant and urging them to support the Farah boycott in their respective dioceses.[80] Bishops across the country responded and began supporting the boycott individually, in their own areas. Thus prepared by their diocesan experience with a boycott, the bishops were ready to take the next step and officially endorse the Chavez boycott when they met nine months later in their annual conference.[81] The bishops as a body had adopted a labor weapon to be used against management and property and they had declared support for a particular and, they felt, moral and liberal social policy.

An even more significant example of the Church's changed attitudes toward political issues and the roles played by different sectors of the Church in bringing this change about involves the bishops' decision in 1971 finally to condemn the Vietnam war. The Church had earlier given uneven but often strong support to labor, so perhaps the 1973 boycott endorsements can be seen to have some precedents in Church history. The denunciation of the Vietnam war, however, reversed all previous Church actions in regard to American wars and is clearly a policy break with the past.

Throughout American history the Catholic Church and its bishops were probably the biggest hawks in our skies. Dorothy Dohen documented Catholic hawkishness and the reasons for it in her 1968 book, *Nationalism and American Catholicism*. She pointed to the influence in the Church of historical factors: the predominance in the American Catholic world, and especially in its hierarchy, of the Irish who came from the Mother Country with an established commitment to a fusion of religion and national feeling; the threat of the recurring, anti-Catholic nativist movements which made Church leaders fearful of even the appearance of anti-Americanism, of anything less than total allegiance to the nation; the fear of disintegration caused by the ethnic pluralism of the American Catholic Church, leading the hierarchy to renewed stress on assimilation and conformity to American speech, values, and traditions; and finally the ardent Church opposition to Communism, difficult for the Church to abandon when confronted by the rhetoric of the Vietnam war.[82] In Dohen's assessment, these factors help lead to a situation in which "religion will be used to sanction the nationalist goals, to support them, and to encourage adherence to them," and one in which "leaders of a religion will use religion to support nationalism not simply to keep their Church acceptable in the pluralist society but out of the same need for identity and the sense of belonging that motivates all people in a given society."[83]

Dohen pointed out that until 1968 the Catholic hierarchy had supported every war in our history. Even the Spanish-American war, felt by some of the hierarchy before its declaration to be an unnecessary conflict and one, moreover, involving fellow Catholics as opponents, was, once declared, wholeheartedly supported by those previously troubled bishops. At the Vatican Council itself, after speaking the week before in support of religious liberty, Francis Cardinal Spellman rose in opposition to a Council proposal reaffirming the right to conscientious objection. "Military service," he declared, "can certainly be made obligatory and it should be made clear that the individual cannot arrogate to himself the right to accept or refuse obedience."[84]

In the early years of massive buildup of United States troops and their engagement in the Vietnam war, the American hierarchy maintained its traditional support for American wars. Asked his opinion on American involvement in the Vietnam war, Cardinal Spellman answered by paraphrasing the words of Stephen Decatur, a nineteenth-century naval hero: "My country, may it always be right. Right or wrong, my country."[85] When in early 1966 the respected Catholic weekly, the *National Catholic Reporter*, sent questionnaires to 225 bishops asking for their comments on the goals and conduct of the war, it received six replies, only three for publication and those all voicing support of the administration.

For the first time in American history, however, substantial numbers of Catholics were coming to question the morality of an American war. World War I produced only one American Catholic conscientious objector; in World War II, there were only 200, nearly all of them followers of Dorothy Day's Catholic Worker movement. But when Congress sought during the Vietnam war to pass legislation specifically forbidding the destruction of draft cards, it was a young Catholic, David Miller, a follower of Dorothy Day and a former student of Daniel Berrigan, who first publicly burned his card. In the summer of 1964 Jesuit Daniel Berrigan helped form the Catholic Peace Movement, designed to educate Catholics in regard to long-forgotten Church traditions on peace and war. In November 1964 his brother and co-chairman of the Catholic Peace Movement, Father Philip Berrigan, frustrated with the lack of political and religious response to conventional forms of dissent, decided the time had come to move from dissent to "dramatic and costly resistance."[86] With three associates he poured blood over the draft records in the Baltimore customhouse, an act for which he was later sentenced to six years' imprisonment.

Hundreds of young Catholics were stirred into a reevaluation of war and Christian conscience by the speeches and deeds of this new prophetic element and by the questions raised in the documents of the Vatican Council regarding the morality of war, especially under the conditions of modern warfare. By the late 1960s Catholic attitudes had changed so dramatically that the greatest single percentage increase in conscientious objection occurred in this hitherto most supportive religious group.[87]

Church experts and eventually the hierarchy as a whole were challenged by the moral stance of the prophets, by their own study of pertinent Council documents and the encyclicals of Popes John and Paul, and by the plight of these young Catholic conscientious objectors. James Finn, in an article on Catholics and the Vietnam war, pointed out that moral leadership within the Catholic community on the issue of the war depended less upon the institutional authorities of the Church, its hierarchy, than upon "those who have established their authority through experience, study or personal charisma [the experts and the prophets] and . . . upon the documents of the Vatican Council and the statements of John XXIII and Paul VI."[88]

Throughout the late 1960s pressures grew greater and greater upon the bishops to speak out against the war. Within the USCC a thorough study began of the ancient Catholic "just-war" theory and how it might apply to the Vietnam conflict. The first institutional Church actions taken in opposition to the war were initiated by a few bishops acting independently, such as Bishop Fulton Sheen's call in 1967 for immediate withdrawal by the United States from Vietnam.

By 1968 hundreds of young Catholics were being forced into prison or exile because draft boards were refusing their claims to conscientious-objector status on the basis that Catholics in this country had not traditionally been associated with religious pacifist convictions. Stirred to action by this phenomenon, the National Conference of Catholic Bishops issued a pastoral letter that asked an end to military conscription and a modification of the Selective Service Act to permit conscientious-objector status for Catholics. Moreover, they questioned the justification of the Vietnam war in the light of Catholic moral principles regarding warfare. They particularly questioned whether or not the principle of proportionality, central to the Catholic just-war theory, was not violated by the "inhuman dimensions of suffering" involved in the Vietnam conflict. The Catholic just-war theory, of medieval origin, holds that a Catholic must judge whether or not a war is "just" and his participation in it morally permissible according to several criteria. The war must be declared only as a last resort by a lawful authority, for a just cause, using just means, and with reasonable expectation of success. Most important, the military action cannot produce a greater evil than it seeks to correct. Hence the principle of "proportionality." However, the bishops gave no answer to the questions they themselves raised regarding Vietnam, although in their letter they specifically stated that every citizen should in conscience examine for himself the decisions and actions of his government.[89]

A bishop, commenting on this letter in his interview, said, "In a document they themselves put out . . . the bishops declared that every citizen had the obligation to analyze government acts and act accordingly. But we couldn't get the bishops to do this in regard to the war. They said they didn't know enough, that they had to trust our national leaders, even though they themselves had issued a document saying every citizen had an obligation to analyze government acts. It's just not a responsible way for leaders to act."[90]

The bishops, however, were continually being pressed toward

greater responsibility in regard to the war by the increasing resistance efforts of the prophets and their young followers, by the series of statements published by the USCC on Catholic just-war principles and their application to the Vietnam war and Catholic conscientious objection, and by the growing numbers of their own colleagues in the hierarchy who were taking public stands in opposition to the war and urging an official, collective statement.[91] Finally, at their annual meeting in November 1971 the National Conference of Catholic Bishops issued a *Resolution on South East Asia*, declaring the war unjust and demanding its end. "At this point in history," the bishops said, "it seems clear to us that whatever good we hope to achieve through continued involvement in this war is now outweighed by the destruction of human life and of moral values which it inflicts. It is our firm conviction, therefore, that the speedy end of this war is a moral imperative of the highest priority."[92]

Thus, the Catholic Church and its hierarchy, in this period of Council reforms and of a rejuvenated, enlarged leadership, had come to reverse its traditional position in regard to perhaps the most crucial of all political questions: the issue of war and peace and support for the nation's wars. The *Resolution on South East Asia* represented an attitude completely at variance with such earlier hierarchical statements as that of the influential Archbishop John Hughes, "There is but one rule for a Catholic, wherever he is, and that is to fight on the side where he finds himself," or that of the even more influential John Cardinal Gibbons, who demanded "absolute and unreserved obedience" to the nation's call.[93]

The effect of this decision of the bishops and the process through which it was finally achieved was to spur an additional decision to support unconditional amnesty for war deserters and resisters. The following year the NCCB denounced the continuing war in even stronger terms and urged amnesty for war resisters and deserters. The statements were reiterated on the diocesan level by individual bishops, and the USCC began lobbying congressional committees to argue for unconditional amnesty.[94]

The decision to oppose the war had perhaps a more significant effect on the institutional Church's attitude toward political participation in general. At least during the year 1973-74, when these interviews were conducted, there seemed to be a feeling among many Church leaders that it spelled a kind of declaration of independence for the Church. Church leaders, they now felt, would be much readier than they had been in the past to challenge political actions they believed morally wrong.

Except for abortion, the issue of war and peace was the single issue most often introduced into discussion by those I interviewed. More than half spontaneously introduced this subject in some way. In three cases the references were slight: reiteration of the belief that the Church should be more concerned with the issue of war, and recognition of the Berrigans and their movement as "uniquely Catholic" in inspiration and values. In nine cases, however, the issue constituted a major part of the interview and the interviewees attributed real significance to it as an example of Church social and political concern. Four people described from personal experience how Catholic nuns, priests, and brothers were slowly drawn into the antiwar demonstrations and became part, therefore, of the prophetic movement urging a formal Church stand; they also described the agony of the bishops as they slowly and hesitatingly came to reverse the tradition of Church support for American wars, and the hostile and baffled reactions some found among their own people when they took such stands on the issue.

Five interviewees went beyond this level to assess, explicitly and lengthily, the impact of the decision on the Church's future attitudes toward war and, perhaps, toward political issues in general. All five volunteered their opinions, unprompted by any interview questions. They represented about a fourth of the institutional interviewees, and four of them held the highest Church posts among all interviewees. Two were bishops, a third was considered one of the two most influential men in the USCC, and the fourth had been a division director for the USCC for seven years. The fifth did not hold an official Church office to rank with these but did represent an important segment of Catholic opinion as a leader of the conservative Catholic movement.

All five indicated their belief that the Church could not condone modern warfare or, at least, said one, could not condone some of its tactics. "The search and destroy missions, for example," he said, "are clearly immoral by Catholic ideas of the just war."[95] The others went further, questioning the morality of war in general, in part because such "clearly immoral" techniques seem to be symptomatic of the guerrilla aspects of many modern wars, just as use of nuclear weapons — also widely regarded as prohibited under the just-war theory — would probably be regarded in any world war. One bishop, who had personally lobbied Congress on the amnesty issue, said, "It's impossible today to have the conditions which the Church set up for a just war. A moral, justified war is impossible under today's wars."[96] Another bishop said, "The proportionality is gone and proportionality is central to the Catholic just-war doctrine."[97] One of the USCC officials declared flatly, "The super-patriotic phase is over . . . If a war broke out in South East Asia many more bishops would speak out against it."[98]

One finds the same kind of thinking in Catholic journals. Political scientist and Jesuit Edward Duff wrote in an article analyzing the impact of the Berrigans on Church thinking about the war: "The Berrigans have achieved at least this: they have challenged in the public mind the automatic identification of American Catholicism with the status quo, its alliance with prevailing patriotic causes, its ambition to be accepted . . . The example of the Berrigans raises a doubt that American Catholicism can be counted on to supply acolytes for *all* the shrines of the civic religion that is the American Way of Life."[99] Many Churchmen believed that the experience of Church leaders in taking a public stand against government on this issue, based on their conviction that the government's action was immoral, made much easier the Church's strong, open, organized opposition to government on the abortion issue, also considered an immoral government action.

Surely the institutional Catholic Church and its leadership have gone through an enormous transformation in the past fifteen years. The Church, under the impact of general Catholic upward mobility affecting its own ranks and of the reforms instigated by the Vatican Council, developed a new, more heterogeneous, more widely shared leadership base and a far greater concern for political and social issues. Church leaders believed that concerns and participation had increased greatly and tied this development to religious values through their references to the Council and the recent popes and their teachings regarding worldly involvement and Christian love. They also tied it to changes in the sense of security and status of American Catholics generally. Certainly this change toward greater and more independent political concern and participation on the part of the Church is amply, even dramatically, documented by the reversal of Church positions toward war. If a criterion of the prophetic element of religion is its readiness to challenge the state on what it believes to be a moral issue, in the instance of modern warfare at least the entire Church has become prophetic.

To say this is not to deny the heterogeneity within the Church leadership but to emphasize the new, legitimized process of participation in decision making which permits both the resolution of issues and a rather extensive unity. This interplay of expert, prophet, and hierarchy seems also to result in a generally more liberal and certainly a politically and socially more active Church.

3

The Catholics in Congress

I N THE DEMOCRATIC LANDSLIDE of 1958 Catholics were finally elected to the United States Congress in numbers approximating their percentage in the American population. Ninety Catholics were elected to the House of Representatives and twelve to the Senate, making them the largest single religious body in the Congress.[1] The sudden election of such a large number of Catholics combined with increasing expectations that a Catholic, John Kennedy, would run for the presidency in 1960 caused interest and concern on the part of the public, the press, and the academic world.

The *Congressional Quarterly* for the first time in 1960 published tables showing the religious makeup of the Congress. The political scientist John Fenton explained that his book *The Catholic Vote*, published also in 1960, grew out of this concern. "The election," he wrote, "of such a large number of Catholics to Congress raised the question of their possible effect on public policy decisions made by the national legislature. In other words, many wondered whether Catholic Congressmen would vote as a bloc."[2]

The elections of the 1960s and early 1970s showed a slow, uneven, but continuing increase in the numbers of Catholics elected to the Congress. In 1960, 100 Catholics were elected (89 to the House and 11 to the Senate); in 1964, 107 (93 to the House and 14 to the Senate); in 1966, 108 (95 to the House and 13 to the Senate); and in 1970, 113 (101 to the House and 12 to the Senate).[3]

In the Ninety-third Congress (1973-1974), the numbers rose again.[4] There were 14 Catholics in the Senate (10 Democrats and 4 Republicans) and 100 in the House (69 Democrats and 31 Republicans). Interviews were conducted during this period with six senators and nineteen congressmen. Former senator Eugene McCarthy was also interviewed because of the unique position he has held during the last fifteen years as a political leader of national status, a senator and presidential aspirant, and a spokesman for what has been called a kind of Catholic intellectualism. In a few cases additional interviews were also made with legislative aides who had worked with congressmen or senators on bills with specific Catholic import, such as aid to parochial schools and abortion.

Interviewees were chosen from the two major parties in approximately their percentage strength among Catholics in the Senate and the House. Both the liberal and conservative ends of the philosophical spectrum were represented, as were both newcomers and senior members, party leaders and committee chairmen. Catholic politicians of Irish, Italian, Slavic, French, German, English, and Spanish-speaking origin were interviewed.

An examination of Catholic congressmen and senators reveals that Catholic congressmen resemble their non-Catholic colleagues in most characteristics. The congressmen as a whole in the Ninety-third Congress averaged fifty-one years of age; the Catholics averaged slightly more, fifty-two years of age. Lawyers made up 51.8 percent of all congressmen, while 51 percent of the Catholic contingent were lawyers; 33.3 percent of all congressmen declared themselves businessmen and only a slightly smaller percentage of the Catholics, 28 percent, listed business as a former occupation; 12.2 percent of all congressmen and 12 percent of Catholic congressmen listed teaching as a former profession; 6.5 percent of all congressmen and 4 percent of Catholic congressmen listed journalism.[5] In only two cases did Catholics notably diverge from their fellow congressmen in regard to occupation. Congressmen as a whole were three times more likely than Catholic congressmen to have been engaged in agriculture (9 percent of all congressmen versus 3 percent of the Catholics). Catholics were two and a half times as likely to have spent their entire careers in public service, listing no other occupation, as were congressmen as a whole (9 percent of Catholics gave this listing versus 3.7 percent of all congressmen).

Catholic congressmen also resembled their House colleagues in their length of tenure in the legislature. Like the House as a whole, slightly more than one-third of the Catholic House contingent were first elected to that body in 1968 or later (35 Catholics in the 1968 or subsequent elections, 65 Catholics before 1968, compared to 155 members overall in the 1968 or subsequent elections and 277 members overall prior to 1968; three seats were vacant at the start of the Ninety-third Congress, leaving total House membership at 432). Catholic seniority patterns, then, resemble those of their colleagues in general.

Catholic congressmen did differ from their colleagues in their educational backgrounds, especially because of the likelihood of their having received part or all of their higher education in Catholic schools. Forty percent of the Catholic congressmen received at least part of their higher education in a Catholic college or university, with twenty percent of these men or women receiving all of their higher education in Catholic institutions.[6] Catholic congressmen were also significantly less likely than their colleagues to have attended one of the prestigious Ivy League schools. Only nine percent of the Catholics in the House went to an Ivy League school as compared with nearly twenty percent of House members as a whole.[7]

Catholic members of the Senate present a very different picture. The Catholic senators resembled neither their fellow Catholics in the House nor their Senate colleagues.

In the Ninety-third Congress the average age of all senators was just over fifty-six years. The average age of Catholic senators, however, was only fifty years. Not only were the Catholic senators on the average significantly younger than the average of their colleagues, but they represented to a great degree the more recently elected of the senators. Fully half of the entire contingent of Catholic senators had been elected to the Senate in the 1968 or subsequent elections. At the beginning of the Ninety-third Congress in 1973, seven of the fourteen Catholic senators had not yet served one full term in the Senate. Only two Catholics (John Pastore and Michael Mansfield) had served for twenty years. Only five Catholics had served ten. By contrast almost two-thirds of all senators (62 out of 100) present in the Ninety-third Congress had been elected before 1968 and a little more than a third (38 out of 100) had been elected in 1968 or later.

The Catholic senators also differed markedly from both their Catholic colleagues in the House and from senators in general in their educational background. Only one of the senators, Joseph

Montoya, received all of his higher education in Catholic universities. One other, Philip Hart, had a mixed higher education, with a bachelor's degree from Catholic Georgetown University and a law degree from the University of Michigan. The other twelve Catholic senators had been educated exclusively in secular institutions of higher education. Furthermore, what differentiates Catholic senators most from their House counterparts is not just the overwhelming extent to which they were products of secular universities, but the extent to which they were products of the country's most prestigious secular universities. Half of the Catholic senators were graduates of Ivy League institutions: two received part or all of their education at Yale, two at Harvard, one at Cornell, one at Dartmouth, and one at Princeton.[8] By contrast, only 9 percent of Catholics in the House were Ivy League graduates. In the Senate as a whole only twenty-eight senators, slightly more than one-fourth, were Ivy League graduates.

Another indication of Catholic senatorial distinctiveness can be seen in the fact that 85 percent of all Catholic senators listed law as their former profession, compared to 65 percent of senators as a whole. No Catholic senator was without higher education and only one of the fourteen (Dewey Bartlett, B.S., Princeton) stopped his education at the bachelor's degree level. The one other non-lawyer, Michael Mansfield, went on to get a master's degree.

Finally, Catholic senators seemed to differ from their senatorial colleagues and their Catholic counterparts in the House in the degree to which they were political liberals. Rating the first session of the Ninety-third Congress, for example, the Americans for Democratic Action listed no senators as achieving a score of 100 percent, but nine senators achieved an ADA score of 90 percent or more. Four of these nine were Catholics: Edmund Muskie, John Tunney, Edward Kennedy, and Thomas Eagleton. Thus, 35 percent of the Catholic membership of the Senate were rated highly liberal by the ADA as compared to 9 percent of the membership of the Senate as a whole. No Catholics were among the ten senators rated at 0 percent by the ADA. In the House, only two Catholic representatives—2 percent of all Catholic congressmen—were among the ten House members receiving ADA ratings of 100 percent.[9] Similarly, 2.3 percent of all House members received this rating. These comparisons indicate again the extent to which Catholic congressmen resembled their House colleagues and the extent to which Catholic senators differed from both their Catholic congressional counterparts and their non-Catholic senatorial colleagues.

There is no doubt that Catholic senators had not achieved the degree of power exercised by Catholics in the House. A Catholic, Michael Mansfield, did serve as Majority Leader of the Senate in the Ninety-third Congress just as a Catholic, Thomas O'Neill, served as Majority Leader of the House. However, Catholic senators did not hold committee chairmanships in the Senate to the extent that Catholic representatives did in the House. Of the eighteen standing committees in the Senate in the Ninety-third Congress, only two were chaired by Catholics; one chaired a minor committee, the other, a major. Senator Thomas Eagleton chaired the Committee on the District of Columbia and, toward the end of the Ninety-third Congress, Senator Edmund Muskie was named chairman of the newly created Budget Committee. By contrast, in the House Catholics chaired nearly a third of all its standing committees (seven out of twenty-two, including two of the four most prestigious House committees, Rules and Armed Services, and five minor committees: Judiciary, headed by Peter Rodino, which conducted the impeachment hearings; Merchant Marine and Fisheries, led by Leonor Sullivan, a Catholic and the only woman committee chairman; Post Office and Civil Service, headed by Thaddeus Dulski; Public Works, headed by John Blatnik; and Standards of Official Conduct, chaired by Melvin Price.

Certainly this relative lack of Catholic power in the Senate committee system is a reflection of their newness to the body. However, congressional scholars have long recognized that power and influence can take a form in the Senate which, in recent times at least, has not existed in the House. To paraphrase Leroy Rieselbach, "Presidential candidates come from the Senate and Senators take the role of serving as national spokesmen on issues."[10] Using this criterion of power, a rather different view of Catholic senators emerges. On the basis of their presidential or vice-presidential efforts and their roles as acknowledged spokesmen for liberal (and, in one case, conservative) ideas, fully half of the Catholic senators could claim influence as national spokesmen: Edward Kennedy, Edmund Muskie, Michael Mansfield, Thomas Eagleton (because of his brief vice-presidential role), John Tunney, Philip Hart, and James Buckley.

Thus, a new Catholic force seems to have developed on Capitol Hill, and two characteristics of this force seem significant in the Ninety-third Congress. First, it was made up partially of Catholic congressmen who resembled their House counterparts to a great extent and who held many party and committee leadership posts; second, it was made up partially of young, liberal, ivy-league-educated Catholic senators who differed from their senatorial colleagues and their Catholic House counterparts, and who played a large role as national spokesmen in comparison with their total numbers.

Self-Consciousness in the Capitol

To paraphase John Kennedy's statement to the Dallas ministers' meeting, let us now try to determine if these 114 men and women were Catholic congressmen and senators, or congressmen and senators who happened to be Catholic.

No one need fear a Catholic cabal. That is the first and most easily drawn conclusion from the interview data regarding Catholic congressmen and senators. The cabal predicted by the old nativist organizations would presume recognition of numbers and strength and unity of principles and goals. Yet nothing in the political interviews is so clear and dramatic as the interviewees' own professed ignorance of the numbers and leadership positions of Catholics in Congress and their lack of cohesion. None of the twenty-six senators and congressmen interviewed acknowledged knowing that Catholics formed the largest single religious group in the Congress. Few seemed to have any realization that their numbers had been growing steadily over the past fifteen years. Two of those who were aware of these data were of Italian-American descent, and they expressed their recognition of Catholic growth in terms of changed nationality rather than religious makeup of the Congress. One congressman, after saying the rise of Catholics was evident, explained, "Well, you follow the elections. You see who's there. You see an Italian elected in this district in place of someone else."[11] Only one political leader displayed an accurate idea of Catholic numbers in the Congress and he added, "It would have been a guess [and] I would have guessed the Baptists or Lutherans were larger."[12] None seemed aware of the degree of Catholic power in the party and committee leadership, especially in the House. When our conversation switched to

Catholics holding committee chairmanships, the congressman who accurately estimated Catholic congressional numbers asked in a puzzled tone, "You mean subcommittee chairmen, don't you? You don't mean there are many Catholic chairmen of full committees?"[13]

Their comments seemed to indicate their ignorance of and surprise at my figures regarding their numbers in Congress. Typical was the remark of one House member: "I've been in Congress fourteen years and I didn't know the number of Catholic legislators has been rising. I am friendly with a number of congressmen and I am never aware of what their religious beliefs might be. Sometimes I've only learned them after years of knowing them."[14] An important committee chairman said, "I've been in Congress thirty-six years and I don't know anyone's religion."[15] Another congressman, clearly intrigued by the figures, acknowledged, "I didn't know that. I suppose it's the influence of John F. Kennedy. I wouldn't have believed it. I've never given it a thought."[16]

Catholic politicians seemed also to have only the vaguest idea of who their Catholic colleagues were. For the most part, they did not seem to think about their fellow congressmen and senators in terms of their religious adherence, even when this was Catholic. Only four of the political leaders identified a large number of other politicians by their Catholic religion. Former senator Eugene McCarthy knowledgeably discussed the role Catholics had played and were playing in American political life, recognizing and assessing as Catholic political leaders John, Robert, and Edward Kennedy, former Speaker of the House John McCormack, Senate Majority Leader Michael Mansfield, and House Majority Leader Thomas O'Neill. And Congressman Lawrence Hogan, sponsor of an antiabortion Constitutional amendment in the House, in estimating the chances of his amendment's passage, displayed wide recognition of the religious faith of his colleagues. He discussed Congressmen Robert Drinan, Harold Obey, Peter Rodino, and John Dent. Another politician did the same thing in discussing John F. Kennedy's aid to education bill and the Catholic legislators' response to it. Finally, a very young congressman displayed wide recognition of Catholic congressional membership in a long discussion of differences between political generations, mentioning and contrasting the older Catholic working-class, immigrant generation — the Tip O'Neills — with, in his opinion, the younger, better educated, less self-consciously Catholic generation—the Michael Harringtons and Paul Cronins.

Beyond these four, there was little apparent tendency to recognize or think about colleagues as Catholic or non-Catholic. Only President John Kennedy was widely discussed in these terms, with eight of the twenty-six men mentioning the breakthrough role they saw him as having played. Of Catholics in the Ninety-third Congress, only the Jesuit priest and congressman Robert Drinan was widely identified and discussed as Catholic. Six politicians spontaneously discussed him, in all but one case negatively. To them, he was apparently a thorn in the side, and they especially objected to his practice of wearing his priestly garb on the floor because of the anger this aroused in their colleagues in the House. The most negative sputtered, "I was telling a colleague the other day, the more I see Drinan parading around in that collar, the more I think I should become an Episcopalian . . . Everytime I see him with that damned collar it makes me mad!"[17] Others mentioned their doubts about the legitimacy of a priest's holding political office, and two expressed their irritation with what they saw as Drinan's proabortion stance. The only other legislators identified by their colleagues as Catholic political leaders were Senators Edmund Muskie (so identified by one senator), Edward Kennedy (by two politicians), Congressman Lawrence Hogan (by three congressmen, all in relation to his human life amendment), and Congressman James Hanley (by one congressman).[18] Four politicians also mentioned and identified as Catholic the Jesuit priest and Nixon spokesman Father John McLoughlin, all in negative terms similar to those used in regard to Father Drinan. Of the 114 Catholic senators and congressmen serving in the Ninety-third Congress, only 12 were identified and discussed as Catholics by even one of their colleagues.

One congressman from Massachusetts and two from New Jersey commented on the Catholic predominance in their state congressional delegations. "A big part of our population and our congressional delegation is Catholic," said a New Jersey congressman.[19] Only two spontaneously mentioned the one organized Catholic activity on Capitol Hill, the First Friday club, a group of Catholic legislators who meet for mass and Holy Communion on the first Friday of every month. Neither indicated any real degree of participation in the group. "Friday," remarked one, "is a bad day for congressmen. Everyone's eager to get home or play golf that day. I've only gone to a few meetings."[20] There was more awareness of the nondenominational but largely Protestant prayer breakfasts and Bible meetings. Three of the Catholic legislators mentioned them, two saying they had been invited but had never attended, one describing himself as a participant. "I don't attend as conscientiously as I should but I take part."[21]

A number of Catholic legislators volunteered opinions on the reason Catholics were being elected to office in greater numbers. All saw it as a natural enough reaction to assimilation and a decrease in anti-Catholic hostility. "One of the real gifts John F. Kennedy gave the country," remarked a Republican congressman, echoing the sentiments of a number of others, "was that he caused people to change their fear and hostility toward Catholics in politics."[22]

"It's not surprising, the numbers elected," said a man who reflected on fifteen years in the House, "because there's been a real movement to wipe out cronyism. 'You can't vote for him, he's a Catholic,' and so forth. That's been broken up. Not just for Catholics but all kinds of groups are here now that were not here when I first came . . . How many Italians do you think were here then? There are now two Italians from my own state and they were not elected on the basis of being Italian because there is only 11 percent Italians in my state. But now people look at candidates more than ever before not as members of one group or another."[23]

Another emphasized the assimilation process. "We're reaping the harvest now of the education of the ethnic. After all, the two dominant ethnic groups in our country are the Irish and the Italians. They early adopted politics as a way out of the ghetto. Now their grandchildren are getting degrees and shooting for higher office."[24]

A senator said, "I wasn't aware [of the number of Catholic legislators] and you say most congressmen and senators aren't and I'll tell you that's the reason it happened. We don't pay attention to each other's religion anymore." He added, later, "I think we would be in serious trouble if suddenly the Catholic group in Congress was meeting together."[25]

Finally, two congressmen pointed out that the percentage of Catholics in the national legislature is still only about equal to their percentage in the population. "I don't think it's surprising," said one. "Catholics are also the single largest group in the United States, so why not in Congress? Their percentage in the House is about the same as their percentage in the country."[26]

All but one of the Catholic political leaders interviewed insisted, many vehemently, that senators and congressmen were indifferent to and usually ignorant of one another's religious affiliation. A Republican congressman, the son of a Catholic mother and a Protestant father, who is himself married to a Protestant, said, "I look at individuals in Congress. Four hundred and thirty-five members — a small community. They say water seeks its own level and you tend to form friendships not along religious lines but philosophical, and also through the people you're thrown into contact with in committees, for example. Four hundred and thirty-five people from all walks of life, denominations. We're all under one roof, thrown together . . . We have learned acceptance, respect for one another."[27] A senator said, "[Religion] doesn't come into play. We don't look at each other here through religious or ethnic eyes. That's the wonderful thing about the Senate, I think, its cosmopolitanism."[28] An influential committee chairman insisted he had not realized Catholic numbers were rising in the Congress because "I have never viewed Congress in that aspect. I've never been aware of the denominations of the members."[29]

Only one interviewee demurred from this general description of ignorance of or indifference to members' religious adherence. A Republican Catholic congressman, after saying, "As far as I can tell there is no feeling in the House about members' religion," added, "Oh, some representatives make cracks about Catholics like they do about blacks . . . Oh, in the cloakroom there are a few digs by some of my colleagues. I think because Catholics are interested in social problems. They are sniping not at being Catholic, really, but at being liberal."[30]

It is not easy to judge the sincerity of the Catholic politicians' professed ignorance of or indifference to Catholic congressional numbers and power. Tending to support their sincerity is the seemingly genuine surprise with which, almost without exception, Catholic politicians greeted my recital of their number in the House and Senate and in House chairmanships. After my first two or three political interviewees seemed to show little conception of how large a percentage of the Congress Catholics composed, I changed interview tactics to begin sessions by announcing that one factor leading me to undertake the study was the large and steadily growing numbers of Catholics being elected to the Congress and the number of chairmanships they were assuming. Surprise bordering on shock often greeted this statement. Politicians even displayed a kind of eagerness to know more — the exact number, how fast the Catholic percentage had been growing. I began to wonder if I was inducing a kind of Catholic consciousness raising in Congress.

On the other hand, several facts led me to question how genuine the professed ignorance and indifference to Catholic congressional power really was. Interviewees claiming indifference to Catholic congressional power and insisting that their religion had played no part in their campaigns showed that they had actually thought a good deal about how their Catholicism might affect their elections. They also displayed great familiarity with Church and Church-related groups in their districts and states. Further, this indifference to Catholic numbers in the Congress apparently did not extend to congressional aides. I talked to only nine legislative assistants since my study was focused on the politicans themselves, but every one of them showed familiarity with the religious affiliations of the members of Congress. Three also made the point that aides in their offices were chosen in part to provide a deliberate mix of religious persuasions. A woman working for a senator from the South said, "I'm his Protestant aide and Ms. B is his Catholic aide and we have a Jewish person, too."[31] It is hard to believe that such thorough recognition of religious diversification could persist among staff members without its influencing and being influenced by their bosses' interests.

Probably what we have here is the operation of what David Truman called "the rules of the game." An accepted American political ploy has always been to openly and loudly profess Constitutional separation of church and state and the rightness and inexorable operation of the melting pot while at the same time carefully balancing the ticket. Thus, in these interviews Catholic politicians displayed indifference to their congressional colleagues' religions, but they took an extreme interest in and were very knowledgeable about possible religious influence in their own election campaigns and districts. Truman also emphasized that a member of Congress is expected to look to his constituency but also beyond it to the public interest, and that this dual responsibility inhibits the extent to which the wise legislator will show himself as representing any one group, even one to which he himself belongs.[32] It is perhaps instructive that the two Catholic politicians who displayed most knowledge of and interest in the religions of the congressional membership did not actually hold political power as the time of the interviews. They were former senator Eugene McCarthy and Representative Lawrence Hogan, who was interviewed in the last weeks of a lame-duck Congress, after he had already lost the Maryland gubernatorial primary and had bypassed a congressional reelection bid.

Catholic congressmen and senators probably did not have a precise idea of their numbers and perhaps of their power as far as chairmanships are concerned. But it seems unlikely that they were quite as indifferent to religious currents in the Congress as they tried to appear.

The Influence of Catholicism on Elections and Constituencies

If legislators insisted that generally congressmen had little interest in one another's religion, they did show that they had thought about the effect of being Catholic on their own campaigns and political careers and about the changes in the country and the Church that made their careers, in their opinions, easier. Only one politician said that being Catholic was a negative factor in his political life. A congressman who had been redistricted remarked rather angrily, "I have a new district now and I'm getting letters from constituents saying, 'I didn't know you were a Catholic.' They say they won't vote for me because they wouldn't vote for a Catholic."[33] The congressman was of Spanish-speaking descent and a vocal supporter of such Spanish-speaking causes as the Farah boycott and the Chavez movement. It is possible that the constituent reaction he reported was as much directed toward this as toward his religious adherence.

All others interviewed said either that their religion had never been an issue in their campaigns and had not lost them votes or, in three cases, that they believed they may have even gained votes because of it. No one else reported a personal attack because of his religion. A senator from the same state as the Spanish-speaking congressman quoted above declared, "Anti-Catholic hostility is really pretty much dead. In most political races it's dead."[34] Another senator, echoing the statements of most of his colleagues, insisted, "It never was an issue in any of my campaigns."[35] A congressman from the Midwest said of his campaigns, "I never thought about being a Catholic or a Catholic candidate." Anti-Catholic hostility, he added, was gone now. "Even in 1960 [during the Kennedy campaign] it was really gone."[36] This same man later said he had been supported by "a lot of priests" in his elections.

Three congressmen, insisting religion no longer affected political campaigns, added that even in cases where it may seem to do so, the plus and minus effects of one's religion had a way of canceling each other out. "Catholicism is a minor factor in practical politics. In districts where the Catholic vote is important often both candidates are Catholic, so it's not so much a special factor. It isn't, even in areas where only one candidate is Catholic. Being Catholic isn't so much a special factor."[37]

Another Catholic congressman, who more than any other interviewee wanted greater, more vocal Church participation in politics, illustrated this same point with an example from his last campaign. He, a conservative, had been in a race with a radical, far-left candidate, also a Catholic. "I was in a tremendous battle. More money was spent in that campaign than in any congressional campaign that year . . . I asked for help from the Church and the priests told me they couldn't get involved. Finally, the Episcopalians helped me." The Episcopalians sponsored a testimonial dinner for him, with the governor and lieutenant governor present, to praise the significant legislation he had sponsored. His pastor was asked to give the invocation and agreed to do so but then did not appear. "I was terribly embarrased. Later he told me that he felt he shouldn't get involved but hadn't known how to tell me."[38] A senator remarked philosophically, "My own polls show being Catholic doesn't affect me. For every one I lose, I gain one."[39]

Two Republicans from heavily Democratic states both insisted that religion had not been an issue in their campaigns or in their areas' political life in general. Significantly, though, they both indicated that they thought they might have been chosen to run because their party leaders hoped they might win over some normally Democratic Catholic votes. "Part of my own area is heavily

Catholic. They are generally much more Democratic . . . I think the Republican leaders picked me because, to beat the Democrats, they needed a man from the Democratic area and a Catholic was of some value . . . I have a feeling that Catholics were aware of the fact that I was Catholic, although there was never any discussion of religion and no religious issues. If I got any gains from my religion it was through word of mouth. 'He's a nice Catholic boy. He's got five kids.' Protestants did not seem to be aware of my religion . . . There was no Protestant attack on me."[40]

The second Republican Catholic reported, "My district is 20 to 25 percent Catholic. During the last election seven out of nine of our [Republican] candidates for state offices were Catholics and nobody even mentioned it. We sort of kept wondering if the Democrats would pick it up and point it out but they never did. I believe that one healthy thing now in this country today is that people no longer play on religious biases. But I also think there is a Catholic vote, without the label even being put on a candidate. A bond somehow forms. The majority of Catholics vote for a Catholic candidate more than Protestants [vote for their own], I think."[41]

The examination of institutional Church leaders showed that, overwhelmingly, they believed the Church had been spurred to greater concern for and participation in political issues through, first, the influence of the Vatican Council and, second, the changes in American life effected through assimilation and an end to hostility toward Catholics. The interviews with political leaders demonstrated that Catholic politicians believed they have had easier access to political careers for the same reasons, but they cited assimilation and a lessening of anti-Catholic hostility as of primary importance. Again, only the Spanish-speaking congressman thought that anti-Catholic hostility was of any importance at all in the country in general. The others, in varying degrees, echoed one prominent and prominently Catholic congressman in saying, "It's gone forever."[42] Some said there might still be pockets of hostility here and there, perhaps among fundamentalist groups, but they ascribed little importance to this and felt hostility was disappearing even in these pockets.

Three, including two of the most powerful leaders of the Congress, implied that this was largely because Americans in general are not interested in religion and do not really care anything about it. Religion does not make any difference at all, they insisted.[43] Most political leaders, in discussing the lessening of anti-Catholic hostility, however, tended to stress the gradual assimilation of Catholics into the general society and, especially, what many of them believed to be the effect of John Kennedy's campaign and election. One of the older senators mused, "I think of poor Al Smith and the popery argument — if Smith is elected the Pope was going to come to America. Well, John Kennedy put that to rest when he went to Dallas and talked to those ministers and said that a man's religious beliefs were his own and had no part in government."[44]

One of the oldest and most influential leaders in the House discussed at length Catholic assimilation and the development of what he called "*anti*-anti-Catholicism." He began by telling the story of the "pope's stone."

In 1855 when the Know-Nothings were strong, Congress decided to put up a monument to the Father of our Country. Then they changed their minds. Instead of Congress doing this, it would be better, they thought, if the people did it and so they raised nickels and dimes in all the schools from the kids and they wrote to the ninety-six nations that were in existence then and asked for a stone to put in the foundation. And they wrote to the Vatican, too, and the pope sent a stone. Well, the Potomac came right down to the Capitol then and a group of men crossed the Potomac and they kidnapped the night watchman and they stole the pope's stone. They didn't want the pope's stone in the monument. And that caused a national revulsion. There were thirty-three representatives in Congress then from the Know-Nothing group and in the next election they were all wiped out. That was the first wave that rose against the antireligious forces.

There was no fight then against bigotry until World War I when everybody was sleeping in the trenches together, were buddies and the Catholics did such a good job and everybody realized it. Then you had Al Smith in 1928 but I think the aftermath of that election was that bigotry broke down. Then World War II came along and the Catholic population gained and they saw what the Catholic chaplains did in the war and so forth and people became more broad-minded. And, of course, the final thing, the greatest thing of all, was the election of John F. Kennedy. There are still pockets of bigotry, but that's what they are, pockets.[45]

This congressional leader traced a pattern of gradual assimilation that many of his colleagues also alluded to, and he, as well as they, saw Kennedy's election as the pivotal event resulting in final acceptance of Catholics as equal and legitimate parts of the American political process.

Five political leaders, while discussing the process of assimilation, also pointed to the effect of the Ecumenical Council on that process of assimilation and acceptance. "There's better understanding now, better understanding of the religion and beliefs of other groups. Those are good effects [of the Council]. The whole ecumenical movement is a good thing."[46] "The Ecumenical Council was a good thing," said another. "It made the Church more understandable to non-Catholics and Catholics."[47] The Catholic legislative aide to a Catholic congressman summed up the feelings expressed by these politicians. "There was such an aura of magic about Catholicism before, and the mass. We spoke in a strange tongue and we practiced what looked like oriental rites. We were kind of strange and mysterious to non-Catholics. Now all that's gone and that's not lost on Catholics. There is no overt distance any longer between us and other Americans."[48]

Awareness of Changing Church Concerns

Although there is no discernible Catholic cabal and Catholic legislators not only claimed to be unaware of their numbers and prominence but insisted that religion is little discussed or acknowledged among them, does the Catholic Church, its activities and beliefs, nevertheless exert some kind of influence upon them? Religion can exert influence on politics in at least two ways: through the value formation of its adherents, including, of course, those who make a career out of politics, and through interest group activity—organizing and lobbying to achieve political goals. To determine the extent to which their religion exerts either or both of these influences on Catholic political leaders, I tried to examine five factors. First is the extent to which Catholic politicians were aware of Church political and social concerns, in the belief that they had to have some knowledge of political concern and participation on the part of the Church to be influenced by them. The second factor is the estimation they themselves had of Church influence on politics: was it great or little, in their opinion; had it grown or diminished in the last fifteen years when

Church leaders believed the Church was more aware of and active in social and political concerns? Third is the extent to which they themselves had been targets of lobbying efforts by Church or Church-related groups, on what issues, and with what reaction. Fourth is the Catholic politicians' own analysis of the differences a growth in Catholic membership has had on the Congress. And fifth, I looked at the extent to which Catholic politicians revealed a pattern of Catholic values in their interviews.

I found a very high degree of awareness among political leaders of an increase in Church social and political concerns over the past decade and a half. Only two political leaders failed to comment on this subject. One, the chairman of a powerful House committee, was completely uninterested in the subject of religion, though he had a Jesuit grammar school and high school education. He insisted it had no bearing on politics, would answer few questions on the subject, and treated the ones he did answer as a joke. The other devoted nearly all of his interview to detailing his own religious development, which he described as a progression from a narrow legalistic view of religion to one requiring a commitment to involvement. He implied at least a similar journey for the Church as a whole during the 1960s but never directly commented on the subject. Three other political leaders saw no or little change in Church political and social concerns over the past decade.

The other twenty-one Catholic politicians, or four-fifths of all interviewees, indicated that they believed there had been a definite change in the kinds and extent of Church political and social concerns over the past ten years. Fourteen of them, more than half of all those interviewed, were enthusiastic about the change, viewing it as a positive factor for the Church and the country.

Those who believed there had been a change but reacted to it in a negative or contradictory way did so not primarily because they saw increased activism as a violation of church-state separation strictures but because the change, in their minds, was personified by radical Catholic activists such as the Berrigan brothers and Father James Groppi, of whom they disapproved.[49] One senator, from a state where Mexican-Americans, supported by Catholic Church groups, have become increasingly politicized, said, "Some young priests get a little too militant at times. They have been joining extremist groups. There has been increasing militancy in the area. I don't approve. It grieves me to see priests joining in, trying to disrupt things . . . I've been asked to join and I've always said no. I don't believe in it."[50] Another congressman fulminated, "There have been a lot of radicals in the Church who have been out shouting their positions on things in my opinion they shouldn't have gotten involved with. People like the Berrigans who have destroyed property, burglarized, and then tried justifying illegal acts. In my opinion this kind of thing has been very, very damaging to the Church."[51] Of the politicians who saw and disapproved of Church activism, the overwhelming majority, five out of seven, were conservative Republicans.

The fourteen politicians interviewed (more than half of all those interviewed) who not only saw a change in the kind and extent of Church political and social concern but were enthusiastic about it tended to display detailed knowledge of increased Church activism both on the national scene and in their states or districts. "There've been definite changes," said a Mexican-American congressman. "The Church has finally realized that it has to get off dead center, be more liberal, more inclusive of people and problems. Most of the time the Church has been concerned with people's souls. It hasn't been concerned with their civil liberties, for example . . . This kind of thing should have been done a long time ago. If the Church had taken a position like this in the 1920s we wouldn't have lost the railroad strike . . . but it wouldn't, then. It said you can't mix church and state."[52] "An important thing," said an ex-labor leader and a longtime House member, "and I think a good thing, has happened in the last few years and that is that the Church is increasingly expressing itself on issues that before it normally never would have done. Church leaders before used to talk to politicians, but privately, as persons. Now you don't see that. Now what you see is a publicly expressed Church view on certain issues. It's a fantastic movement. I don't ever remember the Church expressing itself so much and the way they're doing it."[53]

A senator emphasized the effect Pope John and the Ecumenical Council had on increasing Church concerns, an inference drawn by a number in this group. "There's no question about it. Pope John had profound impact and Paul has continued that although perhaps not as rapidly as John could have done. There is a much greater social consciousness on the part of the Church now. The

Church is much more aware of economic and social issues . . .
supporting Chavez, for example, working for the poor. It is almost impossible to find a young priest today without a social conscience."[54]

Two gave examples of new and extensive social concern by the
Church and then mentioned specific local Church political activities. "In going through [Catholic] school, attending Church regularly," said one, "I never heard until the past few years of the
Church participating in politics. Our old archbishop, as a matter
of fact, forbade political meetings in the church or the Catholic
schools or even in the Knights of Columbus halls. There had been
a political meeting at the K of C and some people had protested
having a political meeting there and so he forbade it. But this has
changed recently and the doors are open now to political discussions of candidates and issues."[55]

Most members of this group of interviewees believed, if anything, that the Church was still not active enough in political and
social concerns. After praising Church efforts in the Farah and
Chavez boycotts, one congressman complained that, still, "they
don't take advantage of opportunities to raise the status of their
parishioners, especially minority group members . . . I don't
mean this as destructive criticism of the Church. I mean it as constructive criticism . . . I think separation of church from state is
good. The philosophy of separation maybe has to be, is necessary.
But advocacy of issues is not in my opinion Church involvement
in politics."[56] Another, after praising the increase in social concern and crediting it to the influence of the Ecumenical Council,
added, "I think the Church should be *more* involved with politics." Later, asked if he had ever been contacted by a Church
leader or organization on an issue, he said, "No, the bishops
know where I stand . . . I have to stir them up. I have to bomb
them, whatever."[57]

There seems no doubt that to its adherents in Congress the
Church has definitely projected an image of increased activism
and concern. Further, more than half of the politicians interviewed regarded this as a positive development, one which they
seemed to hope would continue and expand. Those who saw the
change but viewed it negatively—a third of all respondents who
believed change had occurred—were for the most part conservative Republicans. The interviewees who not only saw the change

but viewed it positively were from all parts of the spectrum in age, party, ethnicity, and ideology but the great majority of them were liberal Democrats.

We saw that Church leaders found it difficult to analyze whether, as a result of increased concern and participation, Church influence over political and social life had increased. I found the same difficulty in the political interviews. A number of the senators and congressmen were unwilling or unable to speculate on the question. Nineteen of the twenty-six men interviewed did, though, and the results are intriguing. As in my interviews with Church leaders, there is no connection between believing that the Church had increased its political and social concerns and believing that it had therefore increased its influence. For example, the fourteen politicians who saw and approved increased Church concern were divided in their estimates of its political influence. Four gave no opinion; three believed there had been an increase in political influence; one believed that the Church had never had any influence; and six, almost half, believed that, notwithstanding its increased social and political concerns, the Church had actually declined in influence. Taking into account all nineteen respondents to this question of Church influence, four believed influence had increased; one, who was basically uninterested in the subject of religion and politics, believed that it was about the same; five, that the Church had never had any influence in politics; and nine, that its political influence had declined.

Of those asserting a gain in Church political influence, two, both conservative Republicans, said that the Church had had to try to gain influence to protect its own institutional interests. "The Church," explained one of these men, "has gotten involved in a large number of projects. It's had to. In order to get the money it needs for education and other projects, it had to get involved, had to take an interest."[58]

Two others, liberal Democrats, both men who believed that Church concerns had increased and who approved of this, enthusiastically asserted a consequent increase in influence. Said one, "The Church is more influential now than it was ten years ago because it has begun to take positions now . . . The Church is not always right in the positions it takes, but taking political positions makes the Church more influential because non-Catholics see the political involvement of the Church and they become more involved with the Church. Before John Kennedy, there was no Catholic vote. Then people saw Catholics come out and vote for Kennedy. They became aware of Catholic votes. Now they are aware of Catholic political positions."[59]

Those senators and congressmen who believed there had been little or no change in Church political influence were, with one exception, men who did not believe there had been any change in Church concerns or who saw change epitomized in radical Catholic groups and disapproved of it. Typical were the comments of two congressmen, one of whom strongly disapproved of the changes he saw in Church concerns and one who felt there had been no change. "Catholicism is a minor factor in practical politics," insisted the first. "In Europe when the Church had a chance it has dominated politics. So we're very careful here."[60] The second said, "I don't think really that the Church has ever tried to exert much influence. In the past maybe on the local diocese basis, but not nationally . . . The one best example of that is John F. Kennedy. Some people may have expected him to give aid to parochial schools since he was Catholic and all, but then he comes out opposed to parochial aid."[61]

Most interesting are the men who made up the plurality of respondents to this question, the politicians who believed that Church political influence has declined. Nine believed this, yet the reasons they gave for the decline illustrates a generational split between Catholic politicians which occurred on a number of topics. Those politicians in this group who were older and had served longer in Congress viewed the decline from a historical sense, as stemming basically from the disintegration of the immigrant, working-class Catholic culture, more parochial, more inclined to listen to Church directives. Younger politicians more recently come to the Congress tended to view the decline as resulting from what they believed was a still insufficiently developed and organized Church activism and a corresponding lack of political skills on the part of Church people. The older men, even those who recognized and approved an increase in Church social and political concerns, viewed what they saw as a decline of Church influence on politics with benignity. The younger men viewed it with frustration and anger. They wanted more social consciousness, more political skills, increased Church activism.[62]

Typical of the comments of the first group was that of one of Congress's most powerful men in the House since Harry Truman's day, who observed:

> There was a time when the Church really was a political power, when a parish priest or a monsignor really could be a power locally. But that was, really, before the [Second World] War. By 1950 it had declined already as far as dictating to people goes . . . There is a lot more concern now for social issues. Your young clergymen know so much more now about social affairs, foreign affairs even . . . However, while the Church is participating more, it also respects the views of others now. It's nothing today for a public official to say to a priest in a meeting, "Now wait a minute. I know about this issue and you don't. I'm the expert here." And the parishioners understand that and agree with it. It all changed in World War II with the education surge.[63]

The argument and the tone of the younger men is completely different. Said one first-term congressman who throughout his interview argued for greater Church activism, "Since the Council there's been a lot of talk in the Church about social and political concerns but no Catholic action. We are succumbing to what Pope John hoped to overcome — being stifled by structure . . . It's the Church's fault, for Catholics are not brought up with the degree of political sophisticaion other groups have and therefore when they try to act on an issue like right to life, they are losing, not getting support."[64]

Another of the younger congressmen exclaimed impatiently, "There are things they [the Church] say they believe in but if they believe in them I say they should get involved. They will say they believe in things but then don't go out and organize and work."[65]

A third man, one of the youngest in Congress, in explaining why he felt Church influence had declined, spelled out the differences between his and what he called the "O'Neill-Burke generation."[66] "Different generations have different attitudes toward what the Church should be and the clergy should be, about how you go about meeting needs . . . The Church's sense of involvement is far less [than that of other groups] . . . I think of [John Cardinal] Krol lecturing from hundreds of miles away [to] Drinan on his priestly duties. That generation is going but it is putting a prototype of itself in its place."[67]

We see then that political leaders had the same difficulty as Church leaders in estimating the influence the Church exerts on American political life. Only a small minority felt its influence had increased. The majority of respondents felt either that it had never had any real political influence and did not now or that its influence had actually declined. However, within this majority were some significant differences. Those believing the Church had never had any influence were also, with a single exception, those who saw no change in Church concerns or disapproved of the changes they did see. Those believing Church influence had declined were split along generational lines, the older men viewing this benignly as a concomitant of assimilation, and the younger men viewing it angrily as a result of insufficiently developed political consciousness and skills on the part of the Church.

Catholic Lobbying

While the overwhelming majority (four-fifths) of political interviewees were aware of an increase in Church social and political concerns in the sense of increased support of and participation in social justice issues, poverty, minority group status, and so on, they emphasized different kinds of issues when addressing the subject of direct Church lobbying. Most politicians I interviewed declared that they had been contacted on issues by Church or Church-related organization leaders. The examples they gave, however, indicate that, at least in their experience, much and probably most Church lobbying is done not on social justice but on institutional issues, that is, on issues which would directly benefit a specifically Catholic position or organization rather than the general public.

Many Church leaders and some politicians would probably object to terming opposition to abortion an institutional issue. They see it, especially those who view abortion as only one aspect of an entire spectrum of issues involving respect for life, as part of a humane and human approach to everything that would make life for all people more dignified and more fulfilling. However, the antiabortion stances do reflect a central Catholic belief, and conversation with congressmen and senators indicated that lobbying on this issue has not taken the broader respect-for-life approach but has centered narrowly on abortion itself.[68] It seems difficult, therefore, to regard this as a public interest or a social justice issue rather than an institutional one, especially considering the lobbyists's own approach.

Even if the abortion issue is put aside, the politicians interviewed overwhelmingly cited institutional issues as those on which they had been lobbied by the Church. Part of the explanation for this may lie in the fact that I interviewed only Catholic legislators. As reported earlier, both of the Catholic lobbyists interviewed agreed that, whereas on social justice issues they tended to seek out those legislators with most interest in or in the best position to affect the particular issues regardless of their religious adherence, they did go first to Catholic legislators in regard to institutional issues.[69] I should also note that political interviewees, when discussing lobbying, discussed it entirely in terms of personal approaches to them or their Washington or local offices. They did not seem to consider under the "lobby" framework congressional committee testimony to which the USCC directs major effort.

Only four politicians insisted that they had never been approached by a Catholic leader or organization in regard to an issue before Congress. Two of these were conservative Republicans and two were liberal Democrats. One of the conservatives had no objection to such an approach and was plainly puzzled by its absence: "It's funny. I don't know why."[70] The other took violent exception to the question on lobbying, insisting, "What the bishops say doesn't matter to me. I vote as I think. I don't pay attention to what they say. They don't influence me in any way. I don't even know if there are any [Catholic lobbyists]."[71] Of the two liberal Democrats who also insisted that they had never been lobbied by the Church, one, generally regarded as part of the Catholic Left, intimated that he believed this was because he was so far ahead of the Church that he, rather, had to lobby it. The other had no explanation.

Three other interviewees gave ambiguous replies. One, a powerful party leader and liberal Democrat, indicated that Church lobbying did go on in Congress but cited no specific examples, contenting himself with the observation that he believed the Church did not approach just Catholic legislators but legislators of all religious backgrounds. "It wouldn't be right. The Church wouldn't do that. The Church is more 'catholic' than that."[72] Another interviewee, a former presidential candidate, made no reference to his congressional experience but instead insisted that the Church had not approached him in any way on any issue during his presidential race.[73] The third, a conservative Republican, showed the influence of Catholic values in his career to a degree unmatched by any other interviewee. He had entered politics, he said, in order to seek greater involvement with his fellowmen as part of the Christian attitude. Once in the Senate, however, he became convinced that basic concerns can only be affected through changes within individuals. Therefore, he downplayed the importance of any kind of political action, including lobbying, and only addressed the topic from that point of view.

The great majority of politicians (nineteen) reported that they had been approached on issues by Church leaders or organizations. Twelve specifically said they had been lobbied on abortion. Four others indicated indirect pressure on the same subject. One, for example, said he had not been specifically lobbied but that he was aware of and had been influenced by the bishops' statements on abortion. Another said he had not been lobbied but had been asked to and had addressed a Right to Life organization meeting in his district. On no other issue did such a large number of congressmen and senators report being approached, nor did they feel so much pressure on other issues as they had felt on the abortion issue. Whereas some congressmen and senators resented what they believed to be excessive and illegitimate pressure on this issue, there was no sense of resentment on the part of the legislators to lobbying on other issues.

Abortion aside, the issues most often listed by congressmen and senators as ones on which they had been lobbied by Catholic organizations or leaders were the following: aid to Catholic schools, cited by five; support for the Chavez and Farah movements, citied by three; and support for the Office of Economic Opportunity, cited by two congressmen, both from urban states. One other congressman said he had been lobbied by Catholic groups in support of welfare reform, and one senator said he had been approached on "social welfare" issues, without specifying more. Thus, I found seven reports of Catholic lobbying on issues of public interest. All other instances of Catholic lobbying mentioned, including antiabortion and aid to Catholic education, concerned institutional issues.

Except for antiabortion, aid to education, aid for Chavez and the Farah strikers, and reform of the OEO, other issues were mentioned by only one political interviewee. Examples were the school prayer amendment, aid to Catholic libraries, aid to Catholic hospitals, postal rates for nonprofit publications, a pension bill that would have affected diocesan employees, the rise in oil prices (because of its effect on Catholic schools, hospitals, and old age homes), and welfare.

Individual Catholic politicians seem to have been the objects of lobbying efforts on particular issues for reasons that research on lobbying indicates are true for lawmakers in general. In a number of cases the institution or group wanting the benefit or result represented a more or less powerful organization or interest in the congressman's or senator's district or state. This was true in regard to requests for aid to Catholic hospitals, libraries, and in some cases schools. It would seem also to have been true in regard to requests for support for the Chavez and Farah movements, since all three politicians reporting these efforts were from states with large Spanish-speaking populations and two of the three were themselves of Spanish-speaking descent. In some other cases the congressman or senator said he had been contacted because of his membership on a particular committee with jurisdiction in the area of Church interest. Of the five congressmen reporting lobbying contact on aid to education, two were members of the Ways and Means Committee, which handled the tax credits bill, and one was a member of the Education and Labor Committee, which controls much education legislation.[74] Another politician stressed his committee membership in reporting that, "only one churchman has contacted me in sixteen years and that was on lowering the postal rate on nonprofit publications. I was on the Post Office Committee and Cardinal Cody called me about that."[75]

Committee membership was stressed, too, by the one interviewee who mentioned contact by the USCC's Government Liaison Office. When discussing Church lobbying, this congressman remarked that he was a member of the Ways and Means Committee and then said, "Dick Kelly of the USCC has been in contact with our office, mostly on mundane matters. There was a pension bill before the Ways and Means Committee, for example, which would have affected pensions for diocesan employees and he wanted something done about it. That's not a moral or a religious issue, of course, but it was something they were interested in."[76]

The congressman who discussed efforts by Catholic groups to

alert him to the effects of high oil prices illustrated the combination of district interest in an issue and committee membership which appeared in the comments on Catholic lobbying made by a number of politicians. "I'm under great pressure," he reported, "by Catholics in my district who are upset about oil. I'm on Ways and Means and so I get a lot of pressure. There's a group in my area called CHOP. It means something like Catholics Opposed to Higher Oil Prices. They have really enlightened me on the problems of the price rises in oil on old age homes and schools."[77]

This same combination of district interest and committee membership acting to focus attention on a particular politician seems to have occurred, too, in another congressman's active role in the tax credits bill. The congressman was a high-ranking member of the House Ways and Means Committee and represented an urban (and Catholic) district to which the bill was important. His legislative aide explained, "The congressman was spurred to work for the bill because he comes from X state where a lot of people send their children to parochial schools. The bill was more than a Catholic versus non-Catholic issue. It was more of a big city versus rural issue because the big cities needed the aid. A proof is the fact that Ribicoff [senator from Connecicut, and a Jew] was a co-sponsor of the bill in the Senate and he is a big city representative. The parochial and public schools were in trouble — the parochial schools are in better shape now than they were expected to be — and people felt the option should remain. The bill was going well, gaining more and more co-sponsors. If the Supreme Court hadn't issued its decision, Ways and Means would have passed it out . . . [The congressman] hasn't completely dropped it yet but he's been saying to the people he talks to on it — Ribicoff and the USCC — present us with something, a way to get around the decision. It's not dead but a lot of momentum has gone out of it, of course."[78]

In discussing lobbying efforts by the Church on issues other than antiabortion and the reaction of Catholic legislators, I found much the same situation Lewis Dexter has described regarding congressional lobbying in general.[79] First, there was a tendency for the politicians interviewed to be rather vague about the names and aims of the Catholic groups writing or coming to see them. Echoing the vagueness found in many politicians' discussions of lobbying groups, one congressman said, "Only one group I ever heard of has been to see me, SOS, or some such. They're all Catholics. At least I think so."[80] Second, political interviewees emphasized the cross-pressures to which they were subject on any issue, the lobbying from both Catholic and non-Catholic groups. "When a Catholic hospital contacts me," said one senator, for example, "there's a Protestant or a public hospital contacting me too."[81] Third, they indicated the extent to which they were protected by their staffs from direct pressure. "Of course I may not know about some contacts," remarked a senator. "There may be contacts I'm not aware of. My staff protects me. *Y* is such a big state that of necessity my staff sees most people."[82] Fourth, the political interviewees seemed more attentive and responsive to Catholic groups representing some part of their constituency than to large national organizations. Only one political leader and one legislative assistant mentioned direct contact by the USCC, for example. When discussing political contacts, senators and representatives tended to cite, instead, organizations and people affiliated with the Church but based in their own districts or states.

Two other facts emerged in regard to lobbying by Catholic groups. Three congressmen with earlier tenure in local and state offices indicated that they had felt more pressure on the local and state levels than they did now that they were serving in the Congress. "When I was on the city council in *Z*, I was approached by the legislative advisor of the *Z* archdiocese on issues. Since I've been in Washington, no, I haven't been approached directly."[83] "On the state scene, yes," said another congressman, "on parochial aid . . . I supported aid mainly to help the governor, but some of my friends suggested I pick my issues elsewhere."[84] Also, in discussing lobbying by Church leaders or organizations, political leaders generally tended to try to strip the effort of any specific Catholic or even religious context. "In my time," said a congressman, "aid to education has been a big issue, but even here I've always thought of the issue on a tax basis, not religious. Why should we pay double taxes? What would happen if all Catholic kids had to go to public school? Maybe all that means is that I'm not a good Catholic."[85] "There is no reason any church can't press for legislation on an economic basis, for example," remarked another congressman. "Pressing for a school lunch program, for example, whether it's for St. Aloysius or P.S. 62, it's school lunch. But no one has the right to pressure Congress to leg-islate on religious belief. I wouldn't stand for that."[86] Although most politicians did view the antiabortion issue as one polarized by religious belief, a few extended this attitude even to that issue, giving examples from their experience to show that, as one said, "the right-to-life movement combines various faiths."[87]

Only two interviewees, one who said he had never been con-tacted by a Church leader or organization and one who said he had been contacted, reacted to the question by expressly stating that they believed such contacts were wrong and should not be undertaken by a religious body. "I think religion and politics are separate and should stay that way," said one.[88] The other said that he believed religion could influence a political leader through the general value orientation his early religious training might have given him but not through Church expression of opin-ions on issues. "I'm against abortion but as a result of my own value orientation, because *I* believe it's wrong, not as a result of any bishops' statement . . . I vote as I think. I don't pay attention to what they say."[89] Three other congressional interviewees, while they did not disapprove of Church lobbying and stated that they had been lobbied by Catholic groups, did add a cautious note re-garding the necessity of keeping religion and politics separate. One remarked, "Here in Congress the separation of church and state is always felt. Members of Congress are scrupulously aware of it . . . [I have been approached] by people as individuals, not by Church groups. Catholics, I think, are very careful about the separation stricture. They're very careful about anything like this."[90] Three of these five men, either strongly disapproving of or cautious in regard to religious intervention in politics, were con-servative Republicans.

More significant, perhaps, than the party split on the issue of religious intervention is the generational split. These disapprov-ing or cautious respondents averaged fifteen years of congres-sional or senatorial tenure and fifty-nine years of age. (The aver-age age of all Catholic congressmen was fifty-two and of all Cath-olic senators, fifty.) Otherwise, lobbying by all religious leaders and organizations, including their own Church, seemed to be ac-cepted by the majority of Catholic politicians as natural and even, by some, as laudatory. This generational split may be based on the greater influence among the older men of traditional

American strictures against breaching the "wall" between church and state, religion and politics. Thus, they would perceive Church lobbying as illegitimate.

Political leaders in general stressed that lobbying efforts on the part of religious organizations were made up of their own constituents, and they seemed to justify Church lobbying on that basis. However, a minority of respondents, five, seemed to have a fairly well developed understanding of a somewhat different lobbying process, a process closer to that envisioned and described by Church leaders. They seemed to see, either in operation already or in formation, a process by which the Church hierarchy, after consultation with experts and with those concerned, expressed opinions on issues, opinions which were shared by a socially aware younger clergy making up part of the politicians' constituencies, who then exerted pressure themselves and mobilized other people to exert pressure on issues. Four of the men mentioning and praising this process were liberal Democrats and one was a moderate Republican. "I think," said one, "that the Church can be present on issues. I think it would be correct to be approached by councils representing your area. In Texas, for example, there is something called the Texas Bishops Commission on the Problems of the Spanish-Speaking. It's made up of priests and agencies and so forth concerned with the Spanish-speaking. I think contact by councils of this kind can be correct. It can have influence on civil rights and other issues. It would not be correct for the archbishop to come and contact the congressman, but a group such as the one I've described could."[91] A senator recognized nationally as a liberal Democratic leader described a similar process, stressing first the Church's greater social consciousness and greater awareness of economic and social issues which led to its support for Cesar Chavez and for the poor, and then saying that the political lobbying he had experienced from Catholic groups had been concerned with "social action."[92]

In six cases, too, congressmen and senators indicated that they thought the Church was not yet active enough or skilled enough in organizing and pressuring on issues. A senator, cited above as one of those with a wide concept of what Church lobbying should and could be, said that he was approached by Church groups "no more than by other social action groups. From time to time the Church does have lobbying activities but in my experience those activities are much less apparent on the Church's part than on the part of many other groups."[93] A congressman who believed firmly that the Church should be more politically involved said, "The hierarchy follows the separation stricture absolutely, especially in regard to candidates. Oh, they're quick on abortion where they feel they have a right and something to say, but they never speak on the responsibility of government, for example. The Catholic Church holds politicians at arms length, at a distance, like people held nuns twenty years ago."[94] Five of these six men who wanted more active involvement by the Church were liberal Democrats and the sixth was a conservative Republican. More important, the generational difference appeared here again. Whereas those disapproving or cautious about Church lobbying averaged fifty-nine years of age and fifteen years of congressional or senatorial tenure, those who believed that Church lobbying on social issues, especially, was not yet organized and active enough averaged forty-seven years of age and five-and-a-half years of tenure.

The effectiveness of the Church in lobbying its Catholic political adherents is difficult to judge on the basis of my evidence. Certainly there is no well-oiled Catholic juggernaut in operation here. No straight, simple lines can be drawn between Church pressure on Catholic legislators and the desired result. As yet there has been no vote on the human life amendment. However, Catholic congressmen and senators did vote the "prolife" way in the Ninety-third Congress on five of six minor measures concerned with abortion, but in most of these cases so did non-Catholic politicians, although not always by as heavy majorities. Still, there seems not to have been a much greater tendency on the part of the right-to-life people to lobby Catholic politicians than to lobby non-Catholics.

Both Church leaders concerned with the school aid issue and a number of congressmen and their assistants seemed to believe that the Church would have won a school aid bill, the second most widely cited instance of Catholic lobbying, if the Supreme Court had not preempted legislative decision. On the evidence of statements by Ways and Means Committee members and their aides, this seems to have been due as much to the fact that the issue was seen as a constituency demand, Catholic or not, as it was to congressional response to the pressure of the USCC or the Catholic Church in an institutional sense.

Interviews seemed to indicate that those who requested support for Chavez and the Farah strikers were not so much concerned with legislative action as with a request for the politician's aid in publicity, statements of support, and so forth. Here again, this lobbying seems to have been concentrated on politicians from states with large Spanish-speaking populations, and their positive response was conditioned in great part by that same factor. Lobbying on institutional interests such as financial aid to Catholic hospitals, libraries, and so on was apparently successful, but politicians also indicated that they considered it of small importance and that their reactions were little different from their reactions to similar requests from Protestant, Jewish, and public institutions. The best that can be said in regard to the legislative effects of Church lobbying is that, although it seems often successful, it seems successful with both Catholics and non-Catholics. Catholic politicians seem to view it as simply a part of the whole schema of lobbying by all kinds of groups. When they accede to it, they and their non-Catholic counterparts do so because they view the contact and interest as emanating from groups of their own constituents rather than from the Catholic Church as a national institution. They seem to respond as politicians to constituents, not as Catholic senators and representatives to their Church.

Religion would not seem, at least on the surface, to have much direct, independent effect on American politics, then, in the sense of its effects as an interest group lobbying for particular benefits and issues. At least this seems to be true as far as the Catholic Church is concerned.

The Rise in Catholic Membership

To discover in what ways, other than lobbying, Catholic beliefs and Catholic organizational structures might affect politics, I asked the Catholic political interviewees if, in their opinions, the presence of increasing numbers of Catholic legislators and their increasing predominance in committee and party leadership made any difference to the functioning of the Congress. Does it matter in any way that Catholics now form the largest single religious body in the Congress? Has it affected general political attitudes, votes, anything at all? Congressmen and senators seemed to find the question unexpected and difficult to answer. They tended to pause and to struggle for answers.

One person never really responded to the question at all. Although he displayed as much knowledge of the Church and its teaching and as much religious influence on his life and career as anyone else interviewed, he tended to have a view of religion so personal and so concerned with inner change that he never really explored its applications to his fellow Catholics in Congress and to the Congress as a whole. Nine political leaders said flatly that, in their opinions, the increase of Catholics in Congress had no effect whatever on Congress because religion does not affect politics. "It doesn't come into play."[95] "Religion has nothing to do with politics. I've never known it to."[96] "Religion does not play any part that I can see in politics or in Congress."[97] "Religion to me is a private matter."[98] One congressman who did think that religion might have some effect still said forthrightly, "I think it's fantastic how *little* influence Catholicism has on the senators and congressmen. This is true of all religions except when there are special conditions — among the Mormons, for example, where the whole state [Utah] is Mormon . . . I think the Catholic factor as far as Catholic politicians are concerned is primarily one of Catholic upbringing. It's an accidental factor."[99]

Of the nine men taking the view that the Catholic adherence of a growing number of its members did not affect Congress in any way, one was a senator and eight were representatives. Three were conservative Republicans, one a conservative southern Democrat, and five, including the senator, were liberal Democrats. They can be distinguished from those of their colleagues who believed that Catholic representation did make a difference by no single characteristic. They were divided almost equally between parties and ideologies. They represented five separate ethnic groups and southern, southwestern, midwestern, New England, and Atlantic Seaboard states. The only difference that can be discerned in this group of men is that three seemed to feel that religion did not but *should* exert influence on politics; the others felt that it did not and should not. Once again the split was largely along generational lines: those in the former category tended to be among the younger and more junior members of the Congress, and those in the latter category were all older, more senior men.

With the exception of these nine men and the one who failed to respond to the question, the other sixteen representatives and senators believed that the increase in numbers and position of Catholics in the Congress did make a difference, did affect the way the Congress functioned. However, their answers were hesitant and tentative and in some ways perhaps partly wishful thinking. Two interviewees illustrated this in their struggle to respond. Both men are known to be personally devout and to work for causes important to their Church, although one was a conservative, politically and theologically, and the other a liberal. Said the liberal in a puzzled tone, "I think it does make a difference that a lot of senators and congressmen are Catholics but I don't know how . . . I think it should but I don't know how."[100] The conservative politician said, "Of necessity [the rise in Catholic membership] has to [affect the Congress], something has to be added by the Catholic background, although I'd have a hard time pinpointing how . . . I'm not sure how religious belief . . . translates itself pragmatically."[101]

The representatives and senators were better at selecting and explaining areas where they felt religion and their own and their colleagues' religious adherence were not important or at describing factors counterbalancing religious adherence than they were at designating areas and situations in which religion was important. A number of interviewees stressed that a politician's district or state might have as much influence on his actions in Congress as his religion, or more. "In general a congressman reflects the area he's from. A Bible Belt congressman is going to reflect the Bible Belt whether he's Catholic or Protestant," said one politician.[102] Another agreed: "The area [the congressman] comes from matters too. For example, members from areas where labor is strong are almost compelled to vote for labor measures and whether they're Catholic or Protestant doesn't matter a bit. The same with a rural district or other members from small towns."[103]

There was also a division of opinion on whether or not religious belief and adherence affected voting on issues. Most interviewees insisted, like one congressman, that, "there is no group voting on issues on the basis of religion."[104] Four stressed strongly that even such issues as school prayer, school aid, and antiabortion were not really Catholic issues and did not result in group voting. "In the past three years the issue which could best be called a religious issue was the prayer amendment—that was as close as we came to having a religious issue and that had as much support from Protestants as from Catholics."[105] A small minority, however, did believe that religious influence had been or was apparent in votes on some, although they all said very few, issues. These included civil rights, aid to parochial schools, and especially antiabortion. Two congressmen mentioned the influence on Catholics of the clergy's stand on civil rights, three mentioned abortion, and one mentioned aid to education. Said a congressman, "Sometimes an issue will have Catholic influence because the issue is important to Catholics. Abortion, though, is the only one I can think of. Maybe some people are going to vote on that issue on religious lines."[106] Another remarked, "Catholics are more inclined to permit the restriction of abortion, more inclined to protest the experimentation on fetuses."[107]

In only two ways did political interviewees indicate any clear evidence of an influence stemming from their Catholicism. Five cited the importance of Catholicism's history in the United States as the religion of the immigrant, the poor, the "outsider." A Mexican-American, an Italian-American, and a Polish-American congressman all expressed similar feelings. Their national-origin and religious identities were closely intertwined, being referred to by these men almost as one throughout their interviews, and this natio-religious background was linked to a particular (and liberal) Catholic approach to political and social issues. A liberal Democrat from a large midwestern city spoke with some bitterness of the resentment he felt directed against him as a Catholic and a Pole in campaigning in the South for John F. Kennedy. "With a name like mine down South they were more struck by that than by anything else. They'd say, 'Hey, you Polish?' Huh! My ancestors have probably been here longer than theirs. If you're Polish, people keep expecting you to wear a miner's helmet."[108] Similarly, the Spanish-speaking congressman associated his people with discrimination and with Catholicism and then linked recent Church efforts to support their labor union struggles with his own efforts to support those struggles and with his political approach. A senator from a New England state explained, "I was born with a silver spoon in my mouth but I remember my father talking about the 'No Irish need apply' signs. I think most Catholics have this kind of memory and it affects how we act in politics. Once, after I spoke on an issue, somebody said, 'Oh, you're just a bleeding heart,' and I said, 'I'd rather be a bleeding heart than a stone wall.' "[109] His statement that "most Catholics have this kind of memory" seemed to have been true for at least a fifth of the politicians interviewed.

The most common answer given by politicians who believed that the rise in Catholic numbers and power in the Congress affected it (cited by eleven, more than half of the interviewees responding positively to this question) was that the influence of religion on politics was exerted mainly through value formation and orientation.[110] Other than the Church's possible influence on votes on a few issues, and the natio-religious historical memory just discussed, this was the only influence factor widely cited or discussed. More agreement existed on the importance of religion in forming character and values and thus one's approach to specific issues and politics in general than on any other circumstance involved with this discussion of religious influence on politics.

"You can't be like Solomon dividing the baby," insisted one congressman. "You can't divide a person's beliefs and his actions. The way you make political judgments is affected by the moral and religious training you received as a child. Catholicism does make a difference — not in the fact that we would pass a law mandating religion, but in our standpoints, our foundations."[111] Additional testimony on this subject came from a non-Catholic legislative assistant who discussed the thought processes her Catholic politician-boss went through in making decisions on the abortion issue.

> The Senator was not raised a Catholic. He became a Catholic when he married a Catholic. He comes from *L* City, which is the only part of the state which is heavily Catholic. The rest of the state is not. On the state level, he plays down his Catholicism, in part because he embraced his religion as a result of his wife. It has molded his personality. He's a Catholic in a non-Catholic place and he's proud to be Catholic. It has, in a way, affected his sense of independence; it makes him different from most of the people around him. On an issue like abortion, for example, he immediately takes a certain stand predicated on his education and constituency. Then you can see him pull back, think, "I'm a Catholic. Should I take a Catholic position?" He regarded abortion at first as an [the aide paused] objective person would react but then he looked at it again as a Catholic would look at it. He hasn't made a judgment because he has two different views on the subject . . . Catholicism at different times is part of his conscious and his subconscious.[112]

Two of the politicians who suggested that the influence of religion on politics was primarily that of value formation gave their opinions in a casual, almost abrupt manner. They did not go on to describe what they meant. These were two of three men who had little interest in the subject of religion. Their answers to this question helped to confirm that opinion and seemed to be given because they expressed the opinions most people would expect. Said one, "We're all influenced to some extent by our background. What we do goes back. Those of us who are religious, of course. Not everyone is."[113] This same man was described by two other interviewees, one a Catholic politician, the other a Church leader, as an example of the Catholic legislator who is probably not much affected or influenced by his religion. "I don't know, for example," said the Church leader, "to what extent [Senator *B*] in his thinking reflects Catholic social values or simply [*D* state]. I've never heard of him having contact with any Church organization or views."[114]

The other nine political leaders who cited the influence of Catholicism in shaping values gave detailed answers and they described different effects and processes. Six looked upon the value formation of Catholicism as that of making one a better, more ethical, more humane human being; the other three felt that Catholicism provided them with guidelines, rules, a set of standards. Illustrating the first point of view, a congressman said, "I think religious, ethical values should perhaps make you less opportunistic, affect the ethical way you look at your job."[115] A senator, after saying, "The ethic in religion is terribly important to me," went on to insist, "Maybe it sounds crazy to talk about spiritual needs but I don't know how to divorce spirit from the structure of society to promote the commonwealth."[116] A representative spoke in this same vein: "I think in general that it's good to have religious training in your background. It is always helpful in legislation to have a sense of compassion, of needs, a tendency to appreciate the needs of others."[117] Two other senators spoke of the role of religion as that of "trying to change the spirit,"[118] and "making you a better person,"[119] giving examples in their interviews to indicate that they meant a humane, tolerant, charitable person concerned with poverty and injustice.

Two interviewees, and probably a third, although his response was somewhat ambiguous, defined the value formation effect of religion as that of providing rules, guidelines, and discipline. Said a senator, "The important thing to me is the conviction that

[Catholicism] is the truth. Once one is convinced of this, one has a set of standards as a guide for one's actions, a measure for your own performance. It's harder to temporize. If one believes in absolute standards, it is harder to excuse straying from them. Religion has an effect on one's performance. Lately I've been thinking of writing an article on the founding of our nation. I've been going back to that, thinking about it, its founding on natural law. I think it's easier for Catholics to accept this now than for others who have perhaps become more relativistic. We are more disciplined."[120] A representative sharing this view said, "Religious training in youth gives you a general value orientation which influences how you think about life and problems . . . [It] gives me a sense of values, a code of conduct. I can situate myself in regard to life as a result of my religious training."[121] A second representative said religion provides one with standpoints and foundations, and then he gave, as an example of that, the Catholic inclination to restrict abortions. By implication value formation in his view, like that of the men quoted above, meant developing a set of unwavering codes and standards.

In their response to the role of religion as a value former, we again find a division between conservative Republicans, who interpreted value formation as the development of rigid standards of conduct, guidelines, and codes, and, except for one moderate Republican, liberal Democrats, who saw it as the development of a more humane, tolerant human being.

Religious Influence in the Lives of Catholic Politicians

Three political leaders gave little or no indication of religious influence of any kind in their personal lives. One indicated nothing beyond the fact of birth by Catholic parents. Two mentioned Catholic education but then disclaimed that it had influenced them. Of these two, one said, "I am Catholic. I was educated by the Jesuits, but it has not affected me politically."[122] His interview as a whole, which was the shortest recorded, indicated that he was little interested in or affected by religion in any way. The other also said he was raised a Catholic and went to Catholic grade school, high school, and college but constantly stressed the lack of influence he felt religion did and should have in politics and said, regarding his own religious adherence and feelings, "I think my family is more religious than I am. My wife, for example, is strong in religion." He, too, showed little interest in the subject of the interview and seemed to answer perfunctorily and with some embarrassment.[123] Two of these three men were of Irish descent and the other of French descent. One was fifty-two years old and the others were in their seventies. One was a conservative Republican, one a conservative Democrat, and the other a liberal Democrat. Aside from these three, all of the other interviewees did show some interest in or influence by religion in their lives.

The Catholic legislative assistant to a Catholic congressman said to me, "Twenty-five percent of the House of Representatives is Catholic now but they're all kinds of Catholic. We use labels now to distinguish one kind of Catholic from another. You know, he's a Berrigan Catholic; he's a Cooke Catholic, or a Paulist Catholic and so forth. And they don't listen willy-nilly to the hierarchy or the USCC. Maybe they tend a little bit to listen to the other people who are the kinds of Catholic they are."[124] Former senator Eugene McCarthy sounded a similar theme when he contrasted himself and Robert Kennedy as Catholics and politicians. "I felt we represented different strains of Catholics. I think 1968 was a transitional campaign." He then went on to say that he tended to agree with David O'Brien's description of Robert Kennedy as the ethnic, urban-machine, group-oriented Catholic and of himself (McCarthy) as the "new-breed" Catholic."[125] "Bobby," McCarthy explained, "I wouldn't say exploited the old group commitments. It was natural for him to operate this way. It may be a difference in backgrounds. We from the Midwest are not conscious of being an oppressed minority. I don't have to recall how my grandmother was maid to the Saltonstalls as Kennedy did."[126] Three other interviewees also stressed the fact that, as one said, "there are all kinds of Catholics."[127]

In examining the extent and kind of religious values that pervaded the interviews with political leaders, nothing showed more clearly than the truth in these remarks. There is indeed no one way to be Catholic; it seems clear that the Catholic Church with its rich and complex history, traditions, and teachings provides a variety of reference points for its adherents. Senators and representatives seemed to have chosen from among several equally genuine, equally valid Catholic traditions and built their lives and thinking around them. There is then no single thrust that

Catholic religious influence takes in the lives and thinking of the Catholic sector of Congress.

The extent of apparent influence varies from the examples of the three men cited above, where it appeared to be negligible, to five other men in whose lives religion seemed, from the interviews, to have extraordinarily large, perhaps even paramount, importance. Even among these men, that influence, although in each case very strong, took different directions and seemed to have resulted in somewhat different effects. In interviews with these five men the religious theme ran throughout. They returned to it again and again in explaining answers to questions on all kinds of topics and they discussed it readily, with no sign of self-consciousness. All showed a much greater and more detailed awareness of what has been happening in the Church in the past fifteen years than was shown in the often sketchy allusions in most of the other interviews. All five, too, showed a conscious and thoughtful relationship between their religious and their political lives.

One was Catholic in the European, Christian Democrat tradition. His Catholicism was displayed especially in learning. He demonstrated far more knowledge of the Church, not just in the present day but in its historical and intellectual changes and contexts, than any other political leader. In his youth he had studied under several of the great Catholic scholars, both European and American, and he had read the others. He was familiar with the papal encyclicals and analyzed the differences in their usages as explanations of and agendas for social change in the labor battles of the 1930s vis-à-vis the peace movement of the 1960s. He discussed knowledgeably the Ecumenical Council reforms in their liturgical and social implications. He was quintessentially the erudite Catholic lay scholar, common to much of Europe but relatively uncommon in American Catholicism.

The second leader, also a senator, displayed unusual religious interest and influence and was what might be called a Council Catholic. He, to a much greater degree than was true of the other political interviewees, resembled the Church leaders interviewed in their constant references to the Council and its reforms and to the theme of Church involvement in the world and its problems, of social consciousness and social concerns. He was obviously a deeply religious man and had no hesitancy in proclaiming and explaining himself as a man to whom religion was of immediate importance. "I believe," he declared, "in Christ as the Son of God . . . I believe Christ was communicating the Word of God that means our salvation . . . I have been exposed to many religions and I believe that God for the Jew is meaningful to him in the Jewish context, but I happen to be a Catholic and so I believe in the truth, the Word of God, as transmitted by the Catholic Church." Yet, again, as I found in interviews with many of the Church leaders, he interpreted the role of religion as that of acting as a force for social and communal humanitarian goals. Again and again in his interview he talked of the Church in terms of increased "social concerns," "working for the poor," "working for social change," developing in its people "greater social consciousness," developing greater "involvement in the world." Asked if he thought there had been changes in the Church in the last ten years, he declared enthusiastically, "There's no question about it . . . There is a much greater social consciousness on the part of the Church now . . . There used to be a gap between the deeds and teaching, before, of a parish priest, for example. Now you find priests and the Church working for the community of God on earth."

He showed greater and more detailed knowledge of the Council and subsequent Church reforms than any of the other political leaders. Yet he never saw the Church as merely a social action movement. The religious and the spiritual element behind the movement was real and important to him. He demonstrated this particularly in delivering what was almost a paean to two values important to many of the Catholics influenced by the Council and subsequent reforms: a sense of humanity and reverence for it and a strong commitment to the development of community.

"We have failed in this country," he began, "in translating economic prosperity into community, into harmony. The only way we can have community is to realize that God is not Mammon. We must not genuflect all day long before Mammon. That's why I say the government can help but it is individuals who will have to make the difference . . . No individual who is hungry or cold can believe in the system that keeps him that way. After we have provided the basic things necessary to life, I believe the work of the government to be over to a large extent. Then it's up to the people themselves to form local ties, communities, to fulfill spiritual needs . . . I don't know how to divorce spirit from the structure of society to promote the commonweal. We have too much emphasized Mammon and not enough emphasized brotherhood."

Later he returned to these same themes by telling me about his bicycling experiences. "What with the energy crisis and all, I've started bicycling into the office and back two days a week. A lot of people are doing it and as we stop for red lights and so forth we start talking. A whole philosophy of fellowship seems to have developed among us. Lots of times you see the same people. While in the steel cocoon of your automobile I find you become aggressive, you try to dominate the other fellow, while bicycling, without the cocoon, is quite different. I think this is just one example of where technology, development, have led us. We have allowed ourselves to become alone, isolated. We are lonely because we have become almost too skillful. We have lost a sense of community, of neighborliness."[128]

The influence of religion in the life of the third man, again a senator, took still another form. Religion for him was highly personal, highly emotional, a continuing search for personal salvation and Christian perfection. Indeed, he attributed his decision to go into politics in the first place to this motive:

Let me begin by saying that I had the conventional education of a Catholic. It was legalistic in the extreme. It didn't show me how to relate myself to my fellowman as part of the Christian attitude. I knew how to take care of my own salvation . . . There was no early prompting to get involved, to fulfill my responsibilities on a broad scale. As I got older, the Christian Family Movement and the *Cursillo* movement had an impact on me.[129] A concern for others grew. But not of ways of displaying this, however. At first I tried to fulfill this growing sense of concern, of involvement, by trying to be a better family man. But I kept thinking about how I might, in a maximum way, be of benefit, be a solver of problems. This might not be the total way I came to politics, but I did see politics as a far more appropriate way to seek greater involvement. Now this is good in a lot of ways. A lot of good stems from that kind of feeling. But it has a negative side. You believe when you get up there you can change things to benefit people. But now that I'm up here, I see basic concerns changing from down there.

Later he spontaneously began to discuss Watergate and again applied his religious framework: a search for perfection and salvation.

> In terms of morality, as far as politics goes, in Watergate we've seen only the tip. And this is the second point I wanted to make . . . There's another level that says this is the way things are, everybody does it, that accepts the way one gets money for campaigns, for example. I truly believe Watergate will be good if it explodes. If it leads us all to say, "I don't give a damn what was the way things were done, how things were done. This is the way we must do things from now on." In Christian teaching the perfect love of God is counterposed to damnation in Hell. We should act out of love of God but if we don't, fear of damnation is there too. We in politics have a double standard. We have high social motives but we are content to play the game. Fear might have the effect of a cleanup of how we get elected, for example. It could do that . . . In the last ten years we've [Catholics] had a higher motive to get involved but as we did that we didn't purify the process. If we apply morality — and the fear of Watergate — perhaps we can do that.[130]

A fourth political interviewee also showed extreme religious influence in his life in this same highly personal form.

Finally, a fifth interviewee exemplified the Jansenist tradition of, especially, the Irish Catholic Church. Religion obviously was central to his life but it was an austere religion. Religion to him meant doctrine, discipline, and a set of rather rigid standards against which he constantly measured himself and others. Religion "has been an influence; the grounding I had from Catholic school and from my family shaped me . . . not in the sense of ceremony or religious position in politics but on basic moral influence." He went on to define politics in moral terms. "I take a moral view towards politics, too. You can't extricate your own moral values from your profession, whatever it is, and sometimes that means the easy way out is not for you." His interview was full of references to religion, always in a sense of moral standards and duties, and he tended constantly to judge others by these moral standards. He opposed, for example, the laxity that he believes has crept into the reforming Catholic Church in the last decade. "I think Catholic schools have changed and they're not doing the job anymore." He indicated a censorious attitude toward many of his Catholic colleagues in the House because they failed, in his opinion, to maintain Catholic doctrines and standards. "I don't know how much [the rise in numbers of Catholic legislators] means because some who call themselves Catholics are the strongest proabortionists in the House. Dent and Obey, for example, getting up on the floor and saying they are against abortion but they didn't think they had the right to impose their views on anyone else!" His interview, like those of the other four men whom I have characterized as greatly influenced by religion, men in whose lives perhaps religion is paramount, was full of references to religion; he returned constantly to the subject throughout the conversation, and always in the austere, disciplined, rigorous Jansenist Catholic terms.[131]

Although these five men showed religious influence operating in their lives to an unusually great extent, all but three of the political leaders inverviewed showed some religious influence. They showed the influence of Catholicism operating in their lives in seven ways, all of them with some political significance, some of them with much. The politicians thus were either intellectuals, Council Catholics, Jansenists, ritualists, personalists, nationality Catholics, or transitional Catholics.[132]

Three of the politicians interviewed were the kind of Catholic epitomized by the unusually religious, erudite senator who was in the European intellectual tradition. Only he could probably be justly termed a true Christian Democrat, but two representatives' interviews reflected strongly the same themes perfected in his. These men declared, unlike him, that religion was not particularly important to them. "Religion doesn't really occupy my conscious mind," said one.[133] Yet these men were unlike the three who showed no evidence of religious influence; those men were uninterested in the whole subject of religion, indeed were uneasy with it, and showed little knowledge of religion. These two representatives were quite different in their reactions. They were two of the men who showed most interest in and ease with the subject. Yet their interest, like the Christian Democratic senator's, was primarily an intellectual interest. They, like him, also displayed detailed knowledge of the Church both historically and in its activities since the Ecumenical Council reforms. Like many European Catholic intellectuals and unlike most Americans, they were perhaps not practicing Catholics, but they had no fear of the

Church and they did have an intense knowledge of it and an intellectual interest in it. One even described himself by saying, "I guess you can say I'm a European Catholic."[134]

Three men were what might be called Council Catholics. The senator already discussed as a Council Catholic and two representatives showed particular concern with and influence by the religious and social changes in the Church occasioned by the Council. Comparison of the views of the men termed Council Catholics shows shared reactions. All indicated strong approval of the Ecumenical Council and its emphasis on greater involvement with the world and its concerns; all strongly approved the American Church's greater participation in social and political concerns, and all tended to discuss religion in terms of its applications to social betterment. The phrases "social consciousness" and "social awareness" recurred throughout their statements on religion and on the Church's role in society.

Three were Jansenists. I have already discussed one of these, a representative, who showed Jansenist influence to an unusual extent, but two others, one a representative and one a senator, showed the same emphasis on Catholicism as a largely puritanical affair of strict codes and rules. All three, two of them strongly, were critical of the Ecumenical Council and its effects, especially what they saw as its tendency to move away from strict rules and discipline. One, for example, said, "One sad thing was that the opening up of the Church came just when youth really needed stern guidance, direction, a stern code to live by. There aren't any rules anymore. When the kids needed a code of living, the Church wasn't there anymore to give it to them . . . There's too much permissiveness."[135] They were critical of many of the Church's efforts toward increased social and political participation. Their discussions of religion were full of references to "discipline," "set of standards," "guides for one's actions," "measure of your own conduct," and so on. All three of these people were conservative Republicans and all three were of Irish descent, making the direction of influence which religion seemed to have taken in their cases perhaps natural enough. The Irish in Ireland and America have generally been considered the proponents of Jansenism in the worldwide Church.[136]

Three of those interviewed, including one senator already quoted at length, demonstrated religious influence in their lives that led them into searches for personal perfection and salvation. They are the personalistic Catholics. For all of them, religion was a deeply felt, intensely private matter, although two, particularly, seemed to believe that private perfection led to larger, more general consequences and, indeed, was probably the only way in which real changes in the world could be made. One said, "I can't think of a better way to say it than Lincoln did when he said, 'Sometimes I've nowhere to go but down on my knees.' " He spoke of religion in terms of prayer and salvation. "I want to feel inspired in Church, awed."[137] The same intensely personal terms were emphasized by another congressman whose interview was replete with references to religion. He made a distinction between Catholics in Congress: "Of course you have Catholics identifying themselves as Catholics and you have *real* Catholics — those who are not practicing their religion in a physical sense, not just in the physical sense, but who carry out their tenets in practice." By "carrying out tenets in practice," his interview showed that he meant not the strict code of conduct of the Jansenist nor the understanding of religion largely as a social movement of the Council Catholics, but rather the practice of personal virtues: "compassion," "spiritual input," following the example of the Founding Fathers who "were so deeply steeped in religion, 'God' in everything they did," "saving your soul" through good works.[138] For all three of these men religion had implications for the larger world, but first and foremost it acted in terms of an intensely felt personal search and relationship. There was an emotional intensity in their interviews found in no others.

Four Catholic politicians demonstrated religious influence as acting upon them in what might be called ritualistic, traditionalist, family-oriented ways. In discussing religion they tended to say such things as, "I guess I am typical of my generation of Catholics . . . I come from a typical Polish Catholic family."[139] They emphasized Catholic school, Catholic family traditions, the importance of mass and confession attendance. They talked of religion almost exclusively in terms of school, family, and ceremonies. When questioned about religion, they tended to revert often to descriptions of childhood memories. Religion seemed to have had little new impact on their adult lives. It remained a matter of memory and continued observances of attitudes and practices inculcated in them as children. Said one, "The old things stay with you. I remember as a little boy going to bed about seven-thirty or eight o'clock and hearing the last streetcar rumble past the house and, hearing that rumble, I'd be scared and wonder if it meant Judgment Day was coming. I can't shake off the rules that were given me when I was young. Some Sundays I'd just like to lie around the pool, but I can't. I can't. I've got to get up and go to mass."[140]

Three representatives reacted to religion almost exclusively through their sense of nationality, or national origin. One was of Italian descent, one of Irish, and the other of Spanish-speaking ancestry. So completely did their ancestral culture and history seem blended with the Catholic religion, forming such an important part of them, that these politicians literally made no distinction between them. Their interviews showed that religion and national origins were of primary importance to them and that they did not separate the two. One interviewee immediately launched into a long description of the Catholic (and Irishman) as "outsider" and of his struggle for acceptance of his religion and national origin. Nearly his entire interview was devoted to this theme, to which he returned again and again.

All three men answered almost every question on religion with references to their national origin. Yet the interviews showed that this did not mean religion was not important to them. They showed a good knowledge of the Church, its beliefs and activities — better and more detailed than that of many other political leaders. To give an example, one spoke approvingly of changes over the last ten years in the Church's concern for social and political issues, especially issues vital to the Spanish-speaking masses, and of the numbers of Spanish-speaking bishops in the Church hierarchy. Asked if he felt the increase in Catholic senators and representatives had made any difference in the Congress, he immediately switched emphasis from religion to national origin, answering, "Yes, it makes a difference in the sense that it makes it possible for people to know the Mexican *sarape*. People in Boston, for example, don't know the Mexican-Americans and their representatives didn't know us . . . Now, because we are here, people are beginning to know about Mexican-Americans."[141] The Italian-American representative answered the question in the same way, leaping from the question of a rise in Catholic representatives and senators to a discussion of the increase in Italian-Americans. Throughout their interviews, these legislators simply fused religion and national origin as their forebears had for centuries.

Three representatives seem best described as transitional Catholics. They were men who retained some of the Jansenist emphasis on religion as restriction, yet also generally approved the Church's emphasis on social and political concerns and were apparently willing to consider a religion more heavily stressing social consciousness as a valid Christian obligation. To a greater degree than the Council Catholics they seemed to have retained pre-Conciliar stresses on absolutes and on discipline, but were not, as the Jansenists seemed to be, locked into this position. They were aware of and approved a more open and activist form of Catholicism. For example, one representative said, "I don't like the new doctrines of the Church—the promiscuity, going to mass on Saturdays, for example. I needed religion as a kid because I needed discipline. I see the changes in my own kids—lack of discipline"; yet he also said he saw and approved some of the changes in Church concerns, such as the increased activism. He could perhaps be open to the changes because he showed that in his own mind he associated this new kind of social and political activism, which he described in approving detail with examples from his district, with the concern he remembered priests showing him and other kids when they were growing up in a Chicago ghetto. "I like the participation of the Church," he declared. 'I remember growing up in the ghetto. The priest used to come to the candy store and round us up and take us to the parish hall to play pool. It helped keep me straight."[142] The other two men I have described as transitional Catholics demonstrated a similar ambiguity and apparent openness to their changing Church.

It is difficult to know why the political leaders making up the various groups selected those particular facets of Catholic tradition or thought on which they based their faith. Presumably there should be patterns—people sharing a religious disposition should have had similar family, schooling, experiential, and generational factors in their backgrounds that account for the way in which religion came to exert influence in their lives. National origin is certainly not the factor. With the exception of the Irish background of the Jansenists, I found no pattern of national origin in any group. The ritualistic group, for example, included legislators of Polish, Irish, and Spanish-speaking descent; the transitionalists included Irish, English, and Polish. Nor does type of education seem the key. Catholic education results in no one "kind" of Catholic. The Council Catholic group included two Yale graduates and a man whose entire education was Catholic. The group showing no religious influence of any kind in their lives included one man whose education was completely secular, one who went to both Catholic and secular institutions of higher education, and one who had been educated by Jesuits through high school with secular education thereafter. Occupation also played no discernible role. Lawyers form part of each group but monopolize none. In only one group does occupation perhaps play a role. Two of the three men described as nationality Catholics, unlike the other political leaders with the same ancestry interviewed (Italian and Spanish-speaking), spent their formative years in work among poor people of their own national origin group — one as a labor leader, one as a social worker. This experience probably strengthened their sense of nationality and helped lead them to closely associate religion and national identity. The third leader in this group grew up in a heavily Irish-American area where memories of discrimination were strong and spent his formative years as the protégé of still older Irish-American politicians who had participated in the struggle to wrest political control from the "Yankees."

There is, however, one interesting tendency to be noted. Age and length of time in Congress seem to correlate with the extent and kind of Catholic influence these men demonstrated. The three men indicating no religious influence in their lives had on the average longer service in Congress than most of the Catholics interviewed. Two of the three were the oldest men interviewed (and among the oldest of the Catholic membership in Congress in general). One of these men had been elected to his post in 1940, the second in 1952. The third was elected in 1960, but even he exceeded in seniority all but seven of the Catholics interviewed. Two of them were in their seventies, nearly twenty years older than the average age of all the Catholics interviewed. The third was younger, fifty-two, the average age of those interviewed. Those politicians making up the transitional and Council Catholics, those open to the greater participation of the Church in political and social concerns, form another generation. These men on the whole were among the youngest members of the Catholic congressional contingent. They ranged in age from thirty-five to fifty-three. Only two of the six were over forty-five. Their average age was forty-four. They also have only recently come to the Congress. One of the six was elected in 1958 and one in 1966. All four of the others were elected after 1970. A Church leader discussing the USCC remarked that "new men are coming here. Men who have themselves been formed by the Council." That seems true of the Congress, too.

When religious influence in the lives of Catholic political leaders is examined, the many rich traditions of the Church among which they chose becomes clear. One can also see the more general influence of the institutional Church and the Catholic community in which the politicians were raised and lived. The experiences through which their Church and community have passed affected Catholic political leaders. For example, despite the fact that they related to different strands of Catholicism, the nationality, transitional, and Council Catholics all reflected the pattern I have shown before. Earlier group experiences with discrimination and poverty wedded to the more recent development of Church emphasis on social concerns resulted in these men's being open to Church participation in social concerns, indeed urging more participation.

The fact is that many strands in the Church's rich web seem to push people in the same direction. The Christian Democratic movement was in a way an earlier Council experience, with the efforts of its founders to bridge the gap between Church and world and to effect a Christian concern for social and political problems.[143] I found these concerns in the political and social attitudes of what I have called the intellectual, or Christian-Democrat politicians, all of whom were extreme liberals. Even in the case of the political leaders I have called personalistic Catholics, two men particularly indicated that meditation on the true meaning of religion and salvation had brought them to an understanding of religion as implying, at least in part, compassion and involvement. There is a common basis of experience in the American Catholic community, a common mirror through which one sees the world reflected. The reflection of renewed Church concerns emphasized in many politicians' interviews, backed by their experience of belonging recently to the poor section of society, may be leading political leaders, regardless of the particular Catholic tradition to which they seem most attuned, to see and emphasize in that tradition the strands which impel concern and involvement. Only those leaders I have turned ritualistic, traditional, family-oriented Catholics and those I have called Jansenists seem immune from this.

Religion seems to come into play in regard to Catholic politicians in three minor ways: election campaigns, possible group voting on a few issues, and lobbying. Its main role, however, seems to lie in value formation. Further, the possible, overt influence of religion on politics seems to be checked by what Truman calls the "rules of the game," societal and congressional strictures opposing it.

While many Catholic representatives and senators insisted that most congressmen are ignorant of and indifferent to one another's religions and that their Catholicism had not affected their political campaigns, I found some indications of a lack of candor here. A few politicians, not in power at the time of the interviews, and all staff people interviewed showed wide acquaintance with the religious backgrounds of the members of Congress. Most political leaders also showed interest in the possible effect of their religion on their elections: some conducted polls to determine constituent response to their Catholicism; they welcomed the support of the Church and of priests in their districts, and so on.

Most congressmen insisted that there was little or no religious bloc voting in the Congress. Several did suggest, however, that Catholic beliefs and Church positions might have been an influence on Catholic members' votes on a few issues, such as civil rights, school prayer, and especially abortion. There has been little research on ethnic (religious, racial, or nationality) bloc voting in the Congress. It may be, however, that, while ethnic bloc voting is rare, certain issues of particular relevance to an ethnic group may catalyze such a vote.[144]

Church lobbying in a direct sense, such as a Church leader or organization approaching a congressman, seemed to be fairly widespread and generally accepted by Catholic politicians as legitimate. While lobbying by Catholic groups appeared often to be successful, Catholic congressmen seemed to regard most of it under the constituent rather than the religious rubric, except, again, abortion lobbying. Most congressmen also reported that direct Church lobbying occurred far more often on institutional than on social justice issues.

Politicians at the same time showed keen awareness of changes in Church attitudes toward and participation in wider social concerns. Whether they approved or disapproved of the changes, four-fifths of the political interviewees indicated an awareness that the Church in the last fifteen years had become much more concerned with social justice issues. In this wider sense, then, Church lobbying seems to be going on, with Church concerns being communicated to politicians indirectly through media reports, bishops' statements, and the changes politicians discern in their own parishes and among Catholic organizations in their districts. A USCC official remarked, "The congressmen and senators you mentioned . . . as Catholics are for the most part liberals. If influential Catholic liberals advocate issues, I think it challenges us to speak out on them, too."[145] I would posit that the reverse is also true and that Church "lobbying" in the wider sense cited above reinforces the particular religious and political values and efforts of many Catholic politicians.

The Catholic congressmen themselves believed that more than in any other way the influence of religion on American politics lies in value formation and orientation. Certainly, a number of senators and representatives demonstrated that Catholicism had entered deeply into their lives and influenced their political views and activities.

With its rich cultural and social as well as religious history, Catholicism provides many different philosophies and traditions to which one can adhere. As examples revealed, the value orientations important in the lives of these politicians stemmed from various of the Catholic traditions. Two themes seemed to dominate: a religious formation that emphasized strict codes of conduct, rules, and guidelines, a rather rigid, puritanical devotion to duty and order; and one which stressed Christian love, compassion, and concern for one's fellowman, especially the poor, the helpless, and the unfortunate. This second theme probably grew out of a combination of American Catholic history as an immigrant, recently poor, and discriminated-against people, and the emphasis on compassion and concern occuring in several Catholic religious traditions.

Finally, the inhibiting influence of American societal norms stressing church-state separation and of congressional norms downplaying representation of any one group and emphasizing the importance of the general or "public" interest was clearly revealed. Norm influence probably strengthened the denial of interest in or knowledge of congressional colleagues' religious affiliations, the insistence on the lack of bloc voting, the tendency to see Catholic lobbying under the constituent-relationship rubric, and the difference in attitudes on these and other points constantly displayed between younger and older Catholic politicians. What may be particularly important here is the attenuation of these strictures among the younger Catholic politicians who have more recently come to the Congress. It is these leaders, scions of an upwardly mobile Catholic people, entering politics in the post-Kennedy, post-Conciliar era, who seemed most at ease with the idea of their public identity as Catholics and urged more, not less, Church political activism.

4

The Catholic People

"THINK ABOUT HOW VILLAGES were laid out," said a Catholic community leader.[1] "The old New England village was strung out along a road, houses one after another, a church, more houses, all side by side in a line. People here are separated out, each facing, not one another, but forward, alone. The Italian or Mexican village, though, has a completely different shape. It takes the form of a circle, the houses forming around a central piazza . . . In Catholicism there has always been the sense of a Catholic community, communalism."[2]

This man, like most of the Catholic community leaders I interviewed, displayed the conviction shared by many Church and political leaders that Catholics still remain a particular group, with their own values and their own attitudes toward life. Survey data both confirm some differences between Catholics and other Americans and illustrate the ways in which especially white Catholics of European descent resemble their northern white Protestant neighbors.[3]

When most Americans talk or write about American Catholics, they generally refer to white Catholics, children of the European immigrants, the Irish-, the Italian-, the Slavic-Americans, and so on.[4] There is a certain justice in this, for white Catholics of European heritage make up the great majority of the American Church. Although there have been slight changes lately, Catholic leadership, both in Congress and in the Church itself, is also made up largely of white Catholics. The American Catholic Church does contain, however, a small number of black Catholics, estimated at 855,000—less than 2 percent of the Catholic population—and a much more significant number of Spanish-speaking people. The Spanish-speaking group makes up 21 to 33 percent of the Church and figures prominently in the thinking of Catholic congressional and Church leaders.[5] For the most part, since this is a study of American Catholicism as a whole, analysis of the Catholic people will concentrate on the majority of that group, the white Catholics of European descent. Although white Catholics trace their ancestry to a large number of European countries, and differences among Catholics of various national origins do exist, the real split within American Catholicism, both in demographics and often in attitude, seems to lie between majority white and minority black and Spanish-speaking Catholics and not between Catholics of different European derivations.[6]

To set the analysis in context, white Catholics will often be compared with their nonsouthern white Protestant neighbors, since these two groups most closely resemble one another: they are both large, politically significant portions of the white population, they inhabit the same parts of the country, and they are fairly similar in socioeconomic status.[7] By nonsouthern I mean all white Protestants living outside the Deep South and the border states. For brevity's sake I shall often refer to them as northern white Protestants.

Demographics

Few white Catholics of European descent live in the American South — only about 10 percent were born and grew up there. White Protestants are far more evenly distributed; nearly 40 percent are native-born southerners. Region makes little difference among white Catholics, but a decided difference among Protestants. Northern and southern white Protestants differ greatly in status and in attitudes, especially concerning civil liberties and race. Southern white Catholics differ only marginally from northern white Catholics in either status or attitudes.

White Catholics also tend to live in about the same kinds of places in the same percentages whether north or south. Although Catholics throughout American history have generally been considered big-city dwellers, Catholics are actually as likely to live in small cities and towns as in big cities. They are slightly more likely than white Protestants to be suburbanites. Catholics are notably absent only on farms. As far as dwelling place goes, perhaps the most significant fact about white Catholics is not that they are large-city dwellers, but that they are the only racial-religious group in America which in large percentages lives in small cities, large cities, and suburbs. Thus, by residence, they have become a kind of middle people. They share the small-town life of many white northern Protestants, the big-city experience of Jews and blacks, and the suburban lifestyle of, especially, white northern Protestants and Jews.

Catholics vary more in political and social attitudes by residential type than they do by region. Suburban Catholics tend to be notably more liberal than Catholics as a whole on civil liberties questions and somewhat more liberal on racial issues and in political ideology. Rural Catholics are more liberal on race than are other Catholics; those living in medium and large cities, presumably nearest blacks, least liberal. White northern Protestants also vary in attitude by residential type. Most important is probably the way in which the large numbers of Protestants living on farms depress general Protestant indices on political ideology and civil liberties (table 4.1).

Ethnicity

Andrew Greeley estimates that about 60 percent of all white Catholics of European descent are now at least third generation Americans.[8] White Catholics, however, are still more likely than white northern Protestants to be foreign-born. Surveys from the 1970s show that 5.4 percent of white Catholics are foreign-born, compared to 2 percent of white northern Protestants.[9] Surveys also show some evidence of a continuing consciousness of national origin. Asked to specify from which country their ancestors came or with which they identified, 83.5 percent of white Catholics give a specific national origin; 81.2 percent of white northern Protestants do.

White Catholics trace their foreign roots to four major countries with very different histories and cultures: Ireland (17.0 percent), Italy (17.0 percent), Germany (13.3 percent), and Poland (8.7 percent). The next largest group of Catholics traces descent to Mexico (6.4 percent). White northern (and southern) Protestants in similar percentages mention only three countries which are much more closely tied in culture and history: Germany, England including Wales, and Ireland. Differences do persist among white Catholics of different national origin. Irish-Ameri-

Table 4.1. Social and political attitudes by type of residence (in percentages).

Type of residence	Support civil liberties	Support improvement for blacks	Liberal in political ideology
WCED[1]			
Open country	68.7	79.2	20.0
Farm	47.8	78.6	26.5
Small city	66.8	75.0	30.0
Medium city	72.5	69.8	29.5
Large city	68.7	68.3	27.9
Suburb	86.6	76.8	30.6
All	67.7	73.3	27.6
WPNS[2]			
Open country	63.7	80.0	33.9
Farm	47.5	75.4	12.1
Small city	66.3	72.5	20.3
Medium city	68.8	79.4	33.0
Large city	70.7	72.0	33.3
Suburb	80.2	72.6	32.5
All	63.2	74.8	24.7

1. WCED: white Catholics of European descent.
2. WPNS: white Protestants, non-South.

cans, followed by German-Americans, enjoy a higher socioeconomic status than do other white Catholics. Italian-Americans show signs of recent strong upward mobility and are beginning to approach Irish and German Catholic levels of educational and economic status. Only Polish-Americans among major white Catholic groups lag behind. The German-Americans are the most rural, least urban of the major white Catholic groups. They and Polish-Americans are the most likely to be religiously devout. Italian-Americans are least religious and show least confidence in the major public and private institutions of the country such as the Supreme Court, the press, and the medical establishment.

Religiosity

It is more difficult to determine religiosity from survey research data than from interviews with Church and congressional leaders. In hour-long personal interviews with these men and women

I could determine what Glock and Stark called the essence and function of religion: what religion is to them, what role it plays in their lives. National surveys seldom ask such open-ended questions as, "What does religion mean to you?" Attempts to determine religiosity through survey research must rest upon what Abramson calls "visible religion," questions dealing with apostasy, conversion, in-group marriages, and church attendance.[10]

The signs of visible religion demonstrate both weaknesses and strengths in the American Catholic Church. Catholics have a somewhat higher apostasy rate than do their white Protestant northern neighbors. Surveys show that 16.1 percent of Americans who were raised as Catholics profess another or no religion when they reach adulthood. Among white nonsoutherners raised as Protestants, 13 percent later choose another or no religion. Catholics, though, make up a great deal of that loss through conversions, more than the loss made up by Protestants. When apostasy and conversion rates are calculated — "leavers" and "joiners" — Catholic and white Protestant northern group strength remains about the same.

Group unity is also affected by the extent of in-group marriage. For a heterogeneous society containing peoples of many different religions, races, and national origins, endogamous or in-group marriage rates in America historically have been high: Catholics generally marry Catholics, Protestants marry Protestants, and Jews marry Jews. In the 1970s three-quarters of all white Catholics are married to spouses of their own faith, although this percentage is still not as high as the percentage of endogamous marriage among white northern Protestants (85.4). When white Catholics and white northern Protestants do marry outside their faiths, they generally tend to marry one another. Eighty percent of white Catholics married to non-Catholics are married to Protestants, only 1.9 percent to Jews. Seventy percent of white Protestants married to non-Protestants are married to Catholics, 2.5 percent to Jews. The rest largely are married to spouses professing no religion.

Younger people today are much more likely to have married outside their faiths than older generations, and the rate is especially high among young Catholics. Young Catholics are two-and-a-half times as likely to have married non-Catholics as are Catholics fifty years of age and older. Thirty-six percent of Catholics eighteen to twenty-nine years old have non-Catholic spouses but only 14.4 percent of Catholics fifty and older. Among white northern Protestants, 24.3 percent aged eighteen to twenty-nine have non-Protestant spouses; 10.6 percent of those fifty and older. The percentage of endogamous marriage among Catholics is still high, but the decline is obvious, especially when measured against the smaller decline evident among white northern Protestants. Somewhat surprising is the fact that the institutional Church has scarcely taken any public note of this rise in outgroup marriage; certainly it has made no public outcry like the public expressions of concern, even anguish, with which some Jewish leaders have responded to similar increases in exogamous marriage among their young people.

Responses to questions concerning religious attendance provide more indication of continued Catholic religious unity and distinct Catholic-Protestant differences. There is no doubt that Catholic devotion, as measured by attendance at the central ritual of the mass, has declined in the last decade. Scholars writing on religion in the 1950s all noted the extraordinarily high rates of churchgoing among Catholics as compared to Protestants and Jews.[11] Weekly mass attendance also held and probably still holds a different value for Catholics than does weekly church or temple attendance for, especially, northern white Protestants or Jews. Weekly mass once was the *sine qua non* of American Catholic religiosity. "Theologically," wrote Harold Abramson, "the Catholic Church is very much concerned with associational involvement, through liturgical requirements of weekly attendance at Mass and other defined standards. These are clearly expressed requirements, especially in contrast to the less formalized expectations of Judaism and Protestantism."[12] By 1974, however, only 53 percent of American Catholics believed that missing weekly mass is "certainly a sin."[13] An Irish-American community leader illustrated this new attitude toward church attendance when he told me, "I consider myself a good Catholic. I don't go every week but I go to mass two or three times a month."[14]

Various scholars and writers have suggested a number of different explanations for the decline. Most have focused on the effect of the Ecumenical Council. The mood engendered among Catholics or the specific reforms emanating from the Council are variously blamed: the emphasis on Christian living rather than on specific, formal obligations; the changes in ritual procedures, especially the change from Latin to the vernacular as the language of the mass. Other commentators have insisted on what Greeley calls the "it-would-have-happened-anyway model." They attribute the decline in Catholic Church attendance in part to the demographic and educational changes which have taken place since World War II, causing, in their view, Catholic acculturation into American society and the collapse of the immigrant subculture. Greeley, after complex analysis of data on Catholics compiled in 1964 and then again ten years later, rejects both the Council and the assimilation explanation. Instead, he insists that statistical analysis demonstrates the decline in mass attendance and in other indicators of religious faithfulness to be the result of disillusionment engendered among American Catholics by Pope Paul's 1969 encyclical maintaining Church condemnation of most forms of birth control.[15]

Whatever the reason, the decline in such signs of religiosity as church attendance is clear. Clear, too, is the fact that despite this decline, white Catholics of European descent still are considerably more apt to be faithful churchgoers than their white Protestant northern neighbors. A comparison of responses regarding churchgoing can be made between two national surveys conducted in 1954 and those of NORC surveys from the mid-1970s.[16] In the 1950s, 81.3 percent of white Catholics reported attending church at least monthly; in the 1970s, only 64.6 percent so report. Regular churchgoing among Catholics declined by about 15 percent over the past twenty years; yet the rate of regular churchgoing, monthly or more, is still 15 percent higher than it is among white northern Protestants. In the 1950s, 54.4 percent of Protestants reported attending church at least monthly; in the 1970s, 49.1 percent do.

Detailed analysis of the 1970s survey results demonstrates that today white Catholics are half as likely as white northern Protestants never to attend church or attend less than once a year (11.2 percent of Catholics versus 21.1 percent of Protestants). They are twice as likely to be assiduous churchgoers, attending services once a week or more (48.2 percent of Catholics as opposed to 24.8 percent of white northern Protestants).

Despite the assertions of some recent commentators that declining church attendance is in part the result of Catholic upward mobility, including educational mobility, church attendance is actually highest among the best educated of white Catholics (table 4.2). White Catholic college graduates are less likely than their less educated brethren and much less likely than white northern Protestant college graduates seldom or never to attend church, although the college-educated are also the most faithful church attenders among white northern Protestants.[17] In fact, regular churchgoing (monthly or more) remains at a very high level among white Catholics at all but the lowest level of education. Only 58.3 percent of Catholics with less than a high school education attend church regularly—a rate, even so, equal to that of white Protestant college graduates. Since it is the college-educated which usually provide a group's leadership, the continued strong adherence of the well-educated among Catholics seems an important indicator of the continued strength and unity of the group.

On the other hand, significant also may be the lower levels of attendance demonstrated by young Catholic adults in comparison with the levels demonstrated by their elders. Some writers believe that the "shake-out" engendered by the events of the last decade has concluded and that a new period of stability and even

Table 4.2. Religious attendance by education (in percentages).

	Attend church		
Education	Never or less than once yearly	Once to several times yearly	Monthly or more
WCED			
College graduates	8.4	20.2	71.4
Some	8.7	24.5	66.8
High school graduates	9.2	23.7	67.1
Less	15.9	25.8	58.3
WPNS			
College graduates	13.9	27.6	58.5
Some	18.3	31.5	50.2
High school graduates	20.7	30.2	49.1
Less than high school	26.3	29.3	44.4

growth in Catholic religiosity may be approaching. They point, for example, to the success of the 1976 Eucharistic Congress in which 1.2 million Catholics participated.[18] Andrew Greeley, also, in his 1974 study of American Catholics, found somewhat mixed results in analyzing current religiosity: a decline in some traditional religious practices, particularly weekly mass attendance and regular confession, but also strong support for liturgical changes, especially the English-language mass, a sharp upsurge in weekly communion reception, and widespread participation in newer forms of religious life—charismatic or pentacostal prayer meetings, religious discussion groups, home liturgies.[19]

Still, the lower attendance of young adults at the central ceremony of the Catholic faith could be important, especially if it presages their life-long behavior and the training of their children, rather than simply evidencing the greater tendency of the young not to be as involved as their elders in all sorts of organized behavior, such as political party organization and voting. As table 4.3 indicates, the rate of regular churchgoing drops more than 20 percentage points between that of Catholics over fifty and Catholics under thirty. Rates of regular churchgoing decline also among young white northern Protestants, but here the decline between young and old is not as sharp.

Table 4.3. Religious attendance by age (in percentages).

	Attend church		
Age	Never or less than once yearly	Once to several times yearly	Monthly or more
WCED			
18-29	11.0	35.8	53.2
30-49	11.2	24.0	64.8
50 and older	11.8	13.0	75.2
WPNS			
18-29	19.3	39.9	40.6[1]
30-49	21.0	29.5	49.1
50 and older	22.1	24.3	53.2

1. Rest, "don't know"/no answer.

Steep as is the decline among Catholics, young Catholics still are much more likely to be regular churchgoers than their Protestant peers. Indeed, their rate of regular churchgoing is as high as that of the oldest and most faithful of white northern Protestants. There is also almost no difference between young and old Catholics in the percentages who never or seldom attend church. Catholics at all age levels adopt this peripheral stance toward church attendance at much lower levels than white northern Protestants.

Attendance is probably a greater cue to Catholic strength and unity than it would be for other religious bodies because of the emphasis placed upon it by the Church and because the parish and the weekly gathering at mass are used by Church leaders as vehicles to reach and influence Catholics on issues with social and political as well as religious implications. Whatever the future may bring, however, there is at present a reasonably large, unified, and fairly strong institutionalized Catholic body, with an educated and devout lay leadership.

Mobility

Both Church and congressional leaders emphasized in their interviews what they felt to have been great Catholic upward mobility in the post-World War II era. Further, they believed that the rise in Catholic educational and occupational status had made Catholics more capable of and more self-confident about participating in the general social and political life of the country. Mobility was frequently mentioned as a factor in greater Catholic activism. Survey data confirm significant educational upward mobility and high income among Catholics. Data also indicate a rather uneven pattern of occupational upward mobility.

White Catholics of European descent have moved from a position in the 1950s in which more than half had less than a high school education to one in the 1970s in which three-quarters are at least high school graduates. Catholic college graduates have more than doubled in the past twenty years, from 6.5 to 14.3 percent. At the community and junior college level, Catholics also doubled their percentages. The percentage of Catholics who did not complete high school was halved, from 55.8 percent in the 1950s to 25.2 percent in the 1970s. Northern white Protestants still have a slightly higher percentage of college graduates (17.4) and a slightly lower percentage of high school dropouts (23.9).

Although these levels of achievement have not yet been attained by Catholics, their upward mobility rate in education has been somewhat greater.

A comparison of educational levels of white Catholics and white northern Protestants for the same age groups illustrates this (table 4.4). There are twice as many Catholic college graduates among the youngest age group (eighteen-to-twenty-nine) as among Catholics fifty and older, and a third as many high school dropouts. The youngest group of Catholics has a lower percentage of high school dropouts than the youngest group of Protestants, and the gap between the youngest group of Catholics and white Protestants in percentages of college and post-college graduates narrows to 2.5 percent, as compared to the 4.0 percent gap in such graduates between Catholics and Protestants over fifty.

Of possible future significance also in these education figures is the fact that the area in which Catholic gains are especially large are at the "some college" level. More than a quarter of all young Catholics list "some college." If all young Catholics and Protestants in this category were to complete their undergraduate education, the percentage of young Catholics with college degrees would surpass that of young Protestants. If, however, they stop with associate or some kind of technical training or degree, they will probably add to the already high Catholic white-collar clerical and craftsmen occupational percentages.

Greeley theorizes that it is the immigrant factor which inhib-

Table 4.4. Education by age (in percentages).

Age	Post-Graduates	College graduates	Some college	High school graduates	Less than high school
WCED					
18-29	5.1	10.2	28.5	41.7	14.5
30-49	4.3	11.1	14.9	46.0	23.7
50 and older	2.5	5.0	12.8	30.3	49.4
WPNS					
18-29	4.9	12.9	21.2	44.4	16.6
30-49	7.6	8.7	17.5	41.8	24.4
50 and older	4.7	6.8	14.1	30.4	44.0

ited earlier Catholic socioeconomic mobility, and survey figures show that this may well be true. It is the oldest Catholic generation, the one most likely to contain significant percentages of immigrants and children of immigrants, which has extremely low rates of educational achievement. The rate begins to change dramatically with the middle-aged group of Catholics, those thirty to forty-nine years old. However, the same phenomenon is apparent, although to a smaller extent, among white Protestants as well. The fact that older generations of Protestants were heavily rural people may have acted to inhibit their educational advance as the immigrant factor did Catholics'. The great change apparent in the middle generation, especially among Catholics, may also be the result of the postwar G. I. Bill, which gave educational opportunities to many people who would otherwise never have had them. Whatever the reason, the fact is that Catholic mobility in education has been real and has been part of a general upward mobility in education experienced by white groups in the postwar period. Figures for Jews and southern whites also indicate upward mobility.

A somewhat similar process has occurred among white Catholics and white northern Protestants as far as occupational mobility is concerned (table 4.5). If farming and service jobs, as largely

Table 4.5. Occupations in the 1950s and 1970s by race and religion (in percentages).

Occupation	WCED 1950s	WCED 1970s	WPNS 1950s	WPNS 1970s
White collar (all)	*44.5*	*54.1*	*44.0*	*53.0*
Professional/technical	11.3	14.7	13.0	15.0
Managerial	15.3	8.1	12.7	11.9
Sales/clerical	17.9	31.3	18.3	26.1
Blue collar (all)	*55.5*	*45.9*	*56.0*	*47.0*
Skilled craftsmen/operatives	37.2	27.1	34.2	24.2
Unskilled manual labor/transport	4.5	5.2	4.3	5.4
Farming	6.5	1.3	11.7	3.4
Service	7.3	12.3	5.8	14.0

manual, are considered as blue-collar work along with craftsmen and factory workers, twenty years ago both white Catholics and white northern Protestants were concentrated at this manual end of the labor spectrum in nearly equal percentages (55.5 percent of white Catholics and 56.0 percent of white northern Protestants). In the 1970s the percentages in manual work for both dropped about 10 percent. The percentage in white collar jobs rose about 10 percent for both. These figures, however, bear closer examination, especially for white Catholics.

White Catholics do show upward mobility in the increased numbers at which they are now engaged at the highest levels of white-collar work, the professional and technical (judges, doctors, teachers, scientists, engineers, and so forth). Indeed, their rate of increase between 1950 and 1970 at this level is one-and-a-half times that of white Protestants. However, in the same twenty-year period the percentage of white Catholics in the next highest category of white-collar work, the managerial, has declined substantially. Harold Abramson, noting the Catholic decline at this level ten years ago, suggested that it was the result of the gradual demise of the mom-and-pop grocery stores and local ice cream parlors, the kinds of businesses typical of the immigrant Catholic (and Jewish) generations.[20] The managerial occupational category includes these small businessmen as well as managers and administrators of public and private enterprises, bank officers, construction inspectors, school administrators, assessors, and so forth. Protestant decline has been slight, indicating that if Abramson's theory is correct, Protestants at this level were and are administrators and managers of enterprises and not small-business owners. Common social science practice is to divide white-collar categories into two groups, which are regarded as requiring very different degrees of training, thinking, and independent judgment: the higher, professional/technical/managerial, and the lower, sales/clerical. Divided this way, white Catholic percentages at the higher level show a slight decline in the last twenty years (from 26.6 percent to 22.8 percent) while white Protestant percentages show a very slight increase. Although there has been a growth in overall percentages of Catholics in white-collar work, much of this growth has occurred at the lower level of white-collar work, the sales and clerical jobs, secretaries, insurance agents, sales clerks, bookkeepers, bank tellers, postal clerks, and so forth. White-collar growth for Protestants has been concentrated here, too, but not to as great an extent.

Examination of blue-collar workers shows that Catholics, never engaged in large percentages as farmers in America, have nearly disappeared from the farms in the 1970s. Their decline has been even sharper than among Protestants. Skilled craftsmen and factory workers among both groups have also declined by about 10 percent. In the last twenty years, after sales and clerical jobs, the occupation in which Catholic percentages have grown most has been service—bartenders, waiters, dental assistants, practical nurses, airline stewardesses, janitors, barbers, and so forth. Growth here has occurred among white Protestants as well.

Thus, upward mobility in occupation is not as clear for Catholics as is educational mobility. There are signs of positive mobility: the increased percentages of professional and technical workers, the overall increase in white-collar work. But there are counterbalancing factors: the decline in private enterpreneurs, the fact that growth has largely been in the lower categories of white-collar work. The importance of the service increase is difficult to determine, given the wide variety of jobs included in this category, of training required, and of status accorded them.

On the other hand, white Catholic economic well-being is clear; only Jews among white groups do better than they economically. White Catholics surpass northern white Protestants, who have a third again as large a percentage of families living below the poverty level, that is, with incomes of less than $5,000 a year (21.8 percent of Protestants versus 14.0 percent of Catholics). A quarter of all white Catholic families (25.5 percent) but a fifth of white northern Protestant families (19.3 percent) report upper level incomes of $15,000 to $25,000 yearly. Catholic families are also slightly more likely than Protestants to have yearly incomes above $25,000: 7.7 percent versus 6.4 percent. However, northern white Protestant family income may be depressed by the larger numbers living in rural areas.[21]

The real significance to Catholics individually and as a group in educational and occupational upward mobility and financial status may lie in their own sense of personal, familial change over recent generations. Church and congressional leaders may have shown the exuberance they did in discussing mobility because they had seen it in their own families and friends, and this is probably an experience shared by many white Catholics. Widespread personal, individual change is evident in surveys. Detailed analysis of respondents in the 1970s surveys demonstrates that 64.3 of white Catholics have a higher level of education than did their fathers; 7.4 percent have less education than their fathers. Half of the Catholics (50.2 percent) holding white-collar jobs had fathers holding craft, factory, or unskilled manual labor jobs. The upward mobility rates of children over fathers are higher among white Catholics than among white northern Protestants, 58.9 percent of whom had higher, 10.2 percent lower, educational levels than did their fathers. Among Protestant white-collar workers, 38.9 had blue-collar fathers.

Of course these are simple measures of mobility rates and not of overall levels of achievement. White Protestants rates are lower in part because educational and occupational rise had already been experienced by the earlier generation. Still, these results seem important because a rise in educational and occupational levels affects family and group pride and sense of accomplishment and progress. The fact that nearly two-thirds of white Catholics have educations beyond that of their fathers probably affects group feeling about the accomplishments of the group as a whole, just as the fact that more than 60 percent of all Spanish-speaking people have not advanced beyond their fathers' education level probably affects individual and group feeling within that minority.

Worrisome factors intrude into this picture, however. Occupational mobility is not as clear as educational mobility. Substantial percentages of white Catholics remain in low-status white-collar work and in what are generally considered low-status service jobs, as well as in ordinary blue-collar work. Stereotyping American Catholics as a whole as nearly synonymous with working class, as many journalists and, until recently, many scholars tended to do, is obviously wrong, but Church and congressional leaders' euphoria over upward mobility may also be overdone. They, after all, are among those many Catholics who have been upwardly mobile. A more realistic picture may have been presented by Catholic survey respondents. When asked to which social class they felt they belonged, equal percentages of white Catholics, 42.1, said working and middle class (2.5 percent said lower, 1.2 percent, upper, and 12.1 percent either did not know or refused to answer).

The Catholic community leaders I interviewed pointedly raised the issue of the still large white Catholic working class and its problems. Although these men and women were not racists and indeed acted with blacks on community problems in many cases, five of the nine contrasted Church concern for minority poor and what they saw as its neglect of white Catholic workers and their families. The most vehement said, "Those in social-issue-taking positions in the Church have absorbed the liberal-WASP-Jewish position, do-gooding for minority groups . . . There's nothing there for Catholic ethnics [the working class]. It's the Irish Church wanting to be like WASPs. The ethnics in the Church have to fend for themselves."[22]

Mobility is one of the most difficult of all questions concerning white Catholics. Certainly Catholics have risen out of immigrant ghettos to take their place in significant numbers among the kind of educated, professional, affluent people who usually provide political leadership and take active part in political affairs. They would seem to have acquired the socioeconomic status in society Truman regards as an important factor in a group's political influence. However, upward mobility, especially occupational mobility, has bypassed many white Catholics, providing a possible factor for disunity within the group and between these Catholics and their Church and, perhaps, political leadership.

Political Partisanship and Ideology

Few subjects have so concerned political scientists recently as the decrease in voting and in political partisanship. The figures illustrating both are clear. In 1960, 64 percent of eligible voters went to the polls; by 1976, slightly less than 54 percent voted. In 1956, three-quarters of all Americans interviewed in a national survey gave a specific party preference; in the 1970s, only about two-thirds did.

A number of reasons have been suggested for these twin declines. Some political scientists attribute the rise in independent status to the fact that during the 1960s the United States saw the confluence of a rising level of education among Americans and of the emergence of a series of critical issues with immediate impact on them, civil rights and the Vietnam war in particular. The result, they believe, was an increased tendency not to vote for leaders because of traditional party allegiances but on the basis of their specific policies.[23] Americans began to develop concern for specific issues rather than for party politics and thus moved away from party allegiance.

Other political scientists attribute the change to alienation. The Vietnam war, Watergate, and unresponsiveness from government all helped to alienate Americans from their traditional party systems, the electoral process, and from government and politics in general.[24] Finally, large numbers of new voters have entered the political system in the last ten years as a result of the extension of voting rights to minorities and the lowering of the voting eligibility age to eighteen. Scholars point out that new voters traditionally go through a period of socialization before they begin to assume a party identification or the habit of regular voting.[25]

Both scholars and politicians have given much attention to the behavior of Catholics in regard to independence and voting. Catholics traditionally have served as one of the major bulwarks of the Democratic Party. As Robert Axelrod comments, "Catholics have formed a large and reliable segment of the Democratic coalition. They have always provided more than a third of the Democratic votes . . . even though they are only a quarter of the population."[26]

Many writers have contended that Catholic loyalty to the Democratic Party began to recede in the 1960s and early 1970s. Richard Krickus insists that acquiring white ethnic, heavily Catholic support was a key element in the Nixon strategy to form a new Republican majority. Writes Krickus, "Like Wallace, Agnew recognized that while economic problems were still of great moment to these traditional Democratic voters . . . they were also concerned about rapid social change and the emergence of people in the Democratic Party who reviled their values, symbols and patriotism."[27]

Surveys from the 1970s do show an increase in Catholics preferring to call themselves independents rather than Democrats and Republicans. They also show, however, a continued strong Catholic allegiance to the Democrats and they show party loyalties in general to be greatest among the most devout group of Catholics, those attending church at least monthly.

The percentage of Catholics claiming to be political independents has increased over the past twenty years slightly more than the percentage of independents among white northern Protestants. Among Catholics, however, the plurality of Democratic identifiers over Republican has remained about the same for the last twenty years; that is, about 30 percent more Catholics did and still do prefer the Democratic to the Republican Party.

Surveys in the 1970s asked respondents claiming independence to which of the major parties they felt closer. When this second question is posed, white Catholic independents are far more likely than Protestants to express preference for the Democrats. Almost twice as many Catholic independents express support for the Democrats as for the Republicans, while Protestant independents split closely between the two parties. The traditional party allegiance apparently still has considerable strength even among Catholics who call themselves independents.

The generally strong, continuing allegiance to the Democrats holds true when political partisanship is analyzed by age group. Young Catholics are more likely than their seniors to say they are independents, but the percentages of young Catholics claiming independence are not as high as those of young northern white Protestants. Young Catholics with party preferences are nearly three times as likely to call themselves Democrats as Republicans, while young Protestants who express a party preference tend to divide evenly between the two parties. The plurality of Democrats to Republicans at every age level among Catholics, in fact, is almost exactly the same—about three to one Democratic over Republican (table 4.6).

Although some Church leaders believed Catholics were disappointed and angered because of decisions which seem to disregard their values, there is no evidence that this, if true, has affected political party allegiance, organization, and voting. Presumably those Catholics most closely tied to the institutional Church should feel most threatened by governmental actions such as the decisions on abortion and parochial school aid. Yet it is the peripheral Catholic, the person never attending church or attending less than once a year, who tends to remain outside the traditional party and electoral systems. The regular churchgoer among Catholics is much less likely to be independent, is more tied in to the traditional party and political organizations, and more likely to be a voter. Survey analysis demonstrates this clearly. Thirty-four percent of Catholics attending church monthly or more call themselves political independents, as compared with 42

Table 4.6. Political preference by age (in percentages).

Age	Democrats	Independents	Republicans
WCED			
18-29	40.2	45.3	14.0[1]
30-49	44.4	38.4	15.7
50 and older	54.1	26.7	18.5
WPNS			
18-29	23.5	51.1	24.2
30-49	33.0	34.5	31.3
50 and older	29.4	26.7	47.4

1. Columns do not add up to 100% because of a small minority of respondents who refused to answer the question or gave other party or "don't know" responses.

percent of peripheral Catholics. More than twice as many peripheral as fervent Catholics failed to cast a vote for President in 1972 (37 versus 17.9 percent). Almost five times as many fervent as peripheral Catholics belong to political clubs (5.4 percent versus 1.2 percent). The difference in political and electoral participation is actually greater between peripheral and fervent Catholics than between perhipheral and fervent white northern Protestants.

Surveys have questioned people about their political ideology as well as their party preferences. Respondents were asked if their political views might be considered extremely liberal, liberal, slightly liberal, middle-of-the-road, slightly conservative, conservative, or extremely conservative. Few white Catholics or white northern Protestants classify themselves at either extreme; both white Catholics of European descent and white northern Protestants call themselves middle-of-the-road in exactly the same (and very high) percentages, 43.3. Catholics who chose the left or the right, that is, those who did not say they were middle-of-the-road, tend to split almost evenly between calling themselves conservative and calling themselves liberal.[28] Protestants are more inclined to call themselves conservative (table 4.7).

Political ideology examined by age group shows a rather surprising result. Catholics and Protestants in their middle years, the

Table 4.7. Political ideology by race and religion (in percentages).

Ideology	WCED	WPNS
Detailed		
Extremely liberal	1.1	1.3
Liberal	13.7	9.6
Slightly liberal	12.8	13.8
Middle-of-the-road	43.3	43.3
Slightly conservative	15.4	16.8
Conservative	9.8	12.3
Extremely conservative	1.7[1]	2.9[1]
Summary		
Liberal	27.6	24.7
Middle-of-the-road	43.3	43.3
Conservative	26.9[1]	32.0[1]

1. Rest, "don't know"/no answer.

thirty-to-forty-nine-year-olds, are nearly identical in political philosophy. However, young Catholics, eighteen to twenty-nine, and older Catholics over fifty are both more likely to be liberal and less likely to be conservative than their white northern Protestant age peers. Older Catholics in particular are much less likely to call themselves conservative than older Protestants (table 4.8).

Thus, in regard to political ideology, there may be an important phenomenon among Catholics: the higher rate of liberalism and lower rate of conservatism found in both the oldest and youngest Catholics may be an example of the New Deal, working-class liberalism of Catholics over fifty united with the new liberalism of the young, highly educated Catholic. Among white northern Protestants, where neither the Democratic, New Deal, nor liberal working-class traditions are as strong, there seems to be no such conjuncture. Instead, in this group there is a strong liberalism among the young but a relatively high rate of conservatism among the old.

Regular churchgoing correlates with a conservative political philosophy among both white Catholics and white northern Protestants (table 4.9). Fervent churchgoing Catholics, those attending once a month or more, are more conservative politically than

Table 4.8. Political ideology by age (in percentages).

Age[1]	Liberal	Middle-of-the-road	Conservative
WCED			
18-29	43.1	41.4	15.5
30-49	22.1	41.3	36.6
50 and older	22.3	49.3	28.4
WPNS			
18-29	39.2	41.2	19.6
30-49	22.1	40.6	37.3
50 and older	18.0	44.4	37.6

1. Of all WCED, those 18-29 make up 27.8% of the group; 30-49; 36.6%; 50 and older, 35.6%. Of all WPNS, those 18-29 make up 21.2% of the group; 30-49, 35.4%; 50 and older, 43.4%. The liberalism of young Catholics, therefore, assumes increased importance for they make up such a large percentage of the total Catholic group (as compared with young Protestants within the Protestant group). For the same reason, the conservatism of older Protestants assumes increased importance.

Table 4.9. Political ideology by religiosity (in percentages).

Religiosity	Liberal	Middle-of-the-road	Conservative
WCED			
Peripheral[1]	20.5	56.4	23.1
Occasional[2]	38.3	44.8	16.9
Fervent[3]	25.8	41.7	32.5
WPNS			
Peripheral	27.0	47.5	25.5
Occasional	28.7	38.8	32.6
Fervent	20.9	39.6	39.6

1. Never attend church services or attend less than once a year.
2. Attend church services once to several times yearly.
3. Attend church services monthly or more.

less faithful groups of Catholics, but they are less conservative than fervent Protestants. Churchgoing and political philosophy correlate in a rather peculiar way among Catholics. Among white northern Protestants conservative percentages increase continually as one moves from those never attending church, to occasional attenders, to the fervent, monthly-or-more attenders. Among Catholics there is a break in the progression: occasional church attenders—those attending church once to several times yearly—are by considerable percentages the least conservative and most liberal of all white Catholics.

Church leaders did not discuss political parties or espouse a particular party, but many of the positions they took on issues were more in accord with Democratic than Republican party positions. Among Catholics in the Ninety-third Congress there were more than twice as many Democrats as Republicans. One could say, therefore, that there is both an implicit and explicit Democratic tendency among much of the Catholic leadership. This does not seem to be out of tune with tendencies among the Catholic people. Although the percentages preferring partisan independence to partisan politics have grown among them, as they have among all whites, white Catholics of European descent still demonstrate a strong preference for the Democratic Party. The ratio of Democrats to Republicans even among young Catholics is little different than that of their fathers and grandfathers.

More of a disunity between Church leaders and people appears in the area of political ideology. Certainly the interviews of most Church leaders indicated generally liberal political philosophies. If asked the same question regarding political ideology posed to survey respondents, most Church leaders would surely have called themselves liberals. White Catholics called themselves conservatives less often and liberals more often than white northern Protestants. However, there is a definite ideological split among the Catholic people. Church leaders espousing a liberal philosophy may be encouraged by the fact that the strong rates of liberalism and low rates of conservatism among the youngest group of Catholics conjoin with those of the oldest in a way not true of Protestants. However, they face a particular problem in that it is precisely the most faithful of churchgoers who are the most conservative of white Catholics.

While it is interesting to note Catholic political ideology and the ideological split in the Catholic world, it must be pointed out that these are merely self-imposed political labels. One of the persistent problems of political science is the great difficulty of explaining how political ideology translates into positions on concrete political issues. A plurality of white Catholics called themselves middle-of-the-road, with a little over a quarter each calling themselves conservatives or liberals. Confronted with a series of economic, civil liberties, and racial policy questions, a large majority proved liberal on civil liberties and a majority liberal on most economic and racial questions, as the following analyses will show.

Government Activism and National Problems

Writers on religion during the 1950s generally described Catholics as economic liberals, supportive of New Deal measures and of a large role for government in social and economic policy. However, more recent commentators have suggested that Catholics have become more conservative, more alienated from and distrustful of big government as they have become more middle class, more suburban, and perhaps more resentful of what they may see as the unequal distribution of benefits from government programs of the 1960s.[29]

Congressional and Church leaders regarded Catholic reactions to politics in a very different way. Political leaders particularly believed that the recent historical experience of Catholics as a largely poor, immigrant group, accustomed to look to government for aid, still affected their view of the role of government in national life. A congressman remarked, "Catholics are Democrats because they are more government-oriented . . . They were the last ones off the boat so they turn more toward government."[30] Both Church and political leaders insisted that increased levels of education and higher socioeconomic status among Catholics had not encouraged alienation but greater government and political interest and activity. Catholic community leaders agreed with these assessments, adding the important point that there still persists in the United States a considerable number of white Catholics who badly need government aid programs. Said the woman director of an Italian-American organization, "Do you know our figures show us Italians are third in New York City in drug addiction, second in high school dropouts?"[31]

There seems to be much truth in Catholic leadership views.

Surveys in the 1970s show very high levels of support among white Catholics of European descent for active government intervention to solve national problems. The pattern of Catholic support is consistent, demonstrated at every age level and at every degree of religious fervor.[32] Catholics may now be more middle class than they were twenty years ago but they seem to have maintained their position as economic liberals. Certainly they are more inclined toward this position than white northern Protestants.

Surveys asked respondents if they felt that we were spending too little, too much, or about the right amount of money on a whole series of national problems: health care, the environment, the problems of big cities, rising crime, drug addiction, education, the condition of blacks, defense, welfare, and others. White Catholics of European descent in every case are more inclined than white northern Protestants to think present government spending levels to solve problems are too low and to want more, not less, government action. Catholics are particularly more likely than Protestants to want more money spent on what might be called general economic issues (health, education, the environment), issues which affect the American population in general and their own group and which differ little with what have been considered the traditional issues of economic liberalism. Three-fifths of all white Catholics think too little is being done by government on these issues. Large numbers of both Catholics and Protestants think more should be done in regard to law and order issues and few think more should be done about defense. Differences between white Catholics and white northern Protestants are least on the issue of minority welfare, programs generally perceived as affecting only certain portions of the population (table 4.10).

Both white Catholics and white northern Protestants perceive the same five problems as most in need of government solution: crime, health care, drug addiction, the environment, and big city problems. In every case higher percentages of white Catholics than of white northern Protestants think more government action is needed. Differences are small between Catholics and Protestants in regard to halting crime and solving the problems of drug addiction: 72.1 percent of white Catholics and 70.4 percent of Protestants want more action on halting crime; 63.6 percent of Catholics and 63.3 percent of Protestants want more done about

Table 4.10. Attitudes toward government spending by race and religion (in percentages).

Issues	WCED		WPNS	
	Too little spending	Too much spending	Too little spending	Too much spending[1]
General welfare[2]	60.7	7.0	53.3	10.1
Minority welfare[3]	21.8	39.9	20.5	39.9
Law and order	67.9	4.6	65.8	6.2
Armaments and defense	15.5	37.9	13.5	34.2

1. Respondents were given three choices: too little spending, too much, and about right. The "about right" responses have been eliminated from this chart. Categories therefore do not add up to 100%.

2. Includes: health, education, the environment.

3. Improving the condition of blacks, welfare.

drug addiction. Much larger percentages of white Catholics than of white northern Protestants think more should be done about health care (67.5 percent of Catholics verus 60 percent of Protestants), the environment (65 percent of Catholics versus 57 percent of Protestants), and the problems of big cities (59.1 percent of Catholics versus 51.1 percent of Protestants). Nearly half of all white Catholics, but considerably fewer white northern Protestants, also believe more money should be spent on education.

Attitudes toward government spending to solve problems show that white Catholics at every age level are more inclined than white northern Protestants to want increased spending. The seriousness with which Catholics and Protestants view specific problems reveals distinct differences between the two religious groups, especially among the middle and older Catholic and Protestant generations. The youngest generation of Catholics and Protestants see the same six problems as so important they require even greater levels of government spending, and they assign these problems virtually the same priority. In every case but one, however (solving the problem of drug addiction), larger percentages of young Catholics than of young Protestants want increased action. The differences are particularly striking in regard to solving the problems of big cities, of crime, and of education.

WCED ages 18-29

Environment	80.5%
Big cities	70.5
Crime	67.6
Health care	66.5
Drugs	59.3
Education	58.9

WPNS ages 18-29

Environment	78.0%
Big cities	64.8
Crime	62.4
Health care	64.8
Drugs	60.3
Education	51.9

Problems listed are those on which 50 percent or more of respondents in the groups favored increased government action.

Among the two older groups, white Catholics tend to see a larger number of problems as serious enough to warrant more government action than do Protestants in the same age groups. Both Catholics and Protestants in their middle years believe crime, health, drug addiction, and the environment to warrant government action, and Catholics, but not Protestants, want government to do more about big cities and education.

WCED ages 30-49

Crime	70.6%
Health care	70.2
Drugs	67.7
Environment	63.8
Big cities	54.5
Education	50.9

WPNS ages 30-49

Crime	68.8%
Health care	61.0
Drugs	65.6
Environment	60.8

Protestants fifty and older view only three problems as serious enough to warrant more action — crime, drugs, and health. Older Catholics would add big cities and the environment.

WCED 50 and older

Crime	77.6%
Health care	65.0
Drugs	63.5
Big cities	54.0
Environment	53.7

WPNS 50 and older

Crime	70.9%
Health care	57.1
Drugs	62.6

Even in cases where middle and older generations of Catholics and Protestants name the same problems as important, larger percentages of Catholics than Protestants want more government action. Thus, in all age groups Catholics consistently support government action in problem solving to a greater extent than their white northern Protestant neighbors.

Peripheral Catholics, who are the most marginal of the Catholic group in terms of political party and electoral systems, are overall more supportive of government spending to relieve problems than are churchgoing Catholics. Still, white Catholics of European descent at every degree of religiosity are more supportive of government spending than their northern Protestant counterparts. On the basis of religious attendance, Catholics tend to support government action in greater percentages and in regard to more problems than white Protestants in all but one instance: Protestants who are only occasional churchgoers support spending to control drug addiction to a greater degree than occasional Catholics. Catholics of whatever religious fervor regard the same five problems as important enough to warrant more government effort: crime, health, the environment, the problems of big cities, and drugs; a majority of occasional Catholics would add education to the list.

WCED peripheral		*WCED occasional*		*WCED fervent*	
Crime	74.6%	Health care	73.0%	Crime	71.9%
Health care	68.9	Environment	72.9	Drugs	65.0
Environment	67.0	Crime	71.3	Health care	64.9
Big cities	63.9	Drugs	60.4	Environment	61.3
Drugs	62.6	Big cities	60.3	Big cities	57.6
		Education	56.7		

WPNS peripheral		*WPNS occasional*		*WPNS fervent*	
Crime	66.7	Health care	60.0%	Crime	69.9%
Health care	68.0	Environment	60.6	Drugs	64.1
Environment	56.8	Crime	67.0	Health care	58.2
Big cities	55.0	Drugs	64.5	Environment	54.8
Drugs	58.7	Big cities	54.5		

Attitudes toward national problems on the part of the Catholic Church and congressional leadership cannot be fully compared with those of the Catholic people. Church and congressional leaders talked in interviews about the problems they individually saw as most important. Survey respondents were asked their reactions to a specific list of problems prepared by the surveyers. Some comparisons can be made, however, in regard to general attitudes toward government intervention in problem solving and to priorities given certain problems considered by both the leadership and the people.

Certainly Church and congressional leaders seem to be correct in their belief that Catholics generally want action from government in regard to national problems, and that they have a politically activist position on issues. Catholics show little tendency to feel that government is doing too much. In general, no matter how the statistics are analyzed, white Catholics of European descent tend to be more supportive of government action than their white Protestant northern neighbors.

Congressional and Church leaders mentioned a number of issues on which they believed it important for government to act. Congressmen listed education, Watergate, racial discrimination, the war and amnesty, school prayer, poverty (including in this the necessity of maintaining antipoverty programs, the problem of unemployment and of welfare reform), the problems of migrant labor and health care. Church leaders were concerned about the war and amnesty and what they called social justice issues, meaning an end to racial discrimination and poverty. They also stressed education, the problems of migrant labor, welfare, health care, women's rights, prison reform, and the Farah strike. Other issues were mentioned by individuals in both groups but those listed above were the ones stressed by a number of people in each.

When problems deemed most urgent by Catholics in general are compared with those raised by their leaders, there is both agreement and disagreement. Neither Church nor congressional leaders to any extent mentioned the environment, crime, or drug addiction as serious problems; yet all three of these seriously concern the Catholic people. Crime and drug addiction were also listed as important by Catholic community leaders. Aid to big cities was raised inferentially by Church leaders. A number of Church leaders, in discussing social justice, talked of improving the quality of life in the cities and of continuing antipoverty and other urban funding. Aid to big cities proved important for white Catholics. Both health care and education were listed as important by Church and congressional leaders and these, too, are widely supported by Catholics in general.

Two issues stand out: one because of the similarity of feeling between the people and their leadership and one because of a possible dissimilarity. Church and congressional leaders both stressed the problems of war and peace, Church leaders most specifically in an antiwar sense, and here they seem in tune with the people. Catholics consistently give lowest levels of support to further government spending on defense and fervent Catholics support defense spending even less than Catholics who are more infrequent churchgoers.

Both Church and Congressional leaders stressed the problem of racial discrimination in America, but here the reaction of Catholics is unclear. A quarter of all white Catholics (slightly more than of northern white Protestants) thought too much money was being spent to improve the condition of blacks. Catholics support levels on this issue and on welfare spending were lower than they were on any other issue except defense. However, 73.3 percent of white Catholics either supported present spending levels for blacks or thought even more money should be spent.

Civil Liberties

One of the areas in which Catholics have apparently experienced a great change of attitude over the past twenty years is civil liberties. Although the view was not unchallenged even then, a number of scholars in the 1950s believed that, because of Catholics' religious training and home upbringing, they tended to be authoritarian, enclosed in their own communities, convinced of the rightness of their religious and communal values, and fearful of outsiders, especially of those who were much unlike them. In the views of these scholars, this made Catholics more inclined than other Americans to fear and hate nonconformists. Catholics were thus less willing than other Americans to believe nonconformists such as atheists and Communists should be granted Bill of Rights guarantees.

After discussing the lower levels of tolerance displayed by Catholics as compared with white Protestants and Jews in surveys in the Detroit area, Gerhard Lenski warned that in an America in which Catholics would, in his opinion, become an increasingly larger part of the citizenry, there would be a subsequent narrowing of latitude for free speech and other civil liberties.[33] Samuel Stouffer found in his study *Communism, Conformity and Civil*

Liberties that church attendance correlated with lower civil liberties support and then demonstrated consistently more frequent religious attendance figures for Catholics than for Protestants.[34]

Church and congressional leaders did not explicitly discuss Church or Catholic attitudes toward atheists, Communists, or other nonconformists in their interviews. Both groups, however, spontaneously and at length did discuss the new, more open attitudes toward non-Catholics and the world in general they believed had been generated in the Church, largely through the effects of the Ecumenical Council but also through the breakdown of the ghetto mentality among Catholics and their entrance into the general American society. Said a nun, for example, "We have been opened up (by the Council) and there's no return . . . the process brought acceptance of diversity . . . I think it has been good even in terms of the American dream, helping us to understand the diversity of the country.[35]

Many political leaders made similar statements. Said a senator, "The old rigidity of the Church was broken down, which was absolutely essential if the Church was going to maintain itself in the modern world,"[36] To contrast today's more open attitudes with the more fearful attitude toward outsiders Catholics felt in past years, a congressman reached back to the kind of childhood memory many Catholics have. "I remember when I was a boy I played basketball on a Baptist church team and my parents were kind of worried about this. They felt it might be an opening wedge for getting me away from the Catholic Church. You don't see this kind of thing anymore.[37]

Responses to civil liberties questions show great changes among Catholics between the 1950s and the 1970s. Twenty years ago both churchgoing and nonchurchgoing Catholics were almost always less willing to support civil liberties for nonconformists than were white northern Protestants. Today they are always more willing to support them.[38] Although Stouffer in his book considered only the gross categories of Catholic, Protestant, and Jew, the way in which responses were collected and coded allow them to be broken down into the racial-religious categories dealt with here. NORC in the 1970s repeated the exact wording of the Stouffer civil liberties questions. Thus, comparison can be made between the responses of white Catholics of European descent and white northern Protestants twenty years ago and today.

As table 4.11 illustrates, in regard to atheists and Communists, both white Catholics and northern white Protestants have become much more liberal over the past twenty years. The change toward liberalism, however, is particularly dramatic among Catholics. Tolerant responses to the idea of rights for socialists were already high among both groups in the 1950s. White Catholics have very slightly increased that high response but, rather surprisingly, it subsequently dropped among white northern Protestants. The 1970s surveys added a question regarding another nonconformist group, homosexuals, and here, too, white Catholics of European descent show themselves more ready to concede civil liberties to this group than are white northern Protestants. Averaging the percentages of "yes" responses to all nonconformist civil liberties questions demonstrates that white Catholics in the 1950s were slightly less tolerant than white northern Protestants. By the 1970s, they were more tolerant by 4.5 percentage points (67.7 versus 63.2 percent).

Important in terms of this study is the persistent correlation Stouffer found between churchgoing and intolerance. "There would appear to be something about people who go to church regularly," he concluded, "that makes few of them, as compared

Table 4.11. Support for civil liberties for nonconformists in 1950s and 1970s (in percentages).

Group	Support civil liberties for:						
	Atheists		Communists		Socialists		Homosexuals[1]
	1950s	1970s	1950s	1970s	1950s	1970s	1970s
WCED	40.8	72.1	27.7	60.4	70.2	70.5	70.8
Change in tolerant response	+31.3		+32.7		+0.3		—
WPNS	42.5	67.8	31.4	56.8	68.5	65.0	65.4
Change in tolerant response	+25.3		+25.4		−3.5		—

1. Question on homosexuals added in the 1970s.

with nonchurchgoers, willing to accord civil rights to non-con-formists."[39] Analysis of his survey results bears him out. Among both white northern Protestants and white Catholics of European descent, churchgoers in the 1950s in nearly every case were signif-icantly less willing to extend Bill of Rights guarantees to non-conformists than were the nonchurchgoers. Churchgoers today among white Protestants and Catholics still have lower tolerance rates than nonchurchgoers. The change among Catholic church-goers, however, has been immense and has been in the direction of increased tolerance, much more than is true among Protes-tants. Also, in nearly every case, Catholic churchgoers tend to approach the higher tolerance levels of Catholic nonchurchgoers much more than Protestant churchgoers approach the higher levels of their nonchurchgoing brethren. Although churchgoing still does correlate with lower levels of tolerance, there seems no doubt that the effect has been much mitigated among white Catholics of European descent (table 4.12).

Table 4.12. Support for civil liberties for nonconformists by religiosity in 1950s and 1970s (in percentages).

Religiosity	Support civil liberties for:						
	Atheists		Communists		Socialists		Homosexuals
WCED	*1950s*	*1970s*	*1950s*	*1970s*	*1950s*	*1970s*	*1970s*
Attend church less than monthly	47.6	77.1	35.8	64.5	74.5	77.5	76.1
Attend monthly or more	39.1	70.6	25.8	60.1	69.2	68.9	67.9
WPNS							
Attend church less than monthly	47.4	73.9	32.1	61.4	71.5	69.5	70.6
Attend monthly or more	38.3	61.9	31.0	55.0	65.8	62.3	60.1

Stouffer found that if religious attendance correlated negatively with civil liberties support, education correlated positively
with it. The same correlation is found today. Significantly, however, Catholics, who in the 1950s were generally below Protestant
levels of support, are now generally above them, regardless of
educational level. Catholic college graduates, high school graduates, and high school dropouts now support civil rights for atheists, Communists, and Socialists to a greater degree than white
Protestants at the same educational level in all but one case:
Catholic and Protestant high school dropouts agree to a Com-
munist's right to speak in about equal percentages. Comparison
of the percentage of support registered by the groups in the 1950s
and in the 1970s also demonstrates that levels of tolerance have
risen more sharply for Catholics than for Protestants at every
educational level in regard to the two most extreme nonconformist positions, Communists and atheists. In regard to socialists
where, oddly enough, there have been some slight decreases in
tolerance over the past twenty years at some educational levels,
the decreases have been less for Catholics than for Protestants.
Catholics also show higher levels of support, regardless of education, for toleration of homosexuals, asked only in 1970s (table
4.13). At every level of education, those who attend church regularly are less tolerant than those who do not. But Catholics who
attend church regularly, whatever their education, are always
more tolerant than their Protestant counterparts (table 4.14).

The fact that Catholic levels of tolerance for nonconformists
are now higher than they were twenty years ago and higher than
those of white northern Protestants, no matter how statistics are
analyzed, reveals two things important for this study. First, Catholics as a whole have developed more open, probably more confi-
dent, certainly more democratic attitudes, as their Church and
congressional leaders maintain. This would certainly seem to
have to affect their view of and their actions in the political
arena. Second, Catholic leadership and people seem fairly agreed
in their more open attitudes, and this would seem to affect the
unity of the group. The difference in attitude toward civil liberties among Catholic and Protestant churchgoers, where a more
supportive attitude is found among devout Catholics, would also
raise at least the possibility that Catholics may have gone through
a particular experience in the past two decades that tends to

Table 4.13. Support for civil liberties for nonconformists by education in 1950s and 1970s (in percentages).

	Support civil liberties for:						
Education	Atheists		Communists		Socialists		Homosexuals
WCED	*1950s*	*1970s*	*1950s*	*1970s*	*1950s*	*1970s*	*1970s*
College graduates	51.5	94.3	37.3	87.9	83.3	90.3	92.0
High school graduates	50.2	76.6	31.2	65.5	76.0	75.3	78.0
Less than high school	31.1	52.1	22.4	36.4	62.9	57.2	48.7
WPNS							
College graduates	69.7	90.4	56.0	80.4	86.2	86.8	86.4
High school graduates	51.4	71.4	31.5	57.7	73.9	70.0	67.9
Less than high school	28.4	45.8	23.9	37.0	58.5	50.1	44.1

make them more open to challenge and to those unlike themselves. Church and congressional leaders may be right in thinking that the Council, with its emphasis on ecumenism and on the world, was that particular experience.

Race

Andrew Greeley has recently devoted much time and effort to refuting the notion that white Catholics are more racist than other American whites.[40] Nie, Verba, and Petrocik insist that white Catholics may have become more racist in the last twenty years than they were earlier.[41] Certainly survey results on race are not clearcut as they are on civil liberties. White Catholics are more liberal on race than white southern Protestants, less liberal than Jews, and about as liberal as white northern Protestants. The degree of liberalism for Catholics (and northern Protestants) varies according to the specific racial issue presented.

Surveys in the 1970s asked the following five major questions on race:[42]

1. BLACKS SHOULDN'T PUSH WHERE THEY ARE NOT WANTED.

	Agree	*Disagree*
WCED	71.0	29.0
WPNS	76.3	23.7

2. THERE SHOULD BE LAWS AGAINST MARRIAGES BETWEEN BLACKS AND WHITES.

	Agree	*Disagree*
WCED	27.3	72.7
WPNS	38.4	61.6

3. IN A CHOICE OF LAWS ON HOUSING, RESPONDENT WOULD VOTE FOR A LAW:

	Allowing home-owner to sell to whomever he pleases, even if he prefers not to to sell to blacks	*Under which homeowner could not refuse to sell to blacks*	*Neither law*
WCED	60.9	37.7	1.4
WPNS	62.6	36.5	0.9

4. RESPONDENT WOULD AGREE/NOT AGREE TO SENDING HIS CHILDREN TO A SCHOOL WHERE HALF THE CHILDREN ARE BLACK?

	Agree	*Not agree*
WCED	78.9	21.1
WPNS	79.1	20.9

5. PRESENT SPENDING LEVELS TO IMPROVE THE CONDITIONS OF BLACKS ARE:

	Too little	*About right*	*Too much*
WCED	26.7	46.6	26.7
WPNS	24.3	50.5	25.2

The majority of both white Catholics and white northern Protestants take antiblack positions on blacks "pushing" where they are not wanted and on open housing. The majority of both groups take liberal positions on interracial marriage, school integration, and government spending to improve conditions for blacks. Comparing the two groups on all these questions shows that white

Table 4.14. Support for civil liberties for nonconformists by religiosity and education (in percentages).

	Support civil liberties for:	
Religiosity and education	Atheists	Communists
WCED		
College graduates who attend church less than monthly	96.6	93.1
High school dropouts who attend church less than monthly	72.7	57.3
College graduates who attend church monthly or more	93.7	87.2
High school dropouts who attend church monthly or more	63.4	52.2
WPNS		
College graduates who attend church less than monthly	93.3	82.8
High school dropouts who attend church less than monthly	67.9	54.1
College graduates who attend church monthly or more	87.7	80.3
High school dropouts who attend church monthly or more	51.1	44.1

Catholics tend to be substantially more liberal than white northern Protestants on interracial marriage and somewhat more liberal on blacks "pushing." On open housing, school integration, and government spending for blacks, Catholic and Protestant positions are nearly identical, with Catholics marginally more liberal on open housing, and Protestants marginally more liberal on school integration and government spending.[43]

For the purposes of this study the most significant differences emerge in analysis of racial attitudes and religiosity. Responses to two racial questions were examined intensively: spending to improve conditions for blacks and school integration. Analysis of these issues demonstrates that northern white Protestants who are regular church attenders are more liberal racially than less devout Protestants. That is not true among Catholics, where correlations between religiosity and liberal racial attitudes are much more erratic. For example, the questions on integrated schools and spending for blacks show that fervent Catholics, those attending church monthly or more, are the most likely of all Catholics to approve government spending for blacks but are least likely to approve integrated schools. Fervent Protestants, on the other hand, are in both cases and by considerable margins more liberal than their less devout brethren (table 4.15).

The same results hold even within age and education groups. Among white Protestants, regardless of age, those who attend church at least monthly are always more liberal on race than less devout Protestants. Among Catholics this is true only half the time (table 4.16). In most instances also, regardless of educational level, the churchgoing among white Protestants are more liberal on race than the nonchurchgoing. Among Catholics, the same correlation does not appear. In most cases Catholic churchgoers, regardless of educational level, have the same percentages or smaller percentages of liberal response than the nonchurchgoers (table 4.17). Whereas fervent Catholics always were more liberal in regard to civil liberties for nonconformists than fervent Protestants, the opposite is usually true with regard to race.

Table 4.15. Attitudes toward questions on race by religiosity (in percentages).

Religiosity	Would agree to sending own children to school where half the students are black	Support present government spending levels to improve conditions for blacks or want higher levels
WCED		
Peripheral[1]	79.1	71.3
Occasional[2]	80.4	70.9
Fervent[3]	78.3	74.6
WPNS		
Peripheral	77.1	70.3
Occasional	75.9	70.6
Fervent	81.2	79.7

1. Never attend church or attend less than once a year.

2. Attend church once to several times yearly.

3. Attend church monthly or more.

Table 4.16. Attitudes toward questions on race by religiosity and age (in percentages).

Religiosity and age	Would agree to sending own children to school where half the students are black	Support present government spending levels to improve conditions for blacks or want higher levels
WCED who attend church less than monthly		
18-29	83.9	80.5
30-49	78.4	69.5
50 and older	74.0	61.4
WCED who attend church monthly or more		
18-29	78.4	74.6
30-49	75.8	80.3
50 and older	81.1	69.1
WPNS who attend church less than monthly		
18-29	82.8	80.5
30-49	77.6	65.7
50 and older	72.5	67.5
WPNS who attend church monthly or more		
18-29	92.4	92.2
30-49	81.1	74.0
50 and older	76.8	79.6

Many Church and congressional leaders emphasized racial justice and minority rights as prime issues facing America. Church leaders were particularly eloquent on the issue of race; only abortion and the Vietnam war equaled the emphasis they put on this issue. The Church has taken public action to implement its stand on racial justice: early integration of Catholic schools, support for the civil rights law, support for migrant workers' rights, and joint declarations on racial issues by the National Conference of Catholic Bishops. These may have alleviated the potential for a growth in bigotry among Catholics, but neither statements nor action by

Table 4.17. Attitudes toward questions on race by religiosity and education (in percentages).

Religiosity and education	Would agree to sending own children to school where half the students are black	Support present government spending levels to improve conditions for blacks or want higher levels
WCED who attend church less than monthly		
College graduates	79.4	85.7
High school graduates	79.7	71.8
Less than high school	78.0	66.2
WCED who attend church monthly or more		
College graduates	81.2	81.8
High school graduates	77.2	71.5
Less than high school	78.0	70.7
WPNS who attend church less than monthly		
College graduates	84.7	83.3
High school graduates	75.4	67.7
Less than high school	75.7	67.3
WPNS who attend church monthly or more		
College graduates	79.6	81.3
High school graduates	80.8	80.7
Less than high school	79.2	76.4

the Church have apparently been influential enough to make Catholics more liberal on race than white northern Protestants. Catholic churchgoers are in fact generally less liberal racially than Protestant churchgoers.

Some clues as to why the Church is not more influential here emerge in congressional interviews and in interviews I did with Catholic community leaders. These are mere undercurrents but they seem to indicate that while Catholics seem generally favorable to efforts for black advance and for integration, they may also feel a gap between their values and the values they believe held by blacks and they may feel some resentment at what they believe to be Church and government priority given to black problems at the expense of their own.

Among congressmen it was almost always the Jansenists who alluded to this. Said a New England Republican, "We are sanctimonious in our response to problems. In the 1960s you had suburban nuns seeing the light and heading out for the ghetto to work there. They are leaving areas in which they are trained to work to do something for which they are not trained and I think at times they made an awful mess of things. Because they are not subsidizing the [Catholic] schools with their work, schools are closing . . . The generation of Catholic-educated kids who could have supported aid for the ghetto is being brought up unaware of it or their responsibilities."[44] A senator echoed his feelings: "There has been an emphasis on activism, going to the ghetto. Some people are a little concerned about this because if one is involved in this kind of activism it means a lessening of efforts in other areas."[45]

Four people among the nine ethnic leaders with whom I spoke also accented divergent interests between white Catholics and black and other minority people. Said an Italian-American leader, "The economic interests of blacks and their liberal supporters and of white Catholic ethnics [working-class Catholics] are maybe the same, but they diverge on social issues—their values aren't the same. White Catholic ethnics don't have the guilt feelings about the blacks that liberals have. 'Look,' they say, 'we weren't even here [in America]. We weren't responsible for the blacks being slaves.' [White Catholic ethnics'] ways of looking at things are different from the blacks and the liberals, more traditional, more family-oriented."[46] An Irish-American leader declared, "I'm learning every day, perceiving what the ethnic problem really is, where the blue-collar worker in our cities comes from, why he fears his black neighbors. The white non-Catholic has largely moved out of the city. It's the Catholic ethnic who's still there. They had always supported the system, but in the 1960s they saw that they were getting nothing out of it. They got nothing out of the progress of the sixties but they paid for it."[47]

These are minor themes in the interviews but they may be given some credence as clues to feelings among Catholics because reportorial and academic research has also pointed to them.[48] It is important to note and to try to understand some of the forces in operation which may be undercutting the strong emphasis of the Church on racial justice, but I would not want to overemphasize them. The fact of the matter is that there are high levels of racial tolerance among white Catholics on most issues despite the strains, but these strains may explain why leadership seems not as influential here with the Catholic people, especially the most devout, as it may be in other areas.

The racial question may present the greatest divergence in attitude between the leadership and the people in the American Catholic Church. However, it is important also to note that on racial questions generally, white Catholics as a whole are as liberal as white northern Protestants and that on the two questions examined in detail, while fervent Catholics seem to have somewhat lower rates of liberal response than the nonfervent, the percentages are still very high for both groups.

Minority Catholics

In his great history of religion in America, Sidney Ahlstrom perceptively begins not with the English Puritans but with Spain and the Spanish-speaking Catholics in what was to become the United States.[49] The order imposed by history has been reversed in this discussion in order to provide an analysis of the people who have become the majority of the American Catholic world, the white Catholics of European descent. Spanish-speaking Catholics, however, in great part Mexican-Americans, must also be considered, not only because of their important historical role but also because they make up a sizable and growing percentage of the Catholic population. In addition, consideration of the Spanish-speaking is important because they are in the forefront of much of the thinking of Church and congressional leaders.

The Spanish-speaking present a complex picture. By all socioeconomic indices they are among the poorest of American citizens; in their attitudes toward many social and political issues they are among the most conservative.

The differences between white Catholics of European descent and the Spanish-speaking become apparent even in considering geographical and residential patterns. The Spanish-speaking are heavily concentrated in areas with few white Catholics — the South and the West — and they are the most rural of all Catholics.

Measured by religious attendance, the Spanish-speaking Catholic is somewhat less likely to be a fervent Catholic than the white Catholic of European descent. While 64.6 percent of white Catholics attend mass once a month or more, 59.3 percent of the Spanish-speaking do. Church attendance drops among the youngest of the Spanish-speaking as it does among white Catholics. While 81.8 percent of Spanish-speaking Catholics fifty years of age or older attend church at least once a month, 52.9 percent of those eighteen to twenty-nine do, a figure nearly the same as that of young white Catholics (53.2 percent). Endogamous marriage rates are much higher than among white Catholics. Of the Spanish-speaking, 92.2 percent are married to Catholics as compared with 76.2 percent of white Catholics. While this is probably as much a matter of ethnic and cultural intermarriage (Mexican-Americans marrying Mexican-Americans) as of Catholics marrying Catholics, Catholicism is such a large part of the Spanish-speaking culture that the two must be entwined and must act to reinforce one another. It may be concluded that, although the Spanish-speaking have a somewhat lower religious attendance rate than white Catholics, religious differences are not great. Their ties to Catholicism seem strong.

By any standard, the socioeconomic position of the Spanish-speaking is far behind that of white Catholics. Indeed, by most measures it is behind that of black Protestants as well. The Spanish-speaking are poor and there seems some evidence that they are not as mobile even as blacks.

Only 3.2 percent of the Spanish-speaking have college degrees; 60.5 percent have less than a high school education. Both figures are worse than those of black Protestants, 5.2 percent of whom are college graduates and 56.6 percent, less than high school graduates. The Spanish-speaking today have a lower level of education achievement than white Catholics did twenty years ago. Today white Catholics have nearly five times the percentage of college graduates of the Spanish-speaking and much less than half of the Spanish-speaking percentage of high school dropouts.

Further, when respondents' levels of education are compared with that of their fathers, 64.3 percent of white Catholics and 60 percent of black Protestants have increased their educational level above that of their fathers. Among the Spanish-speaking, only 38.6 percent have educations above the levels achieved by their fathers. The advances of the 1960s which have allowed blacks to begin to climb the education ladder have apparently not been effective for the Spanish-speaking.

In occupational status the Spanish-speaking lag behind white Catholics and, by some measures, behind black Protestants. Almost a third of the Spanish-speaking, 32.3 percent, are employed in white-collar work, as opposed to 23.6 percent of blacks. Among blacks, however, almost half of white-collar workers are engaged at the two highest levels of white-collar work, professionals and managers. Among the Spanish-speaking, twice as many (21.2 percent) are employed at the lowest level, clerical work, as are employed at the higher levels (11.1 percent).

In income, too, the Spanish-speaking are below white Catholic levels and by some measures below that of black Protestants. The Spanish-speaking have three times the white Catholic percentage of people living on family incomes below $5,000 yearly. Forty-two percent of the Spanish-speaking live on a poverty income of under $5,000, but this is less than the 50 percent of blacks with family incomes below $5,000. The Spanish-speaking, however, have only about half as many people with large yearly incomes of above $15,000: 5.3 percent of the Spanish-speaking but 9.3 percent of blacks.

In regard to socioeconomic status, then, the Spanish-speaking are definitely disadvantaged as compared with white Catholics and in some ways even as compared with blacks. While by some measures they seem to be ahead of blacks in occupation and in income, they are seemingly stuck in the lower levels of white collar work and of family income to a greater extent than blacks.

While the Spanish-speaking are poor, as such things can be measured through survey research, they seem fairly well integrated into the political party system and the institutional system of American society. They are in fact less likely to be independents politically and more likely to be Democrats than are white Catholics of European descent. More than a third of white Catholics, 36.2 percent, but only 20.8 percent of the Spanish-speaking call themselves independents. Less than half, 46.6 percent, of white Catholics but 71.7 percent of the Spanish-speaking call themselves Democrats.

In party preference the Spanish-speaking resemble black Protestants more than they do white Catholics. Blacks, too, are little inclined to call themselves independents (16.5 percent) and much inclined to prefer the Democratic Party (73.2 percent). Although the young among the Spanish-speaking, those eighteen to twenty-nine years old, are less inclined than their elders to support the Democrats and more inclined to be independents, they are still 20 percent more supportive of the Democrats than their white Catholic age peers.

The rate of support which the Spanish-speaking give to American institutions can only be called surprising in a people who would seem to have received so little from them. In 1970s surveys, the Spanish-speaking have higher percentages of respondents voicing "great" confidence in the leaders of America's private and public institutions than any other major racial-religious group surveyed. A smaller percentage of the Spanish-speaking than of either white Catholics or black Protestants are willing to say they had "hardly any confidence" in the institutions.[50]

Although in response to the question on their political ideology the Spanish-speaking call themselves liberals more often than did white Catholics, they do not take a notably more liberal position on specific social and political issues.[51] Their responses to questions on government spending resemble those of white Catholics more than those of black Protestants. On questions of civil liberties, they are much more conservative than white Catholics.

Sixty-five percent of black Protestants believe that on an overall basis the national government is still spending too little money to solve America's problems, but only 48.8 percent of the Spanish-speaking took this position (as compared with 48.4 percent of white Catholics). The Spanish-speaking are less inclined than black Protestants or even white Catholics to support government spending on general welfare issues (education, health care, the environment). They are less inclined than either group to support spending on law and order issues (solving drug addiction problems and problems of rising crime). They are more inclined than white Catholics but much less inclined than black Protestants to want more spending on minority welfare issues: Only 37.8 percent of the Spanish-speaking think more should be spent to improve the condition of blacks and only 30.8 approve more spending on welfare. The difference from blacks is significant, with 83.8 percent of blacks wanting more money spent to improve their condition and 54 percent wanting more spent on welfare. In general, then, in regard to many specific problems, the Spanish-speaking seem to be economic liberals to a lesser extent than white Catholics and certainly than America's other large minority, black Protestants.

The winds of change sweeping through the Church which may have affected white Catholic attitudes toward civil liberties seem to have affected the Spanish-speaking to a much smaller degree. The Spanish-speaking tend to have low levels of support for civil liberties guarantees for nonconformists. They would concede rights in large percentages only to socialists. Otherwise, their tolerance levels are lower than those of white Catholics and, regarding Communists, lower than those of black Protestants also. Civil liberties for atheists are supported by 72.7 percent of white Catholics but only 54.9 percent of the Spanish-speaking, for homosexuals by 70.8 percent of white Catholics and 57.4 percent of the Spanish-speaking, a percentage equaling that of black Protestant support, and for Communists by 61.5 percent of white Catholics, 51.6 percent of black Protestants, and only 44.6 percent of the Spanish-speaking.

It is difficult to assess the racial attitudes of the Spanish-speaking since most racial questions were asked only of whites. Responses are available on these questions only from those of the Spanish-speaking labeled as white by surveyers or as a result of their own responses to a query about their race. However, Spanish-speaking response to the question of spending for blacks, asked of everyone, indicates that they are somewhat more sympathetic to blacks than are white Catholics, at least on this issue. Thirty-eight percent of the Spanish-speaking but only 26.7 percent of white Catholics feel more money should be spent to improve the condition of blacks.

If minority status consists not just of racial or ethnic differences but of a distinctly disadvantaged state of educational, occupational, and economic development, certainly the Spanish-speaking form such a group within the American Catholic world. They show several other distinct differences from American Catholics in general and also from Church and congressional leadership.

Large numbers of them are actually separated spatially from other Catholics. Many live in the Southwest, a part of the country inhabited by relatively few other Catholics. Unlike most other Catholics, they are to a great extent a rural people, which probably affects their attitudes on social and political questions and even their mobility.

They tend not to share tendencies toward economic liberalism and toward civil liberties for nonconformists, which, otherwise, both Church and congressional leadership and white Catholics in general demonstrated. They may share Church and congressional leadership attitudes toward racial justice more than white Catholics.

The Spanish-speaking, however, indicate closeness to the Church. Their degree of religiosity differs little from that of other Catholics. Like white Catholics of European descent, they tend to have confidence in the major institutions of the country and to be even more integrated into the political party systems. All in all, however, the Spanish-speaking in many ways are not integrated into the general American Catholic world, unlike the great majority of white Catholics of European descent. They seem tied to the Church and perhaps to the American Catholic world mainly through their own strong Catholic culture and, perhaps, through the concern congressional and especially Church leaders expressed again and again for this minority sector of the Church.

The American Catholic people present a picture of both stability and change. This is particularly true of the white Catholics of European descent, with whom I have mainly been concerned in this chapter. White Catholics have demonstrated the economic and educational, although perhaps not the occupational, mobility their Church and congressional leaders earlier claimed for the group. In twenty-five years Catholics have become much more middle class and more than a third have attained at least some college education. Thus, white Catholics have achieved the level of socioeconomic status which usually correlates with an increased sense of political efficacy and of political interest and involvement.

While endogamous marriage and church attendance rates have declined, particularly among the young, white Catholics are still much more likely than are other white Americans to be regular practitioners of their religion, and the most educated of Catholics, the group's natural leaders, are the most religiously observant. Lower in-group marriage and religious attendance rates among the young may presage a declining sense of Catholicity in the future. One must conclude, however, that at least for the present Catholics form a strong and fairly unified religious body.

Despite the predictions of some Church leaders of a growing

sense of alienation among Catholics, this seems not to be happening. Indeed, white Catholics seem to be more integrated into our political party and electoral systems than white Protestants and the most fervent of Catholics are the most strongly integrated. Thus, given Catholics' continued unity and commitment as a religious ethnic group, their newly increased social and economic status, and their general integration into American political and governmental systems, white Catholics particularly (that is, the bulk of the Church) potentially hold the political power their Church and congressional leaders assert.

Catholic leadership and the Catholic people do diverge in part on specific issues and on the goals toward which this political power might be exercised. However, the areas of agreement seem wider than those of disagreement. Both Church and congressional leaders stressed continuing Catholic support for economic liberalism and, indeed, survey analysis showed Catholics to be consistently supportive of governmental problem-solving efforts in education, health, the environment, big cities, and so on. White Catholics also demonstrate a dramatic rise in their levels of support for civil liberties guarantees. Thus, they bear out Church and congressional claims of a greater Catholic openness and tolerance towards others, with all the implications the development of such attitudes have for political participation and its modes.

Church and congressional leaders showed little comprehension of the fear of crime and drugs so obviously prevalent among Catholics. Most important, perhaps, in considering areas of divergence between leadership and people is the strong concern voiced by both Church and congressional leadership about racism and discrimination and the smaller degree to which this concern was shared by Catholics, especially by those who are the most observant of church services and, presumably, closest to the institutional Church. The possible divergence on the issue of racism between the bulk of the Catholic people and their leaders could prove important because the American Catholic world contains a large and very poor minority group of its own, the Spanish-speaking.

5

A "Catholic" Issue — Abortion

ABORTION IS AN ISSUE which, although seen by the the Catholic Church as deeply moral, has great political importance and will be decided in the political arena, as Church leaders and other Americans are aware. Partly because of the Church's strongly held position, abortion has become a salient subject of wide public debate. The institutional Church has furnished much of the ideological framework, political leadership, and financial support for the antiabortion movement. Through this movement and through the Church's own dependent institutional organizations it is also attempting to exert massive pressure on legislators and to organize a national educational and lobbying effort among the Catholic masses. If religion, in this case Catholicism, exerts any influence on politics, this influence and the way it is exerted should surely be discernible in an examination of the abortion issue.

The Institutional Church

Interviews with institutional Church leaders showed that there was no other single issue on which they displayed the near unanimity they did on abortion. Only one person voiced any doubts regarding the validity of the Church's position on this issue. "On some of these issues," he said, "like birth control, some aspects of divorce, abortion, I have trouble myself with the Church position."[1] Paradoxically, this man, a lobbyist with a state Catholic organization, was actively involved in trying to elicit antiabortion legislation from a state lawmaking body. Two other interviewees, both priests heading departments for diocesan chanceries, talked of the issue only in terms of political strategy and possible success or failure, without clearly indicating their own feelings on the subject.

All the other institutional Church leaders interviewed (that is, nineteen out of twenty-two, no matter what their particular responsibility in the Church, no matter what their status, clerical or lay, their sex, national origin, age, or location in the country, spoke out strongly against abortion. Half introduced the subject spontaneously before being asked any questions about it. The extent of Church concern and activity in this area was indicated also by the fact that the antiabortion effort had obviously spread far beyond the organizations specifically formed to fight abortion. Excluding leaders of antiabortion organizations, I still found that twelve of the twenty-two Church leaders interviewed had either themselves been drawn into or were among the leaders of organizations which in one way or another had been drawn into the antiabortion struggle. These include the bishops, leaders of USCC divisions whose primary concerns had not earlier been abortion, the lobbyists, the writers and editors (all of whom had written or published articles on the subject), and the leaders of some organizations which ordinarily were chiefly concerned with community and social welfare issues.

Grass-roots institutional Church leadership also showed evidence of the same cohesive attitude on abortion. Frank Traino of the Cornell University Center for Population Planning, in a 1972 survey of priests in eight dioceses in New York State, found that only 6 priests out of a sample of 820 thought that the state's recently enacted liberalized abortion law should be allowed to stand. Of 767 priests responding to the question, 75 percent thought that the old law restricting abortion to emergencies endangering the mother's life should be reinstated or that an even more restrictive law should be passed. Another 7.7 percent said they agreed with the Church's teaching on abortion but thought there should be no laws regarding it.[2]

Almost yearly, from 1969 to the present, the bishops have been issuing increasingly strong statements opposing abortion. These statements and much of the institutional Church's efforts to oppose abortion, including its aid in developing the antiabortion movement, obviously were due in great part to fear engendered first by local efforts to remove restrictive state abortion laws and then by the Supreme Court decision of January 1973 which declared the restrictive abortion laws of Florida and Georgia, and thus the similar laws of forty-four other states, to be unconstitutional.[3] The forceful reaction of the Church, however, and the fact that the Church was not the initiator of all activity among the laity indicate that the proabortion legislative and judicial decisions were seen to threaten a vital element in Catholic life and thinking. The principle which Catholics call "respect for life," although all Catholics do not define it in identical terms, seems to be a central Catholic value, embedded in much of the Catholic world. Both Senator James Buckley and Congressman Lawrence Hogan, for example, sponsors of the major human life Constitutional amendments in the Senate and House designed to nullify the Supreme Court's proabortion decision, insisted that the Church had not prompted their actions. Both declared they had acted independently and on their own initiatives because they felt their own values outraged by the Court decision. Traino also concluded at the end of his study that the prolife movement in New York "grew more from the grass roots than from the Church."[4]

There are even charges that in some cases institutional Church leaders and prominent Catholic spokesmen at first were reluctant to enter the political arena on this issue. The editor of a conservative Catholic magazine said, "Bill Buckley in 1966, although he wouldn't want to be reminded of it now, denounced an official of the New York Archdiocese who had spoken out on abortion, warning him that the Church shouldn't interfere in a political matter. That idea of noninterference had grown to the point where it had sapped Catholics of the courage to do anything."[5] Congressman Hogan said, "A long time ago, at least a year before the Supreme Court decision, I guess in the Ninety-second Congress, I began to recognize a growing problem here. I got a group of people together including Monsignor [X] to talk about it. I told them that this is a national issue and it needs a national organization. And [he] said, 'You can't expect the Church to get involved with a political issue'!"[6]

By 1973 this same Church leader was one of the men directing the Church's education effort on abortion. "We're not going to shut up on this issue," he insisted in an interview, "no matter what our critics say. We're going to be more vociferous, more political. Aid to parochial schools was important, sure, but it's nowhere near the same thing as this. Our critics can deny it until the cows come home but the whole value system of the nation is involved in this."[7]

This man in his interview also talked of a growing Church willingness to act politically, occasioned by the abortion controversy. "Among the bishops there was still a residue reluctant to participate in political action but even the residue was washed away by the abortion issue. That was the real watershed."[8] Certainly Church educational and political action on abortion has steadily increased in the 1970s. In 1969 the bishops simply included several paragraphs in their pastoral letter, "Human Life in Our Day," concerning what they called, "Further Threats to Life." "Reverence for Life," they wrote, "demands freedom from direct interference with life once it is conceived."[9] In 1972 and 1973 they went on to issue major policy declarations on abortion. In 1975 the National Conference of Catholic Bishops issued the *Pastoral Plan for Pro-Life Activities*, a document calling for a large-scale effort to make the Church's views on abortion known and for political activities designed to persuade federal and state governments to restrict abortion as much as possible.

In 1972, also, the National Bishops Committee on Population and Pro-Life Activities began sponsoring "Respect Life" programs designed to inform and activate Catholics in the 18,000 parishes in the country, and the *New York Times* cited Church efforts as major factors in the struggle against repeal of restrictive abortion laws in New York, Connecticut, and Florida.[10] The director of the USCC's Family Life Division in 1973 termed the abortion issue "the single issue . . . that has overshadowed others since I've been here."[11] In addition to these antiabortion activities on the part of bishops, dioceses, and institutional Church organizations, there is also good evidence that the institutional Church helped to organize major sectors of the antiabortion movement.

Robert Lynch, a Catholic, was the former director of CREDIT, Citizen Relief for Education by Income Tax, a nationwide group lobbying for tax credits for parents of children in private and parochial schools. He now heads the National Committee for a Human Life Amendment, organized officially in 1974. A USCC official described the organization in these terms: "Lynch's group was specifically set up by the bishops—that is, it's legally separate from the Church, but it's not really—that's sort of a p.r. thing— to pursue the Constitutional amendment."[12] Lynch concurred, adding, "I was probably asked [by the bishops] to be involved because I know the Church, I know politics, and I know people."[13]

A second national organization, the National Youth Pro-Life Coalition, with charter groups in twelve states, is largely a college students' organization that stresses its nonsectarian membership. However, its first president, Susan Bastyr-Hillgers, and first executive director, Thomas Mooney, were both Catholics. The organization seems to be the only major antiabortion group which views abortion as do the bishops and the USCC—as one among many factors such as poverty, euthanasia, imprisonment, and mental illness which unjustly terminate or dehumanize life. More than any other antiabortion organization, it reflects the "respect-for-life" ideology of the institutional Church at its highest levels.

Apparently the largest and certainly the most visible antiabortion organization is National Right to Life. The organization has a federated structure, with active organizations in nearly every state in the union.[14] *New York Times*'s reports and the organization's own newspaper agree that right-to-life groups began as grass-roots organizations between 1967 and 1969 to fight attempts in several states to liberalize traditional restrictive abortion laws.[15] In June 1973 the present National Right to Life Committee, Inc., was restructured and approved by a national convention of state organizations. It acts as a national coordinator and information center for the state organizations and is largely in charge of lobbying at the national level.

National Right to Life describes itself as an independent organization with a nonsectarian membership, and, indeed, people of diverse religious backgrounds are active in it.[16] Its executive directors have changed frequently, but both its first president, Edward Golden, and at least one of its executive directors, Ray L. White, were Catholics. Catholics also head many of the state and local chapters. *National Right to Life News*, the organization's official newspaper, reported that the informal national committee operating prior to the June 1973 convention worked "in cooperation with the Family Life Division of the United States Catholic Conference."[17] The New York chapter of Right to Life fought for repeal of that state's liberalized abortion laws from offices loaned them by the Archdiocese of New York. "Membership [of Right to Life]," reported the *New York Times* in 1972, "tends to be heavily Roman Catholic with some conservative elements of

Protestants and Jews. In California Catholics are the strongest single voice."[18] In 1978 *Newsweek* agreed: "By one estimate, Catholics make up about half the members of the national movement and contribute hundreds of thousands of dollars to it."[19]

Certainly, the institutional Church was spurred into active, even political opposition to abortion by the sometimes successful fights to repeal restrictive state abortion laws and especially by the Supreme Court decision. Almost a third of the institutional leaders interviewed spontaneously spoke of the catalytic effect of that decision. Said one, "The Supreme Court decision did more to radicalize the Church than almost anything else I can think of. The Church now doesn't care about antagonizing people."[20] There seems evidence, however, that the unanimity of opinion on abortion by the Church leadership and its commitment to fight against it may be due in part to the fact that over the past five years antiabortion has come more and more to be seen as part of an entire respect-for-life ideology; and that ideology, and not the antiabortion principle alone, has come to be seen as threatened.

The *Constitution on the Church in the Modern World*, issued by the Second Vatican Council in December 1965, helped to lay the foundation for this ideology. The USCC underscored this by quoting relevant sectors of the *Constitution* in its booklet, *Documentation on the Right to Life and Abortion*: "This Council lays stress on reverence for man . . . taking into account first of all his life and the means necessary to living it with dignity." It declared that whatever is opposed to life itself, that violates the integrity of the human person or insults human dignity, are "infamies." The Council *Constitution* then listed these life-depriving and life-degrading infamies as not only, or even primarily, abortion but also murder, genocide, euthanasia, mental and physical coercion and suffering, subhuman living conditions, arbitrary imprisonment, and disgraceful working conditions.[21] Both the institutional interviews and the Catholic press indicate a widespread development of belief within the Church in such a total understanding of what "respect for life" entails. Antiabortion is viewed as a key sector of this philosophy and the sector currently under strong attack. The primacy of the abortion issue and the wide spectrum of beliefs in which it is encompassed by the Church is illustrated by a near unanimity of opinion regarding abortion even from the most liberal Church leaders interviewed.

The institutional Church's experts and prophets seem to have been important in pressing for the encapsulation of antiabortion into a larger respect-for-life concept. Spearheading this attempt seem to be the Church leaders, clerical and lay, who have been involved over the last ten years in antipoverty, antiwar, and social action programs. A minority in this category adopted the tactic of angry denunciation. While personally opposed to abortion, they believed the Church was concentrating too much of its energies on abortion and not enough on social action. I found evidence in both documentation and in the institutional Church interviews that the expansion and development of the "life" issue was partially catalyzed by criticisms made against the Church's antiabortion stance by some sections of the Catholic Left and by the urgings of the now large number of social-action-oriented leaders in its own institutional midst.

Asked after the Supreme Court decision of January 1973 if he supported the Church's stand on abortion, antiwar activist Father Daniel Berrigan, in an example of the critics' position, replied only that he could not turn his attention to that issue until the killing of live babies in Vietnam was ended.[22] In spring 1973 one of the most respected and intellectual of Catholic magazines, in summarizing charges by abortion proponents, agreed that "in fact some of the staunchest 'pro-life' advocates are the loudest protesters either against abolishing the death penalty or for bombing the Vietnamese to win the war."[23] Similar statements came from a minority of Church interviewees. A nun, involved in community action work for ten years, illustrated their attitudes:

> I have never seen so much power put behind an issue. The display of power is fantastic on these issues [aid to parochial schools and abortion]. I mean power in a financial and political sense. The flood of literature that is coming out on these issues, going to every parish! The groups that are being formed to fight on these issues! We haven't seen the bishops of the Church exercise this kind of power on other issues, on justice, for example, or poverty. Sometimes I almost forget that I myself am opposed to abortion because I spend so much time trying to bring the whole thing into some kind of balance.[24]

A larger group of Church leaders spoke not to contrast Church action on abortion and on social justice issues but to emphasize their desire that the Church expand its concept of respect for life to encompass everything that will help achieve "a truly and entirely human way of life." A leader in both a social action organization and a political and lobbying group said, "I am horrified about abortion but I think we must also be concerned about the quality of life of the born . . . There's not enough concern about war, poverty, about a lot of issues besides abortion and tax credits." Referring to the Vatican Council reforms, she added, "The Church now says that all of life is the responsibility of the Church and of the individual person in the Church."[25] A bishop who had been a leader of the antiabortion movement which led to rejection of a more liberalized abortion bill in a Michigan state referendum talked explicitly about effecting organizations like those established to fight abortion to struggle for social reforms. "There are other issues which need the impetus of the Church, of individual Catholics. Prison reform, for example, war, poverty. We have issued strong statements on many of these issues but politically there has been no follow-through by the Church. On these issues no organization like CREDIT has been formed." As a model for the rest of the Church, he suggested an educational and organizational network developed by the bishops of his state to fight for welfare and prison reform. "Within the diocese we are trying to set up the kind of network we need to bring institutional change consistent with Catholic values."[26]

The institutional Church, as exemplified by the National Conference of Catholic Bishops and the United States Catholic Conference, seems to have come more and more to the position expressed by the leaders quoted above. The statements and documents issued by the NCCB and the USCC have begun increasingly to demonstrate that the respect-for-life program must include many issues beyond abortion, to include circumstances, for example, which actually deprive people of life (euthanasia, war, capital punishment) or of a full, dignified life (poverty, physical and mental handicaps, harsh aspects of imprisonment). The USCC official most involved with the antiabortion movement said in his interview:

> We are aware of the need to broaden the base of teaching on right to life . . . we realize that if we are going to fight the abortion issue we must have credibility, internal consistency. In the past two-and-a-half to three years the bishops in their pronouncement on

respect for life have shown a specific intent to broaden their concerns in regard to respect for life and this has led to carrying it into areas other than abortion. The respect-for-life statements pursuing abortion continue to be broader and broader in their interpretation of what respect for life means. Respect for life first was extended to abortion, poverty, the aged, youth, peace, and war. Now in the latest statement it encompasses the mentally retarded, population problems, prison reform, health care, poverty, food. Next year this will form the basic core and we'll probably add new topics. Gun control, for example. That's something we really haven't gone into yet but we should, and capital punishment, we haven't done enough on that yet.[27]

Interviewed at the conclusion of the 1973 annual bishops' conference, a prominent eastern bishop confirmed and applauded the hierarchy's decision to expand the respect-for-life issue: "I like the new emphasis. Not antiabortion but prolife, a respect for life in all its forms. There is some justice in the criticism that we are not prolife because we did not speak out against the war. But now our prolife resolution speaks of prolife in, I think, nine different conditions—aging, youth, peace, abortion, family life, and so on. It's a total package. It says we must speak out whenever human dignity is threatened."[28]

Documentation confirms adoption by the NCCB and USCC of a total package on the prolife issue. In addition to the leaders' statements referred to above, the same package is found in the educational materials put out by the NCCB and the USCC on respect for life. Beginning in 1972 the American bishops declared annual "Respect Life" programs to be held in every parish in the country, starting in October of each year. In handbooks issued by the USCC for parish use, respect for life is broadly conceived as concerning everything which unjustly ends or dehumanizes human life. Sermons are preached around these themes, and various religious, educational, and social club meetings are held around them. The 1972 program and handbook was designed to focus attention on the sanctity of human life, including not only abortion but war, violence, hunger, and poverty. The 1973 program and handbook focused on abortion, the mentally retarded, the aging, youth, the family, poverty, social justice at home and abroad, international development, population problems, and peace and war.

Despite the statements and publications on respect for life and right to life of the bishops and the USCC, even those sectors of the antiabortion movement largely or entirely organized with Church aid show almost no conception of this larger respect-for-life stance. Their focus is on abortion per se and not on "everything and anything that unjustly ends or demeans life." The only exception is the National Youth Pro-Life Coalition. Some right-to-life publications do show a growing tendency to link abortion and euthanasia, but this is the only other issue which the leaders of most of the major antiabortion organizations seem to see as connected to a respect-for-life program.[29] The popular media also appears unaware of the larger aspects of the right-to-life issue as it is conceived by the Church hierarchy and the USCC. Numerous articles in the press have appeared on the Church and abortion, but almost without exception they project the issue and the Church's activities regarding it in the narrowest sense.[30]

The narrow focus on abortion by the antiabortion movement, even that section of it largely led by Catholics, seems to be at least in part a matter of political strategy and tactics. A leader of the National Right to Life Committee seemed puzzled at first when asked if her organization was involved with a total right-to-life agenda or only with abortion. After she explained that groups connected with the National Right to Life organization were discussing ideas such as protection of individual rights, rights of old people, for example, and euthanasia, she added, "In the abortion movement the whole idea of ethics, of morals, is ever present. However, the main fight now is abortion and so our effort is concentrated on abortion. What happens afterwards, if we go on to other prolife issues, depends only in part on us. It would also depend on the decision of our board of directors and on what the state and local organizations want to do."[31]

The director of another national antiabortion organization said, "It is true that most prolife groups concentrate simply on abortion per se but I view it primarily as a political strategy on their part and not due to ideological differences. My staff's experience is that the majority of those involved in prolife efforts are deeply concerned with all human life, and have made the conscious decision to concentrate just on the rights of the unborn because their goal is herculean, their numbers are limited, and the other social justice/prolife goals are being pursued by a huge class of liberals in America."[32]

Despite these partial disclaimers, there seems reason to believe that the dichotomy of approach to the right-to-life issue, the differences in understanding it and of projecting it on a wider or narrower basis, may involve more than tactical decisions. Evidence from the institutional Church interviews seems to indicate that different groups in the Church, performing crucially different functions, apparently do perceive the issue differently.

Of the nineteen interviews where remarks were sufficiently clear to permit categorization, I found that nine Church leaders spontaneously spoke of right to life in the broad sense as including not just abortion but everything that unjustly terminates or degrades life. Ten others discussed right to life as involving only abortion. In other sections of their interviews they may have discussed social justice issues and may have favored activity to promote social justice, but they did not seem to link these to the abortion issue in any way. These ten people never spontaneously linked abortion and other social justice issues as did the nine leaders cited above. Two did discuss such linkages but only after direct questions regarding them. Significantly, those viewing right to life in the broader sense of anything that unjustly ends or degrades life were, in general, the bishops and Church leaders whose principal activities had been or were involved with social action. Those who viewed right to life in the narrower sense of abortion only were in general antiabortion organization leaders, Church lobbyists, and some Catholic writers and editors—people whose jobs were most closely linked with publicizing the abortion issue, lobbying on it with legislators, and educating and politically activating the general public on the issue.

Another development in the Catholic Church leadership may help to explain the intensity and commitment of the abortion struggle. Since the Supreme Court decision a significant section of the Church leadership has come to view the abortion issue in terms of a vital conflict between opposing value systems. Those who view the right-to-life issue as involving only abortion seem to express this sense of conflict most explicitly and vehemently, but even among leaders who view right-to-life broadly there are traces of a kind of uneasy sense that "antilife" forces are coming into direct confrontation with the Church.

Russell Shaw was one of the earliest to express publicly what many Catholic leaders are now saying. In an article published in the September 1973 issue of *America,* he asserted that the Supreme Court decisions on aid to parochial schools and abortion "dramatize the growing alienation of American Catholics from American values." The decisions, he wrote, involve "the gut question of whether American Catholics will be accepted in American society on their own terms, or whether the dominant society will define the terms of acceptance for them. Looked at this way the Supreme Court's January decisions can be seen as a blunt assertion by a dominant society that it means to tell Catholics 'just so far and no further.' "[33] Asked in an interview how his article had been received, Shaw answered, "The reaction to my article from bishops and from other people was 'By God, you're right!' I think the bishops, like the rest of us, are going through a period of inchoate realization that something is going on. My article wasn't based on any empirical findings but on something I felt and I seemed to have touched on something others felt."[34]

In the interviews Church leaders showed a strong tendency to characterize the abortion issue as a clash between conflicting value systems; thirteen of the twenty-two leaders made at least an allusion of this sort. Only nine leaders never discussed the abortion issue in terms of divisiveness or group conflict. Four leaders strongly stressed the urgency of avoiding the view of the abortion issue as one of Catholics versus non-Catholics. Cautioned a bishop in this group, "If we allow this to be made a Catholic issue, we'll lose, the amendment will be defeated."[35] Another leader said, "It is a mistake to see the antiabortion issue as a religious, a Catholic issue. It isn't. To put it that way is to lessen the impact of the issue. It is a basic human issue."[36] In interviews with two of the people in this group, however, there were slight allusions to a conflict in value systems. The bishop quoted above also said, "The most important thing is to work to salvage individual, personal dignity, to fight the 'antilife' forces which seem to be mounting in this country."[37]

Eleven people emphasized that abortion was a part of the Catholic value system and that this was now under attack, rather than stressing Catholic and non-Catholic cooperation on abortion. In four cases the allusion was slight. "The Church," said one social activist Church leader, "can't be caught in the prevailing value systems which are not Gospel."[38] With seven leaders the feeling of being under attack was very strong. They believed that the abortion struggle was one between prevailing value systems, and their sense of anger and anguish was compounded by a belief that Catholic acceptance into the general American society in the 1960s might have been a fraud and a delusion, that the Supreme Court's decision mirrored this and had an anti-Catholic bias.

The leader of an antiabortion organization said, "Catholics are pinned against the wall now. The [other] churches have adapted to technology. They have changed their traditions so much recently. The Catholic Church among them stands like a brick wall, invulnerable."[39] A lobbyist declared, "There is still anti-Catholic hostility in areas traditionally opposed to the Church, the area of aid to education, abortion, for example. People disagree with the Church here, disagree for a variety of reasons, but I think reasonable people looking at the evidence would have to conclude that anti-Catholic hostility is a factor here."[40]

A USCC official's interview revealed the depth of feeling toward the Supreme Court and its role. "There is a clash of value systems. The Supreme Court could have decided the issue on much narrower grounds. Historically there would have been precedents for doing so. But instead it said the fetus was not human and so in its decision it is making a moral judgment. Many Catholics and even some bishops are beginning to say that the Supreme Court here is dealing in lawlessness and that if it sustains its position Catholics, through moral conviction, would be justified in civil disobedience. There is definitely growing today in the Supreme Court's decisions an attempt to deny any kind of moral values, to establish a legal system devoid of values and this trend is present in society too."[41]

Coupled with this view of the Supreme Court as central to the attack on Catholic values is the feeling of disillusionment in regard to Catholic acceptance. Said the editor of a conservative Catholic magazine, "Abortion is a clash of value systems. We are being pushed to the wall . . . The theological dream world that liberal Catholics inhabited in the 1960s is now becoming impossible . . . and the fundamental problem of the American political system comes to the fore, its moral neutrality, the inability to define moral truth . . . see the Supreme Court decisions."[42] This was not just a conservative position. One of the youngest and most liberal bishops in the Church remarked, "Sociologists would say that . . . the suspicion of Catholics has died. Of course, the Supreme Court decision finished that."[43] An antiabortion leader remarked sadly, "People in general are more sophisticated but not necessarily less anti-Catholic. The Supreme Court decision mirrors this, mirrors this more sophisticated form of anti-Catholicism." He added, "We had a moment of glory in the 1960s when there seemed to be consensus."[44]

Leadership reaction may seem surprising. Why should the Court's decision have seemed anti-Catholic and the subsequent conflict over the abortion issue have seemed a value conflict in which leaders saw Catholic acceptance into American society called into question? Interviews and Catholic publications indicate that several factors probably influenced the reaction. A number of Constitutional scholars, including Archibald Cox, have questioned the legitimacy of the Court's entry into this area and its strong reliance in its decision on sociological and medical data still being disputed by experts in those fields. Church leaders felt the entry illegitimate also, particularly since a central Catholic teaching was involved. The sweeping nature of the decision was unexpected, as even proabortionists admitted, and came as a psychological shock to Catholic leaders, again, because a central Catholic teaching was involved. Finally, as Church leaders reacted to the decision through intensified political action to counteract it, the legitimacy of the Church's acting politically on the issue was widely and vehemently attacked and the issue labeled by some proabortion as well as some antiabortion exponents as a Catholic/non-Catholic one. These factors, probably combined with memories of rather recent anti-Catholic discrimination, produced feelings among the leadership of a revival of anti-Catholic hostility and of involvement in a value conflict.

The extent to which institutional Church leaders give the abortion conflict the heightened dimension of a clash of value systems is difficult to determine. Of the nine leaders who made no such allusions, six were not based primarily in Washington; this was the only factor they seem to have in common. Of the thirteen making some reference to abortion as a Catholic/non-Catholic value conflict, all of those (seven) who made vehement statements on the subject were Washington-based. The people who most strongly see abortion as a conflict of values, the Supreme Court decisions as anti-Catholic, and Catholic acceptance into American society as perhaps spurious or conditional were the Washington professionals most concerned with lobbying, organizing, and writing on the issue. With one exception, also, they are the people who viewed the abortion issue narrowly, as abortion per se, and not those who incorporated abortion into a whole respect-for-life agenda. They are, with a single exception, writers, editors, lobbyists, and active directors of the Church or Church-related antiabortion organizations. As such, they are in a position to influence strongly both Catholic and general perceptions of the abortion issue and its ramifications.

Among those who incorporated antiabortion into a whole respect-for-life agenda and also made at least some allusion to the issue as a value conflict, there was a tendency to see the conflict not as one of Catholics versus non-Catholics but as a conflict between those — Catholics and non-Catholics — who support a view of life that is nonmaterialistic, compassionate, and humane, embracing both prevention of the killing of a living fetus, prison reform, and aid to migrants, versus those who support a basically materialistic, technological, depersonalized, totally secular society. Although, like the abortion issue itself, the sense of value conflict was somewhat different in these two Catholic groups, what is perhaps most important is how pervasive that sense of conflict was among Church leaders.

One Church interviewee declared that all Church leaders are against abortion.[45] The conservative editor remarked that abortion "may be the one thing that can bring the Church together."[46] Certainly, institutional Church leadership is nearly unanimous in its opposition to abortion, and a large section of the leadership and its organizations, even those one would not ordinarily assume to be involved with the issue, have been drawn into the struggle in one way or another. The Family Services Division of the USCC, committees of the NCCB, and the antiabortion organizations more or less formally separated from the Church but closely tied to it have developed goals and strategies that are much alike. Family Life emphasizes abortion as part of an entire right-to-life philosophy and agenda. Its director describes its activities as having, first, an educative aspect: "We have to begin education in every parish" on the whole spectrum of right to life; and, second, a legislative follow-through: "We have to make our people more aware, more alert to the need for citizen involvement . . . We've got to get involved with political work, campaigning."[47]

Lynch's organization, the Committee for a Human Life

Amendment, formally but not really separated from the institutional Church, follows the same tactics but acts in society in general, not just in the Church and parish structure. Lynch describes its efforts to achieve a constitutional amendment as follows:

> First, we have to get to the clergy and educate them. There is an invidious idea growing. Some members of Congress are saying, "I personally am against abortion. I think abortion is wrong but I can't decide that for other people." [Our] argument for abortion must be (1) not on the basis of moral theology but on the basis of the human rights embedded in the Constitution . . . (2) We must organize throughout the states, sophisticated organizations. Twenty-eight states now have Catholic conferences . . . Twenty-two states with small Catholic populations have no conferences. But we must set up some kind of organizations there, too, because we can't win this fight if we forget twenty-two states. (3) We need to emphasize the role of women in this . . . In the practical political sphere it would be better to show that women are behind this instead of celibate clergy . . . (4) The movement has to involve groups other than Catholic. We must involve non-Catholics and those of no faith.[48]

The National Right to Life Committee, although formally nonsectarian and independent of the Church, has many ties to it and many organizers and leaders of the Catholic faith. The organization and its state and local affiliates have played a leading role thus far in public demonstrations and in lobbying. Beginning in 1974, thousands of its adherents have come to Washington yearly to demonstrate on the anniversary of the Supreme Court decision.[49] Right to Life led rallies in Albany in an earlier effort to repeal the New York State abortion law. It seeks also to educate and activate the general public on the issue through its newspaper and through public meetings sponsored by local affiliates. At the national level, it has lobbied Congress probably more intensely, or at least more openly, than any other antiabortion organization. Along with Lynch's group, it has adopted the strategy of focusing almost entirely on abortion.[50] Its leaders insist that it does not argue abortion on theological or moral grounds but on the grounds of civil rights. Much of its publicity, however, has heavily moral overtones.

The institutional Church organizations immediately concerned with abortion and the more or less independent antiabortion organizations also seem to be in basic agreement on the need for a Constitutional amendment on abortion and on what such an amendment should include. During the Ninety-third Congress, eight antiabortion amendments were offered in the House and Senate, including an amendment by Congressman Edward Derwinski but written by the National Right to Life organization.[51] The other seven amendments were offered by James Buckley and Jesse Helms in the Senate and by Lawrence Hogan, William Whitehurst, James Burke, James O'Hara, and John Dingell in the House of Representatives. Three amendments, those offered by Representatives Whitehurst, O'Hara, and Dingell, would essentially return authority to decide abortion regulation to the states. These states' rights amendments have little support either from the Church or the major national antiabortion organizations.[52]

All of the other amendments would nullify the Supreme Court's ruling and restrict abortion. They were similar in language, scope, and especially intent, when clarifying statements issued by their sponsors are considered. The amendments offered by Lawrence Hogan in the House and Jesse Helms in the Senate were identical and would preclude abortion "from the moment of conception." Buckley's and Burke's amendments excluded abortion "at every stage of biological development." The National Right to Life amendment also uses this language. Buckley, Helms, Hogan, Burke, and Derwinski insisted that they intended by their amendments to prohibit abortion from the moment of fertilization. Language was somewhat different but the time period after which abortion would be restricted seemed identical in all five of these major amendments.[53] Three amendments would specifically permit abortion in the case of danger to the mother's health (those offered by Buckley, Burke, and Derwinski, speaking for the National Right to Life Committee). Although the Helms and Hogan amendment did not specifically state this exception, Hogan said he was in agreement with it and regarded it as implied in his amendment.[54]

The Catholic Church has not officially endorsed any specific amendment. The testimony of the USCC before Senator Birch Bayh's Sub-committee on Constitutional Amendments and the oral testimony presented to it by Cardinals John Krol, Timothy Manning, Humberto Medeiros, and John Cody all urged passage of a human life amendment. Cardinal Krol, President of the

USCC, specifically commended the senators and representatives who had sponsored amendments. Although Cardinal Medeiros pointed out that theologically the Church opposes abortion in all cases, including threat to the mother's life, there is evidence that the Church, realizing the political difficulties of an absolute restriction in a pluralist society, is willing to support an amendment allowing such exceptions.

As Thomas Dillon, a Catholic lawyer who helped to draft the National Right to Life amendment stated:

> The principles of Catholic theology were never totally in agreement with our old anti-abortion laws and in a nation where Catholics are a minority it's a fairly safe assumption that they never will be. This does not mean, however, that the Catholic hierarchy could not support this proposed amendment. Not too long ago, for example, the Catholic bishops of New York State supported the Donovan-Crawford bill which would have repealed abortion except "to save the life of the mother." It would also appear that the hierarchy could support the proposed [National Right to Life Committee] constitutional amendment on the basis that it doesn't, in and of itself, allow a single abortion to take place.[55]

It seems fair to say, then, that there is substantial agreement among Church and Congressional leaders on the specifics of the Constitutional amendment to be fought for. The amendment would preclude abortion from the moment of conception, on the assumption that from that time a human being exists whose rights, including the right to life, are protected under the Constitution. However, the amendment would allow, in accordance with the Constitutional principles of due process and equal protection, with their implied right to self-defense, abortion in the case of serious danger to the mother's life.

The Catholic People

Survey results show clearly that most Catholics are prepared to accept the legal availability of abortion in cases of severe physical or psychological threat to the mother or infant; they are opposed to what is generally called "permissive abortion," or "abortion on demand." That is, the great majority of Catholics would permit legally available abortion when the mother's life is endangered, when the pregnancy is caused by rape, or when the fetus is severely defective. Abortion for economic reasons or reasons of personal happiness is opposed by the great majority. Both white and Spanish-speaking Catholics are more opposed to abortion under all circumstances than other Americans, except southern blacks, and their opposition increases as, in their perception, the reasons for abortion become less severe. Within all education and age groups, Catholics still are more opposed to abortion than most other Americans. The more devout the Catholic, the more strongly he or she opposes abortion in every instance. On this issue, the Church truly seems to have influenced its members, who are strongly united.

NORC surveyed American opinion on abortion in all four years of the combined sample covering 1972-1975. The surveys do not ask Catholics, or Americans of other faiths, any questions on their personal moral approach to abortion, whether they believe abortion to be right or wrong for themselves.[56] They pose instead hypothetical questions involving the legal rights of all Americans. They ask if, in six different cases, a woman should be legally able to obtain an abortion if she wishes.

Posed in this way, the answers demonstrate that 86.0 percent of white Catholics of European descent believe a woman should be able to obtain a legal abortion if the pregnancy endangers her life; 79.1 percent of white Catholics believe that a woman who desires it should be able to obtain a legal abortion when pregnancy results from rape; 76.5 percent of them believe that if she desires it, a woman should be able to obtain an abortion if the fetus is severely damaged. Spanish-speaking Catholics support abortion in these three cases in equal or slightly lower percentages. While Catholic support rates are high, they are much lower than the rates of support for abortion by Jews and white northern Protestants and lower also than those of white southern Protestants and northern blacks. Only southern black Protestants have lower support rates than Catholics (table 5.1).

More significant, perhaps, in terms of the political struggle over abortion is the fact that Catholics are much less willing than non-Catholics to support what is called "abortion on demand," the term used to define the belief that a woman's body is her own and therefore she should be able to obtain an abortion simply because she desires it. As the respected and liberal Catholic magazine *Commonweal* pointed out, "Almost all Catholics are totally

Table 5.1. Attitudes toward abortion by race, religion, and region (percentage favoring).

Group[1]	Serious danger to mother's health	Pregnancy resulted from rape	Serious defect in the baby	Family can't afford more children	Woman is unmarried and doesn't wish to marry	Woman is married but wants no more children
WCED	86.0	79.1	76.5	43.0	39.7	35.6
SSC	86.9	67.2	75.4	29.1	23.7	21.2
Jews	98.1	98.8	96.9	88.6	86.6	84.5
WPNS	94.0	89.0	88.5	59.3	54.6	50.7
WPS	91.8	81.8	84.7	46.8	41.8	38.3
BPNS	88.6	85.1	80.5	52.2	46.3	47.8
BPS	76.4	61.0	59.4	36.1	27.3	29.3

1. WCED: white Catholics of European descent. SSC: Spanish-speaking Catholics. WPNS: white Protestants, non-South. WPS: white Protestants, South. BPNS: black Protestants, non-South. BPS: black Protestants, South.

opposed to the present general permissiveness on abortion . . . we see no evidence of any significant body of liberalizing opinion [in the Church] which would take a passive attitude on abortion on demand, without grave cause."[57] While not showing that "almost all" Catholics oppose "abortion on demand," surveys indicate that Catholic support for legal abortion declines precipitously as perceptions of the gravity of reasons for demanding it decline (table 5.1).

On an average, for example, white Catholics approve abortion in the cases of severe threat to the physical or psychological health of mother or child by 80.5 percent, but they approve "abortion-on-demand" cases by only 39.4 percent. The margin of difference between white Catholics and Jews and white northern Protestants in these less severe cases widens significantly. White Catholic support rates here are even 15 percent lower than those of white southern Protestants, the white group most like Catholics in their attitude toward abortion. Spanish-speaking Catholics disapprove of "abortion on demand" to an even greater extent than white Catholics. Indeed, the Spanish-speaking evince the lowest rates of support here of any major American ethnic group, including southern black Protestants.

Increased education generally has the effect of liberalizing opinion on abortion, but Catholics are less affected by this than other groups. Although southern black Protestants as a whole are less supportive of abortion than are white Catholics, increased education changes this. In regard to abortion for economic or personal reasons, black southern Protestants who are high school graduates support abortion more than white Catholic high school graduates. College graduates among southern blacks are more supportive of abortion in every circumstance than white Catholic college graduates and college graduates in all other groups, black and white, Protestant and Jewish, are far more supportive of abortion than Catholic college graduates. At the lowest level of education—less than high school—some ethnic groups give less support to abortion in certain circumstances than do Catholics. Even high school education, however, begins to correlate with substantially more liberal opinions on abortion for groups other than white Catholics. College education greatly intensifies the liberal trend for all groups but Catholics. White Catholic college graduates are actually less supportive of abortion in cases of severe psychological or physical threat to mother or child than are less well-educated Catholics (table 5.2). Numbers of Spanish-speaking Catholic college graduates are too low for statistical validity and therefore are not included in the table, but the few college graduates among them appear less liberal on abortion than Spanish-speaking high school graduates or dropouts.

Age correlates with abortion attitude among Catholics. Both white and Spanish-speaking Catholics aged eighteen to twenty-nine are more inclined to support abortion than older Catholics. Among some other ethnic groups, people thirty to forty-nine are more or nearly as supportive of abortion as younger group members, perhaps because it is at this middle age that people most feel the demands of family. This is not true among Catholics. Catholic support for abortion declines in a continuous line with age.

Table 5.2. Attitudes toward abortion by education, race, religion, and region (averaged percentage favoring).

Group	College graduates	High school graduates	Less than high school
	Severe physical or psychological threat to mother or child[1]		
WCED	78.4	81.0	79.2
Jews	100.0	96.3	94.1
WPNS	95.3	91.1	85.8
WPS	96.0	88.7	79.2
BPNS	93.6	92.7	74.3
BPS	83.8	78.3	58.1
	Economic reasons or reasons for personal happiness[2]		
WCED	44.4	38.6	36.5
Jews	96.4	81.0	66.4
WPNS	74.3	56.2	40.8
WPS	67.9	43.7	31.0
BPNS	63.4	40.4	42.4
BPS	48.0	44.5	24.7

1. Serious danger to the mother's health; pregnancy resulted from rape; serious defect in the baby.

2. Family can't afford more children; women is unmarried and doesn't wish to marry; woman is married but wants no more children.

Although younger Catholics support abortion in greater measure than do older Catholics, in cases of severe threat to mother or child white Catholics even at this age are less supportive of abortion than young people in any other group except southern blacks. In cases of abortion for economic reasons or reasons of personal happiness, they and young southern blacks have nearly identically low measures of support and the young Spanish-speaking have the lowest support rates of any group of eighteen-to-twenty-nine-year-olds (table 5.3).

The factor that seems sharply to influence opinion on abortion among Catholics, and possibly among black southern Protestants, is religiosity. The more devout the Catholic, the more opposed he or she is to abortion under any circumstance. The Catholic who attends church weekly, in fact, is more than twice as likely to oppose abortion for economic reasons or reasons of personal happiness than is the nonobservant or only occasionally observant Catholic. Even in cases of severe physical and psychological threat to the mother or child, the Catholic attending church weekly is less supportive of abortion by 25 percent than the nonattender (table 5.4).

Table 5.3. Attitudes toward abortion by age, race, and religion (averaged percentage favoring).

Group[1]	Ages 18-29	Ages 30-49	Ages 50 and older
	Severe physical or psychological threat to mother or child		
WCED	86.6	79.6	75.6
SSC	87.8	77.3	56.5
Jews	97.6	99.3	97.2
WP	90.4	89.0	88.7
BP	78.9	80.3	63.8
	Economic reasons or reasons of personal happiness		
WCED	45.8	38.6	36.3
SSC	32.2	21.4	14.2
Jews	87.9	87.8	83.4
WP	56.5	51.9	48.3
BP	44.9	44.8	25.3

1. WP: white Protestants. BP: black Protestants.

Table 5.4. Attitudes toward abortion among white Catholics of European descent, by religiosity (percentage favoring).

Church attendance	Serious danger to mother's health	Pregnancy resulted from rape	Serious defect in the baby	Family can't afford more children	Woman is unmarried and doesn't wish to marry	Woman is married but wants no more children
Never	98.9	91.7	91.4	59.3	57.6	55.9
Less than once a year	96.4	87.1	91.4	57.6	48.8	53.0
Once to several times yearly	94.6	89.9	88.5	61.2	54.4	54.0
Monthly	91.9	85.9	83.1	47.8	41.0	38.3
Weekly or more	76.5	65.5	64.5	25.5	25.0	19.1

Catholic support for legalized abortion generally remains below that of other ethnic groups in the country. White and Spanish-speaking Catholics have significantly lower support rates than Jews or white northern Protestants. Only black southern Protestants have lower abortion support rates than white Catholics, and Spanish-speaking Catholics under some circumstances support abortion even less than blacks. Catholics diverge from other Americans particularly on the issue of abortion for economic reasons or reasons of personal happiness. Only southern black Protestants in two of the three circumstances presented have lower rates than white Catholics here, and Spanish-speaking Catholics are much less supportive than they. Increased education does not tend to liberalize Catholic opinion on abortion to the extent it does that of all other American ethnic groups. Age has more effect on Catholics. Young Catholics are much more supportive of abortion than their elders but even the youngest of Catholic adults are more opposed to abortion than young people of any other group except southern black Protestants. Religious fervor seems a strong factor in Catholic attitudes toward abortion — at least opposition to abortion rises sharply with increased religious attendance.

The Catholic laity seem to diverge from their Church leadership in that large percentages support abortion in cases of rape and a defective fetus, in addition to the widespread support for abortion in cases of danger to the mother — the only condition for abortion to which the Church seems to have given tacit consent. In this the Catholic people may be more in tune with their political leadership (or, perhaps better, the politicians more in tune with them). Catholic politicians in speeches and in their votes have shown fairly wide agreement on acceptance of abortion not just when the mother's life is endangered but in cases where pregnancy is the result of rape or incest.[58] Abortion for reasons of a defective fetus is viewed with disfavor by both the Church and antiabortion organizations formally or informally tied to it, and there is no indication of any extensive support for this kind of abortion by Catholic politicians.[59] There seems strong unity between Church and people — and Catholic congressional leadership — in opposing abortions for economic reasons or reasons of personal choice.

A number of writers, including Catholics, have suggested that

Catholic opposition to abortion may be based on the fact that Catholics, especially white Catholics of European descent, are social conservatives, that is, that they tend to be more family-oriented, more traditional and conservative, and more repressive socially and sexually than other Americans. Their opposition to abortion, according to this argument, is only part and parcel of their opposition generally to more liberal attitudes on sexual matters.

Survey results do not support this argument. Although white Catholics and southern Protestants resemble one another more than other whites in the degree of their opposition to abortion, white Catholics are generally more liberal than white southern Protestants on other questions of sex and morals. Indeed, white Catholics are more liberal on some questions of sex and morals than white northern Protestants. Certainly they cannot be considered less liberal than other white Christians. (Jews are the most liberal of all white groups on sexual and moral issues.)

In regard to pornography, white Catholics are slightly less likely than white Protestants to believe no laws should govern its sale and more likely to believe sales should be prohibited to children. However, they are also less likely than Protestants to believe it should be prohibited to adults. Catholics are much more likely than white southern Protestants and likelier than northern Protestants to believe marijuana should be legalized. They are much less likely than white southern Protestants to think divorce should be made more difficult. Their opinion on divorce differs little from that of white northern Protestants. About 90 percent of white Catholics and white southern Protestants say that birth control information should be available for everyone, but when asked specifically about teenagers, Catholics are likelier than southerners to think that birth control information should be available to them. Catholics also are likelier than either white northern or, especially, white southern Protestants to support the idea of sex education in the public schools (table 5.5).

The concept that Catholics are more traditional, conservative, or puritanical than other Americans and therefore opposed to abortion does not seem to be true. Catholic opposition to abortion, especially abortions for economic or personal reasons, seems to have other roots. Abortion seems to strike a particular chord among Catholics not struck by other moral issues. The reason

Table 5.5. Attitudes toward sexual and moral issues by race, religion, and region on six selected questions (in percentages).

There should be laws prohibiting the sale of pornography to:

	People of whatever age	Children under 18	Should be no laws
WCED	43.4	50.0	6.6
WPNS	46.8	44.5	8.7
WPS	50.0	43.1	6.9

Marijuana should be legalized.

	Agree	Disagree
WCED	20.5	79.5
WPNS	17.8	82.2
WPS	8.9	91.1

Divorce laws should be made:

	Easier	More difficult	Remain as are
WCED	26.4	50.2	23.4
WPNS	24.6	49.4	26.0
WPS	22.9	57.9	19.2

Birth control information should be available for everyone.

	Agree	Disagree
WCED	91.0	9.0
WPNS	94.2	5.8
WPS	89.9	10.1

Birth control information should be available for teenagers.

	Agree	Disagree	Don't know
WCED	78.9	20.8	0.3
WPNS	82.8	17.2	0.0
WPS	74.2	25.8	0.0

Sex education should be available in the public schools.

	Agree	Disagree	Don't know
WCED	83.8	15.4	0.8
WPNS	81.1	18.6	0.3
WPS	71.3	28.5	0.2

may be because of Catholic teachings about the sanctity of human life, for it contains the soul (a belief also of many Protestant groups); it may be the result of recent intensive Church education and activity on the abortion issue.

Catholic Political Leaders

Lewis Dexter wrote that in interviewing congressmen and senators for his study on lobbying and its effect on reciprocal trade legislation, he purposedly began with the broad, innocuous question, "What do you hear from business?"[60] The variety of responses given and the rarity with which reciprocal trade was mentioned helped lead to his conclusions regarding the general ineffectiveness of lobbying and the diffuse quality of legislators' attention, interest, and information. He would have gotten no such response if he had been investigating the abortion issue.

The abortion issue was obviously on the minds of most of the congressmen and senators interviewed for this study. Questions fully as broad and innocuous as Dexter's—for example, on the effect of the rise in the numbers of Catholics in Congress, the changes in the degree and kind of Church concerns over the past decade, the growth of Church influence on politics, the extent to which anti-Catholic hostility still existed in the country—all spurred discussion of the abortion issue by congressmen and senators. Eleven of the twenty-six politicians interviewed spontaneously introduced the issue into our discussions. Also unlike Dexter's experiences with political interviewees on the reciprocal trade issue, these Catholic politicians discussed the abortion issue in great detail and with great emotion. "There are still some pockets of hostility in the country," said one midwestern senator. "The Church's attempt to legislate its moral position, for example, on abortion, doesn't help, especially when attempts are unsuccessful . . . If you play in the realms of Caesar and lose, maybe you've lost on God's fields, too."[61] In another interview an eastern senator, in the middle of a discussion of changes in Church concerns, suddenly said, "The Supreme Court, though. I'm about ready to rebel against the Supreme Court when they say a husband can't prevent an abortion."[62] Only one politician failed to comment at all on the issue. In addition to the eleven who spontaneously introduced the topic of abortion, all of the other fourteen men interviewed discussed it readily enough when asked about it. In general, they too discussed it heatedly and in detail.

Only six politicians seemed to see the issue as not very important or to calmly and rationally assess the pros and cons of the issue. Of those who specifically said they were under pressure from the pro- or antiabortion movement, only two dismissed the pressure. Said an eastern congressman, "I'm being pressured [by Right to Life] but I'm resisting it."[63] Another congressman reported and dismissed even stronger pressure: I don't think [abortion] has strong political impact, regardless of what they say . . . Someone sent me a church bulletin St. Peter's parish [in his district] put out. It lists all the Catholic candidates in W state and alongside my name is 'antilife' and alongside my opponent's is 'prolife.' Only one person bothered to send it to me . . . I haven't heard a word from anyone else."[64]

Most interviewees, however, displayed strong emotion which took the form of either a warm support for the issue or, more often, anger. The anger seemed chiefly to stem from the fact that, unlike other lobbying situations, this one subjected them to intense mail and personal pressure on an issue with great national, state, and district publicity, and their own actions were being watched and reported. Congressman Lawrence Hogan, author of a major human life amendment in the House, commented on his colleagues' reactions. "You've got to understand congressmen, politicians. It's against a politician's nature to want to take a stand on a controversial issue. Because, when you do, you always lose at least some people . . . Every time I take the floor to speak on my amendment, I'm hissed. They don't want to hear about it. They want to avoid the issue."[65]

The targets for the anger and frustration of these interviewees were the Church, both the antiabortion and proabortion movements, and other politicians who had taken action for or against the issue. The following quotations are indicative of their statements in general: "We could discuss the abortion issue rationally. It's the Catholic Church which is polarizing the issue rather than any outside sources."[66] "Both sides say, 'You're against us.' Both sides are using threats. These actions and threats are injuring the image of both sides. But what I care about is that they are injuring the Catholic image and this is important to me."[67] "Then look at the committees. Our chairman, Rodino: he wears a pin that he says came from the Pope, but he hasn't lifted a hand. You'd think he'd be supporting the amendment but he wants to avoid the abortion issue. He goes around wearing this lapel pin and every-time he changes his suit he puts this pin back in his lapel. It's sup-posed to be some kind of papal pin. He's not doing a thing about the abortion issue!"[68] "Right to Life is the most obnoxious group ever to lobby Congress. Any congressman will tell you that."[69] A midwestern Republican most graphically illustrated his own and his colleagues' struggles with this issue. "Abortion? . . . I avoid abortion like the plague. So far I've managed to stay alive on the issue. It's dynamite. I've called for the Judiciary Committee to have hearings and after that I don't know what I'll do."[70]

Twelve of the twenty-six politicians interviewed said they had been targets of intense lobbying. Four others discussed either bishops' statements on this issue or right-to-life organizations and their activities in their districts. "I have been getting letters from both sides asking my position," said one congressman, "and tell-ing me they won't campaign for me or they'll vote against me if I don't agree with their position."[71] A young liberal senator agreed: "I'm being pressed on the issue—by both sides. Both sides have been pressing every congressman and senator."[72] A New York congressman said, "the 'prolife' groups certainly have been in contact with our office. We've gotten mail from all over the coun-try, from various parishes."[73] Ten politicians indicated that they had not been lobbied on abortion.

Antiabortion lobbying groups such as Right to Life, and not the Church hierarchy and the Church as an institution, seemed to have been the source of the politicians' impressions on the abor-tion issue. The politicians' responses differed from those of the Church leaders interviewed, who were nearly unanimous in their outspoken antiabortion sentiment. Only one Church official voiced any doubts regarding the Church's position and only two others failed to assert positively the Church's position. Nineteen of the twenty-two Church interviewees declared themselves against abortion. I heard no such near-unanimous antiabortion declarations from the Catholic politicians interviewed.

What I found more than anything else was caution. Almost half of all the Catholic politicians interviewed discussed the sub-ject but would give no indication of their own position on it. Only one congressman openly declared himself in favor of abortion and only four others, without voicing a personal opinion on abortion, said that they "might not" vote for an antiabortion Constitutional amendment. Four openly declared themselves against abortion and said they would so vote, and three others indicated the same position. Finally, three said that they were personally opposed to abortion but were not sure how they would vote. "I hate abortion," said a Catholic House leader. "I abhor abortion personally, but I don't think I have the right to impose my beliefs on others."[74] Said a midwestern Republican, "I'm against abortion personally but I don't know how I'd vote."[75] Thus, in contrast to the outspoken near unanimity of the Church leaders, I found almost half of the Catholic politicians taking no position on abortion and less than a third indicating an antiabortion belief strong enough to result in their vote for an antiabortion Constitutional amendment. Five of the seven men making up this antiabortion group were Republicans. All of the eight men indicating that they probably would, or at least might, vote against an antiabortion amendment were Democrats.

Even more strikingly at variance with the position of Church leaders was the fact that no politician saw this issue as part of a broader respect-for-life agenda. Notwithstanding the bishops' statements and the literature and statements of the USCC that link an antiabortion stance with peace and social justice issues, no politician seemed to recognize a linkup of the prolife attitude on abortion with attitudes on other issues involved with a more humane life for people in general.[76] The politicians did not use the terms many Church leaders used in discussing abortion, such as prolife, respect for life, right to life, and so on. Catholic politicians spoke in narrow terms of abortion only. Only two politicians even used the term right-to-life, and they used it only as a designation of a lobbying organization, not as a description of a total social justice philosophy. One politician never addressed the subject of abortion and six spoke in terms difficult to classify. Of the other nineteen, though, only seven discussed the issue in terms of morals or values. The other twelve discussed abortion principally in political terms.

The seven men who viewed abortion as a moral issue indicated that they linked this to their Catholic upbringing and the value system it instilled. They made remarks such as the following: "I am against abortion but as a result of my own value orientation, because I believe it's wrong."[77] "I am not aware of Church influence on politics except on the abortion issue, which is a legitimate moral issue."[78] "I suffered some shock from the Supreme Court decision as I think many people did."[79] Half of this group castigated their Catholic colleagues or the Church for not acting forcefully enough in upholding Catholic moral judgment on the issue. "It's frustrating," said one, "if you are against abortion and believe it to be a Catholic position and then this priest [Jesuit priest and congressman Robert Drinan] is for it. What is a Catholic position?"[80] Said another congressman, "I have so much a feeling of disappointment in the Church, in some of the clergy. I've been in church and had a priest say, 'You'll find a petition in your seat supporting the antiabortion amendment and if you happen to believe in that point of view you can sign it.' Well, obviously, that's telling everyone he doesn't believe in it."[81]

The twelve men who spoke of the issue in political rather than moral terms tended to discuss lobbying, constituent reaction, public opinion polls, legislative procedures, and voting, as the following comments show:[82] "Bayh's committee is sort of making an issue of it but I think the House has dropped it."[83] "I conducted a poll among my constitutents."[84] "In politics you learn to be realistic. Hogan's amendment will never get the 218 signatures it needs for discharge."[85]

All seven of the men who took a moral position on the issue were Republicans, and three of the four men who believed themselves ahead of their colleagues and their Church in exercising moral judgment were in the Jansenist group. In contrast, all but one of the men who assessed the issue politically were Democrats.

Finally, the politicians differed from Church leaders who assessed the abortion issue as a supremely vital crisis of conflicting value systems. The belief that the abortion issue was a crucial conflict over values was evident in the interviews of a significant number of Church leaders. They saw the Supreme Court decision on abortion and its aftermath as raising basic questions regarding the continuation of anti-Catholic hostility and the acceptance of American Catholics into the general society only on the condition that Catholic values be subsumed into a generalized system many leaders saw as "materialistic and totally secular." Among the Catholic politicians there was no sense that this issue was in any way a test of hostility toward Catholics by American institutions or society or a supreme clash of Catholic versus non-Catholic or Catholic versus secular value systems. This was true of both the older generation of Catholic politicians, who seemed to have fully accepted the melting pot concept and the separation of church and state argument, and the younger men, who were without any sense of Catholic minority status and believed that the Church should, if anything, be more active and concerned in social and political issues. Catholic political leaders did not believe that this issue would alienate Catholic Americans in any significant way from their fellow citizens, or that Catholics would ever again become or be forced to become an isolated group in American society. In fact, Catholic politicians tended to emphasize how complete is the demise of anti-Catholic hostility and how impossible is its revival.

Only four Catholic politicians suggested the possibility that the abortion issue might in any way lead to a revival of anti-Catholic hostility—three senators and one representative. One of these men, a strong antiabortionist, thought the possibility was there but remote. "Oh," he mused, "I think the old anti-Catholic hostility is definitely gone. Perhaps some has been brought out subliminally by the abortion issue but I think it's really gone and couldn't be revived at this date."[86] The other three also seemed to think the possibility remote but tended to blame the Church for its being there at all. A western senator, for example, said rather angrily, "I don't think [abortion] needs to [revive anti-Catholic hostility]. We could discuss the abortion issue rationally. It's the Catholic Church really which has polarized the issue, rather than any outside sources."[87] Of the twenty-six Catholic politicians interviewed, eighteen discussed the question of the demise of anti-Catholic hostility, many at length, without ever bringing the abortion issue into their discussion in any way. Four made the link between abortion and anti-Catholic feeling but only to insist that, in their opinions, abortion could have no revival effects on hostility. Said one representative, "The Church is part of society now and it's going to stay that way. There may be differences between the Church and some groups on some issues but I can't see them taking on that kind of dimension."[88] A senator agreed: "I can't anticipate any return of real hostility. Not like what was its worst manifestation with Al Smith. I don't think abortion or aid to parochial education can isolate Catholics today."[89]

Further, representatives and senators did not tend to see the Supreme Court as hostile or its abortion decision as an essentially anti-Catholic act, as did many Church leaders. Only four of the political interviewees showed any evidence of this view at all. Both Senator Buckley and Congressman Hogan, sponsors of the two major "prolife" amendments, described their reactions to the Court's decision with the same term—shock. Two other politicians also used this term in describing their reactions to the decision but, even so, went on to say that they were not sure how they would vote on an amendment to overturn the decision. Much more representative of the Catholic politicians' reactions to the Court decision—and their contrast with those of the Church leaders—was a description by a legislative assistant of how a senator was torn between respect for the Court and the law and his moral and religious beliefs.

The senator, reported the aide,

> is also being visited by a steady stream of visitors urging him to lead a constitutional amendment fight against the ruling—not bishops yet, but middle-level priests, in particular from [his state]. He sees them and listens to them but he is protected in a sense from undue pressure by the fact that he is a national leader of the Democratic Party. He is very concerned about the abortion issue. In a meeting he told his staff that he personally opposes abortion from a moral point of view. He felt he had to be consistent. He said if he opposed the Vietnam war and especially the bombings of civilians because of "right to life," because these civilians had a right to life, he had to oppose abortion on a right-to-life basis. I told him I thought if he supported an antiabortion move he would be inconsistent . . . with his earlier stands on respect for the law, for example, his criticism of Southerners and other segregationists for disobeying Supreme Court rulings on civil rights and integration . . . The senator has not yet made up his mind definitely on a public stand. This is just an exploration period.[90]

A final indication that senators and representatives do not take the Church's view that this is a struggle between Catholic and non-Catholic or, as some Church leaders said, "religious and secular" forces, is the fact that these political men are divided in their willingness to see abortion as a Catholic issue at all. Nine Catholic politicians addressed the issue only in political and strategic terms. Of the sixteen politicians responding to the issue in some way in Catholic/non-Catholic terms, only seven believed it to be an issue with particular relevance for Catholics. Four of these men seemed to believe this was so because the antiabortion orientation flowed naturally from general Catholic teachings and values. The other three seemed to believe it was a particularly Catholic issue simply because the Church had chosen to stage a major battle over it. In their opinions, the Church had, by its strong and (they implied) wrong-headed stance, made abortion a Catholic issue. One political leader, for example, declared, "But I think you can say the Catholic Church has no grip, no hold on people in public life . . . Look at the states where antiabortion bills have been up. [The states are] 100 percent or 85 percent Catholic, and it's defeated two to one."[91]

The other nine politicians insisted vehemently that this was not a Catholic/non-Catholic issue: "I'm not sure," said an eastern representative, "that the Church's position on abortion, for example, is much different from that of most non-Catholics throughout the country. Certainly the [polls in my district] haven't shown that."[92] "It's not singularly Catholic," insisted a senator.[93] Both sponsors of major prolife amendments in the Senate and House, James Buckley and Lawrence Hogan, took this position. Hogan declared, "The human life amendment is not a religious issue, anyway. It's a moral issue. It's not a religious issue any more than the Nazi extermination of the Jews was a Jewish issue. It's a human issue. A lot of religious bodies besides the Catholics are against abortion—the Orthodox Jews, for example, the Lutherans."[94]

There was, then, among the Catholic politicians interviewed, a widespread, frank acknowledgment of the abortion issue as one of which they were highly conscious and on which they were being subjected to great pressure. But also among them there were strong efforts to defuse the issue, to lower its emotional quality and impact. This seemed clear through their greater tendency to discuss it in political rather than moral or religious terms and to insist that it was not a narrowly Catholic, sectarian issue but one involving a wider array of people and organizations, non-Catholic as well as Catholic. Politicians' perceptions of the issue differed from those of Church leaders on two important points. Politicians viewed the issue narrowly, as that of abortion alone. Except for the one report by a legislative aide of the struggle of a prominent senator, there were few indications that politicians were even aware of Church leaders' efforts to link abortion with the whole spectrum of issues involved in extending and humanizing life for all people. Politicians also differed from Church leaders in that they did not view the issue as a supreme clash of value systems and certainly not as an attempt to alienate and isolate Catholics from the general culture. Catholic politicians were concerned with trying to lower the heat on a conflict-ridden issue and did not perceive the issue as one dividing religious and ethnic groups.

Examination of the actions of Catholic politicians and the extent to which these actions stem from their Catholic values or from Church and Church-related lobbying efforts is possible only in a limited way. No antiabortion or human life amendment has yet been brought up for a vote in either house of Congress. However, there are some behavioral clues, such as the way in which Catholic politicians addressed the issue in their interviews and the votes of the Catholics interviewed and those of Catholic representatives and senators in general on the twelve abortion-related riders attached to bills in the Ninety-third Congress.[95]

Representative Lawrence Hogan stated that his colleagues were hiding behind "technicalities" as "excuses for not being for [his amendment]."[96] In the interviews I perceived a tendency on the part of those legislators willing to state a position at all not to make a judgment on the abortion issue but to criticize flaws in the amendments or procedures being undertaken to overturn the Supreme Court decision. Only one politician said definitely that he favored abortion and indicated that he would vote against an amendment; only four definitely said that they abhorred abortion and would vote for an amendment. A number of interviewees, however, raised procedural or technical criticisms. A legislative assistant reported that his Catholic boss "was shocked when the [Supreme Court decision] was announced . . . Its ruling provides a legal precedent for genocide . . . The congressman would support strong antiabortion legislation but he also disagrees with the approach James Buckley has taken. He believes that Constitutional amendments should be resorted to as little as possible and only on major, fundamental issues . . . It's like Prohibition all over again. That should never have been in the Constitution and neither should this."[97] A western senator insisted that the issue really was one for decision by the states. "We on the national scene believe that this is an issue which comes under the police powers of the states rather than in the bosom of the national legislature and executive. People can have a clearer voice on the state level."[98]

Lawrence Hogan, unable to persuade the Judiciary Committee, which had jurisdiction in the House, to hold hearings on his amendment, entered a discharge petition and was attempting to gather the 218 signatures needed to discharge the amendment from the committee and bring it directly to the floor for debate and vote.[99] This move was the focus of irritated comments by a number of Catholic legislators, who objected on technical grounds. "For one thing," said a Californian, summing up the objections voiced by a number of his colleagues, "it bypasses the regular legislative process and, secondly, legislation written on the floor is the worst legislation you can have."[100]

Although Catholic legislators as a whole seemed unwilling to join an active struggle on behalf of the abortion issue, the majority of legislators who did take public action were Catholics. During the Ninety-third session, eight Constitutional amendments were offered to nullify the Supreme Court decision, two in the Senate and six in the House. Only two of these eight were offered by non-Catholics (Jesse Helms, Republican from North Carolina, in the Senate and William Whitehurst, Republican from Virginia, in the House). The other six, including the two prominent amendments by Buckley and Hogan, were all offered by Catholics (Buckley in the Senate and Lawrence Hogan, James O'Hara, James Burke, John Dingell, and Edward Derwinski in the House). Finally, there were six votes on riders restricting the use of federal funds and facilities for abortion purposes and restricting experimentation on aborted fetuses in each of the Houses during the Ninety-third Congress. Once again, Catholics tended to be the writers and sponsors of these amendments. In the House, a single Catholic representative, Angelo Roncallo of New York, sponsored four of the six abortion-related riders, Catholic Lawrence Hogan sponsored one, and a Protestant, Harold Froehlich, running a close race for reelection against a Catholic priest, sponsored one.[101] In the Senate, of five riders offered to restrict abortion or experimentation on fetuses, three were offered or modified by Catholics, James Buckley (on two occasions) and Edward Kennedy (on one). Two were offered by non-Catholics Frank Church and Jesse Helms.

The votes on the riders attached to Senate and House bills in the Ninety-third Congress showed Catholics more often than non-Catholics voting in support of measures restricting abortion and fetus experimentation. At best, this is an initial, fragmentary means of analyzing Catholic response to a Church-dominated issue. No votes have yet been taken on the human life amendments themselves. Secondly, except in one case all the restrictive riders were passed by overwhelming majorities in both Houses, majorities composed of the greater part of all legislators, Catholic and non-Catholic. Finally, the vote on riders may be misleading, since on controversial issues legislators may sometimes sponsor and vote for riders in the expectation that these will be lost in the conference committees; they may then reap the benefit of taking a stand desired by powerful interest or constituency groups without also being easily blamed for failure of the measure to result in enactment.[102] Even with these limitations, the rider votes are the only concrete measures available of response by Catholic legislators to what a number of interviewees referred to as "the only religious issue" presently before Congress. There are also distinct differences between Catholic and non-Catholic votes on several of the riders, despite the overwhelming general approval they received.

In the Senate two rider votes were unanimous or nearly unanimous. No distinction, therefore, can be made in these cases between Catholic and non-Catholic voting patterns. On March 27, 1973, the Senate voted ninety-two to one (seven members not voting) to accept an amendment proposed by Frank Church of Idaho which forbade the denial of federal funds to health facilities and individuals refusing to perform or assist in the performance of abortions for reasons of conscience. On March 13, 1974, the Senate voted eighty-seven to zero (thirteen senators not voting) to accept an amendment to a bill on capital punishment providing that in no event shall a death sentence be carried out upon a pregnant woman.[103]

On September 11, 1973, two votes were taken with ambiguous significance. Senator Buckley offered an amendment to the Protection of Human Subjects Act which would prohibit the conduct or support of research on a living human fetus. Kennedy, manager of the original bill, then offered an amendment to the Buckley amendment reading, "Until such time as certification of Institutional Review Boards has been established and the Commission develops policies with regard to the conduct of research on the living fetus or infant."[104] The Kennedy amendment was approved in the Senate by a vote of fifty-three to thirty-five, twelve Senators not voting. The Senate as a whole, then, voted 53 percent for the Kennedy amendment, 35 percent against. Catholic support for the Kennedy amendment was even higher than that of the Senate as a whole, with 64.3 percent of Catholic senators voting for the amendment and 35.7 percent voting against it. (All Catholic senators voted.) Four of the Catholic senators who voted against the amendment were Republicans (Marlow Cook, Peter Domenici, James Buckley, and Dewey Bartlett); only one was a Democrat (Joseph Biden). All of the Catholic senators who voted with Kennedy were Democrats.

This vote could be interpreted as dividing "hard-line" anti-abortion Catholics from those with a more moderate position. However, Senator Kennedy seems to have added his motion because he believed the abortion issue must be met frankly, on the basis of a clear vote on a Constitutional amendment, and not through legislatively inefficient riders, and because he believed that, unless the kind of qualification he made was added, the Buckley amendment might have difficulty in obtaining votes.[105] The Right to Life organization agreed that his motion had at least "bought time" for the struggle against experimentation.[106] Four of the nine Catholic senators voting for it never cast a single proabortion vote, which seems to imply that they, too, accepted Kennedy's reasoning and viewed this basically as a "prolife" amendment. With the Kennedy addition, the Buckley amendment prohibiting fetus research passed the Senate unanimously, eighty-eight Senators voting in favor, none against, and twelve not voting.

Votes on the final two riders of the Ninety-third Congress reveal significant differences between Catholic and non-Catholic senators and some differences within the Catholic group itself. First, on September 17, 1974, the Senate voted on a motion to table an amendment to an appropriations bill for the Labor and Health, Education and Welfare departments which would prevent the use of any of their funding to pay for or encourage abortions. The motion to table was defeated fifty to thirty-four, with sixteen senators not voting. A "no" vote, therefore, is in this case a vote to restrict abortions. As a whole, then, 50 percent of the senators voted the antiabortion position, 34 percent voted the proabortion position, and 16 percent cast no vote. Catholic senators, however, voted the antiabortion position by a distinctly greater percentage: 71.4 percent of the Catholics in the Senate voted to restrict funds for abortion; 14.3 percent voted not to restrict (and 14.3 percent of the Catholics did not cast a vote).[107] Almost a third again as great a percentage of Catholic senators voted to restrict funding for abortion purposes as did senators as a whole. The differences become even greater if the votes of Catholic senators are compared to those of non-Catholic senators alone. In this case 71.4 percent of the Catholics voted to restrict abortion, versus 46.5 percent of non-Catholics so voting; 14.3 percent of the Catholics voted not to restrict, versus 37.2 percent of the non-Catholics so voting. (The remaining percentages are those of senators not voting.)

On June 11, 1974, the Senate voted on a motion to table an amendment to the military authorization bill offered by Senator Jesse Helms of North Carolina. Helms' amendment would have forbade the use of funds included in the military appropriation for the performance of abortions, provision of abortion referral services, or transportation to or equipment of abortion clinics. The motion to table was carried, and thus the abortion restriction defeated, sixty-four to twenty-seven (nine senators not voting). Catholic senators, however, voted in directions opposite those of their colleagues as a whole. The Senate voted 64 percent against restriction of abortion funding, 27 percent for. Catholic senators, however, voted 36 percent against restriction and 57 percent for. Once again, if the Catholic vote is compared with the non-Catholic vote, the difference becomes even more significant. In this case 57 percent of the Catholic senators voted to restrict abortion funding, versus 22 percent of their non-Catholic colleagues so voting; 36 percent of the Catholic senators voted not to restrict abortion funding, versus 68.7 percent of the non-Catholics so voting. (The remaining percentages represent senators who did not vote at all.)

Five Catholics voted against restriction: Senators John Tunney, Edmund Muskie, Michael Mansfield, Philip Hart, and Edward

Kennedy. Eight Catholics voted to restrict abortion funding: Senators Joseph Biden, Thomas Eagleton, Thomas McIntyre, Joseph Montoya, Peter Domenici, James Buckley, Dewey Bartlett, and John Pastore. One Catholic senator, Marlow Cook, did not vote. This is the only antiabortion rider that did not pass the Senate; all others passed by large majorities. It was, also, the only antiabortion measure which a significant number of Catholics (about a third) voted against, whereas only two Catholic senators cast pro-abortion votes on even one of the other riders.

Only five Catholic senators, a little more than a third of the Catholic membership of the Senate, voted against restriction of funding for abortion on the Helms rider, and opponents based their argument against it on the inappropriateness of including such an amendment in a bill authorizing military funding and not on the abortion issue. The somewhat larger Catholic vote against restriction of funding in this case, therefore, may reflect, on the part of Catholic senators so voting, agreement with the argument of legislative inefficiency and inappropriateness rather than support for abortion.

In the Catholic vote on the Helms rider, all five senators voting not to restrict, or voting proabortion, were Democrats. All of the Republican Catholic senators except Cook, who did not vote at all, voted to restrict, or voted antiabortion. The Catholic senators voting against restriction were all Democrats and included all but one of the most liberal of the Catholic Democrats. Their average rating by the American for Democratic Action was eighty-nine. The average ADA rating of those Catholics voting to restrict abortion funding was almost half that figure—forty-eight. This low ADA figure for those voting the antiabortion position was not just a reflection of the Republicans in this group. All but one of the Democrats in the group, too, had ADA ratings below those of any member of the small Catholic group voting not to restrict abortion funding.[108] Age and seniority patterns differ here from those shown before. The older, more senior senators seem to have taken the proabortion position and the younger and less senior took the opposite. The average age of Catholic senators voting against restriction of abortion funding in this case was fifty-four, with an average of thirteen years in the Senate; the average age of those voting to restrict was only forty-nine, with an average of seven years in the Senate. Thus, what may be seen here is a response by older members, those more accustomed to the ways of the Senate, to the argument that such riders attached to a military authorization bill are inappropriate means toward legislative goals, rather than a response to the abortion issue itself, especially since only two members of this group voted against restricting abortion on any other occasion.

In conclusion, the limited means of examination thus far available indicates that Catholic members of the Senate in the Ninety-third Congress did support antiabortion measures in significantly greater percentages than their non-Catholic colleagues and that Republican Catholics always supported such measures; on the one occasion on which any significant number of Catholic senators failed to do so, the defection came from the most liberal group of Catholic Democrats.[109]

The votes on abortion-related riders in the House indicate also that on all but one occasion both Catholic and non-Catholic members voted, sometimes overwhelmingly, for the antiabortion position. Here, too, however, Catholic congressmen voted this position in percentages considerably greater than those of their colleagues. Of the six abortion-related riders offered in the House during the Ninety-third Congress, three were concerned with prohibiting experimentation on fetuses outside the mother's body and three were riders attached to various authorization and appropriations bills to prohibit use of the funds for abortion or abortion-related services. Only one of these failed to pass, an amendment to an appropriations bill for the departments of Labor and Health, Education and Welfare, voted June 28, 1974.

On May 31, 1973, Representative Angelo Roncallo offered an amendment to the Biomedical Research bill that would prohibit experimentation on any human fetus "outside the womb of its mother and which has a beating heart."[110] It passed overwhelmingly: 354 for, 9 against, 69 not voting; none of the 9 "no" votes was cast by a Catholic.

On June 22, 1973, Roncallo offered a similar amendment to the National Science Foundation authorization bill for 1974. It also passed, not by the overwhelming vote of the Biomedical bill, but still by 273 to 73. (Seventy-two congressmen did not vote.) Thus, about 66 percent of the whole Congress voted to prohibit fetus experimentation, 17 percent voted not to prohibit, and 17 percent did not vote. Among Catholic congressmen, however, 74 percent voted to prohibit such experimentation and only 6 percent voted against it (19 percent did not cast a vote). When Representative Roncallo offered the same amendment to the authorization for the National Science Foundation the following year (for fiscal year 1975), Catholics again voted to prohibit in greater percentages than their colleagues. On April 25, 1974, 65 percent of the whole House voted to prohibit experimentation, 13.5 percent voted against such prohibition, and 21.5 percent did not vote. Among Catholic congressmen, however, 76 percent voted for prohibition of fetus research, 8 percent voted against such prohibition, and 16 percent did not vote. If the Catholic vote is compared to the non-Catholic, there is an even more significant difference. Sixty-two percent of the non-Catholic House members voted to prohibit fetus experimentation and 15 percent voted not to prohibit it, whereas 76 percent of the Catholics voted such prohibition and 8 percent voted against prohibition.[111]

In addition to these riders on fetus experimentation, on June 21, 1973, the House voted on an amendment offered by Representative Hogan to restrict involvement of Legal Services Corporation lawyers in proabortion litigation. The measure was passed overwhelmingly, with 69 percent voting to prohibit, 16 percent voting against prohibition, and 15 percent not voting. Among Catholic congressmen, 74 percent voted for the prohibition, only 8 percent voted against it, and 18 percent did not vote.

On May 29, 1974, Representative Harold Froelich offered an amendment to the Community Services Act to prohibit the use of authorized funds for medical assistance and supplies in cases of abortion. Again, the amendment was adopted by a large majority and the Catholic percentage of approval was higher than that of the House as a whole. Sixty-seven percent of the whole House, but 73 percent of the Catholics, voted to restrict antipoverty funding for abortion purposes; 21 percent of the whole House, versus 13 percent of the Catholics, voted against such restriction. (Twelve percent of the House as a whole and 14 percent of the Catholic members did not cast votes.)

Finally, one abortion-related amendment was proposed and rejected by the House, the only antiabortion amendment to fail to pass the House during the Ninety-third Congress. Late at night on June 28, 1974, Representative Roncallo presented an amendment to the appropriations bill for the departments of Labor and Health, Education and Welfare which would restrict the use of funds appropriated for abortion and abortion-related services. The language of the amendment was more detailed, complex, and inclusive than the language of other amendments offered in the Senate and House to restrict funds for abortion services. "No part of the funds appropriated under this Act," read the Roncallo amendment, "shall be used in any manner directly or indirectly to pay for abortions or abortion-referral services, abortifacient drugs or devices, the promotion or encouragement of abortion, or the support of research designed to develop methods of abortion, or to force any State, school or school district or any other recipient of Federal funds to provide abortions or health or disability abortion benefits."[112]

Although Roncallo denied such intent or possible result, several congressmen argued that his amendment, because of its clause regarding prohibition of funds for abortifacient drugs and devices, could have the effect of curtailing funds for birth control services. This argument, plus irritation aroused by the sudden introduction of this complex amendment late at night, caused enough congressmen who had heretofore supported antiabortion riders to change position and defeat it. The *National Right to Life News*, monthly organ of the National Right to Life organization, surveyed the 247 House members voting against the amendment to ask why they so voted. A majority of congressmen responding indicated concern over possible effects on family planning and birth control services.[113] Another reason given was the widespread opinion that the amendment was "hastily drawn" or "poorly drafted"[114] and presented late at night under poor conditions for debate. House members objected to the fact that the Roncallo amendment made no exception for abortions in cases of endangerment to the life of the mother, incest, and rape. Finally, what *National Right to Life News* termed "some hard core proabortionists" said they voted against the measure because they oppose any legislation limiting the Supreme Court decision of 1973.[115] Although the *News* gives no figures for this "hard-core" group, it should be noted that prior to this amendment the maximum number of congressmen voting against an abortion-related rider in the Ninety-third Congress was ninety-one, a little more than one-fifth of the House, on the Froehlich amendment prohibiting use of Community Services Act funds for abortion purposes.

The *News* reported the views of forty-seven representatives by name, including ten Catholics. Reasons given by these members for rejecting the amendment were, in nineteen instances (including four Catholics), that it might restrict family planning services; in ten cases (including six Catholics) that the amendment was badly drawn or presented in poor circumstances for debate; in seven cases including one Catholic, then House Majority Leader now Speaker Thomas O'Neill, that it, in his words, "made no exceptions, either in cases of rape, or incest, or danger to the health of the mother." He concluded, "I could not accept such an extreme measure."[116] Four members, including Catholics Edward Roybal and Henry Helstoski, rejected the amendment as discriminatory against the poor. Fourteen members simply reiterated their general support for the Supreme Court decision. No Catholics were in this group.[117]

The vote of the whole House in regard to the defeated Roncallo amendment was 247 against, 123 for, and 64 not voting. Despite the fact that a much larger number of Catholics voted against this measure, apparently because of what a number of them saw as its ambiguity and legislative inappropriateness, the difference between Catholic and non-Catholic voting positions is clear. With all of the haste involved in the drafting and presentation of the amendment and its extreme nature, 47 percent of Catholic members still voted in favor of it, 34 percent against, and 19 percent did not vote. The Catholic percentages contrast strongly with the votes of the whole Congress (28 percent for, 57 percent against, and 15 percent not voting) and even more strongly with the votes of the non-Catholic members (23 percent for, 64 percent against, and 13 percent not voting).[118]

Out of one hundred Catholics in the House during the Ninety-third session, 29 percent voted the antiabortion position on all six amendments presented, compared with 11 percent of the non-Catholic members of the House. Four non-Catholics (Bella Abzug, Elizabeth Holtzman, Ron Dellums, and Charles Stark) voted the proabortion position on every amendment offered. No Catholics did this. Sixty-two percent of Catholics in the House never cast a "no" vote on an antiabortion amendment. Exactly half this percentage, only 31 percent, of all non-Catholics in the House never cast a "no" vote on an antiabortion amendment.[119] Although no Catholics consistently voted against antiabortion riders, a small number (7 percent) did cast more "no" than "yes" votes. This group presents an interesting anomaly: of the seven Catholics, three are blacks (Ralph Metcalf, William Clay, and Charles Rangel), one is Spanish-speaking (Edward Roybal), and two are generally considered Catholic radicals (Michael Harrington and Robert Drinan). The other was a white Georgetown University graduate, James Jones of Oklahoma.

Within the Catholic House membership, party correlated with degree of support of antiabortion measures in the same manner as in the Senate. Age and seniority did not. The twenty-nine Catholics always voting the antiabortion position averaged fifty-four years of age and eleven years of seniority. They included eleven Republicans and eighteen Democrats, that is, nearly one-third of all Catholic Republicans versus one-quarter of the Catholic Democrats in the House. Twelve Catholics voted the proabortion position on at least two of the six abortion-related riders. All of these Catholics were Democrats; none was Republican. They averaged forty-seven years of age and seven years of seniority. The seven Catholics who voted the proabortion more often than the antiabortion position were, again, all Democrats. They averaged forty-seven years of age and had an average of four and one-third years of seniority. Those few Catholics, therefore, who were more supportive of the proabortion position than the overwhelming majority of their colleagues were Democrats and were on the average younger in age and more junior in seniority than the strongly antiabortion House Catholics. On the only vote in the Senate in which a significant number of Catholics voted proabortion, one-third, the proabortion votes came from the older and more senior members. This may have been more of a test of Senate norms than of abortion sentiment.

Leroy Rieselbach and Lewis Dexter made the observation that when politicians are under strong cross-pressures on a particular issue, their tendency is to vote their own opinions. They also point out that under strong cross-pressures politicians will seek out those interests and those sectors of their constituencies which accord with their own previously held beliefs to legitimize their actions. Wrote Rieselbach, "Lawmakers seem to be prepared to pick and choose according to the situation at hand and in light of their other role orientations. Relevant considerations would, of course, include . . . the views and activities of the relevant congressional committees, legislative parties, constituents and the in-

volved pressure groups."[120] Dexter made a similar point when he
described relations between a congressman and his constituency
(both voters and pressure groups) as transactional rather than in-
teractional. Congressmen, he pointed out, cannot possibly be in
constant communication with all sectors and interests in their districts. They tend to have their own particular beliefs about policy
and attitudes toward politics and political activity and to hear
from people of like views; when they act on those views they convince themselves that they are acting in accord with the national
interest or at least with constituency desires.[121]

When considering the motives of Catholic politicians in voting
on the abortion-related riders, that is, whether they acted on the
basis of religiously instilled values or under the influence of antiabortion (and Church-related) lobbying pressures, one discovers
that something much like the process Rieselbach and Dexter describe seems to have occurred. Certainly values played a role.
Both Senator Buckley and Congressman Hogan insisted they had
introduced their amendments out of their own sense of shock and
concern over the Supreme Court ruling. They voted on each
abortion-related rider and always voted the antiabortion position. One representative was equally frank in stating his own proabortion beliefs and voted that position on four of the six abortion-related riders. (However, he voted against experimentation
on fetuses and did not vote on the sixth rider.) Four interviewees,
who declared themselves personally against abortion and said
they would vote so, did vote the antiabortion position persistently
on the riders. Three who, without such specific declaration, indicated personal opposition to abortion and the probability of so
voting also voted that position consistently.

Seven interviewees, however, showed uncertainty about the issue: they either said they were personally opposed to abortion but
were not certain how they would vote or indicated uncertainty
and said they "might not" vote what one called "the Church position." This group may reflect the complex interaction of personal
values and constituency and lobbying pressure that many Catholic politicians not firmly decided for one position or the other may
have gone through. Three men in this group seem not to have
been able to reach a stable accord between their personal values
and the pressures of lobby groups and constituencies. Two said
they had been under heavy lobbying pressure, particularly from

the right-to-life proponents. They were personally opposed to abortion but admitted having moral qualms about some aspects of the abortion debate. One was worried about "the right to impose my beliefs on others";[122] the other was concerned about the legitimacy of cutting off abortion funding for the poor while the nonpoor could still obtain abortions.[123] Both represented heavily Catholic districts, one in a state in which a liberalized abortion bill had been defeated in a referendum. Both voted inconsistently on the rider amendments. They each voted the antiabortion position three times, did not cast votes twice, and voted the proabortion position once. The third man expressed personal feelings that were more pro- than antiabortion and also said he was under strong lobbying pressure. From a heavily Catholic district, he finally cast one vote against experimentation on fetuses and simply did not vote on any other rider.

The other four men in this undecided group seem to have been able finally to reconcile personal values with lobbying and constituency pressures. A California representative, for example, indicated a more pro- than antiabortion attitude and showed more anger over abortion-related lobbying than any other interviewee. He also said that he believed substantial anti-Catholic hostility existed because, after a recent redistricting, he was receiving letters from new constituents saying they would not vote for a Catholic.[124] In the end he was one of seven Catholics who voted fairly consistently the proabortion position. An eastern Senator who remarked in his interview that he "may not go along with the Church" on abortion, earlier expressed his personal shock and anger over the Supreme Court decision. He also remarked on the high percentage of French-Canadian Catholics now making up the population of his state (and party). In the end, he did "go along," voting the antiabortion position consistently.

A midwestern Representative said that he was not sure how he would vote on abortion, that he "may very well not vote the so-called Catholic" position.[125] During his interview, however, he showed a great love for the Church of his boyhood and a clear sense of his largely Catholic constituency. He finally voted the antiabortion position consistently on the riders.

It should be noted that five of those seven Catholic congressmen who did vote a fairly consistent proabortion position (that is, voted more often pro- than antiabortion) probably were strongly influenced by the views of their constituencies. Three were black and represented heavily black, nonsouthern districts. Their votes correlate much more closely with those of other black congressmen than with those of white Catholic congressmen. Since many of the riders essentially restricted government funding for abortion purposes to military personnel and antipoverty recipients, these black congressmen probably would have had difficulty voting such restrictions, since these would strongly affect their many poor black constituents.

Two of those seven congressmen largely voting proabortion were the radical Catholics Michael Harrington and Father Robert Drinan. Although both represented heavily Catholic Massachusetts, both ran against more conservative Catholics and both apparently derived their winning margins from the non-Catholic sectors of their districts.[126] Their votes were probably in accord with their particular constituencies. In addition, Michael Harrington seems to have had a long-time personal commitment to a proabortion position; Father Drinan, to the view that the Supreme Court decision must be obeyed.

The other two Catholics who voted more often pro- than antiabortion were Edward Roybal of California and James Jones of Oklahoma. Roybal was a Spanish-speaking congressman from a heavily Spanish-speaking district. He may have been influenced by the fact that these riders would discriminate against the poor, even though surveys showed low support for abortion among the Spanish-speaking. I do not know why Jones voted as he did. His vote seems anomalous since the Oklahoma delegation as a whole has generally voted antiabortion. I did not interview him. In the past two years he has tended to vote antiabortion.

Certainly my interviews indicate that Catholic politicians were most comfortable when their personal value systems, whether anti- or, in a few cases, proabortion, were in conjunction with or could be perceived as being in conjunction with their constituencies. This accords with much scholarly research on the Congress. The happy conjunction of personal and constituency attitude toward abortion probably represented reality for many Catholic congressmen. Harold Abramson, in his book *The Ethnic Factor in Catholic America*, noted that 72 percent of the American Catholic population lives in the New England, Middle Atlantic, and east north central states.[127] Seventy percent of the Catholic members of the House come from the same states, along with half of the Catholic senators. The strong antiabortion Catholic vote in Congress apparently is the combined result of personal value orientation reinforced and legitimized by constituency agreement. Like the Catholic people, Catholic politicians are ready to accede to legal abortion in the case of danger to the mother, or rape. The issue of abortion in the case of a defective fetus did not emerge clearly in either Congressional interviews or votes. Both the Catholic people and the Catholic politicians in strikingly similar percentages seem opposed to "abortion on demand" or "permissive" abortion. The internalized values of the Catholic politicians, forced to a declaration by the Church and Church-related antiabortion lobbies, are apparently reinforced by their correlation with the beliefs of their heavily Catholic constituencies.

Catholicism seems to have exerted considerable influence on the political issue of abortion. According to my interviews the Church leadership is almost unanimous in its belief that abortion is morally wrong and is united in working actively to make its views known to the Catholic people and political leaders. As a result of this influence, there are distinct differences between the attitude toward abortion held by Catholic and non-Catholic Americans. Catholics are less likely to support abortion than are non-Catholics, except in some cases southern blacks, and the more frequent churchgoers among Catholics are consistently more opposed to abortion than are the less frequent churchgoers. With a few interesting exceptions, Catholic political leaders showed a significantly greater tendency than non-Catholic politicians to sponsor and vote for abortion-restricting legislation.

Certainly the experience of living in a pluralist society, exposed to other than Catholic points of view, has had an impact on every part of the Catholic world. Catholic willingness to accept the availability of legal abortion in certain cases of extreme hazard to the physical and psychological health of the mother or child is striking evidence of that. Equally striking is the willingness of Catholic political leaders, even those of the strict Jansenist persuasion, to write some such exceptions into their abortion-restricting bills. Even the Church leadership, with its more total commitment to religious life and its involvement in daily professional Church work — certainly the sector of the American Catholic world most self-contained — still seems prepared to accept the political if not theological necessity and correctness of abortion laws allowing exceptions in cases of extreme danger to the mother.

Does Catholicism exert its influence on the abortion issue through inculcation of a particular value orientation or through direct political action by organizing and acting as an interest group? The data and examination are incomplete, but there is evidence of the importance of value inculcation. The greater tendency of churchgoers than of nonchurchgoers to reject abortion indicates this importance, as does the willingness of those politicians who stated that their values were outraged by the Supreme Court decision to sponsor restrictive amendments and to declare a voting position early.

The role played by Catholic interest group activity, however, seems to have been vital also. Political interest group activity and value orientation are not either/or propositions. They enhance one another and greatly strengthen the impact religion and religious adherents have on political issues. Most Catholics in the country and in the Congress felt that abortion for economic or personal reasons in particular violated their beliefs. The institutional Church and Catholic-dominated antiabortion organizations undertook widespread efforts to publicize their point of view and to fight against abortions in the political arena, constantly reminding Catholics throughout the country and particularly in Congress of Catholic values pertaining to abortion. The theological basis for those beliefs was continually explained to them and action was finally forced, despite what Congressman Hogan called a politician's "natural" inclination to avoid an issue on which there are cross-pressures. Most Catholic politicians were able to accommodate their personal values and the pressures exerted on them by antiabortion groups and their largely Catholic constituents.

Within the Catholic world, however, there were also some evidences of strain. While young Catholics oppose abortion more than most young Protestants, their disapproval rate is less than that of older Catholics. Young people, as more irregular churchgoers, perhaps have not been exposed to Church teachings and values as have their elders. With increasing Catholic economic, social, and educational mobility, younger Catholics, especially, are more open to the value systems of the general society. Within the institutional Church, despite its near unanimity in opposition to abortion, different attitudes toward the issue have complicated the Church's efforts to fight it.

The concentration especially by antiabortion organization leaders on abortion per se indicates a different perception of the issue than that held by many Church social activists, who view the issue as part of a whole prolife agenda. Although all antiabortion leaders have strenuously denied this, it may also indicate a fear that adoption of the more inclusive prolife stance will alienate conservative groups and others, including some Catholics, opposed to such issues. Among a small group of congressmen, too, there is evidence of conflicting loyalties. Black Catholic congressmen, all but two of whom represent largely black northern, not southern districts, seem finally to have been moved by racial and constituency rather than religious influences. And among some Catholic politicians there is evidence of conflicting loyalty to congressional rules of the game.

No human being is encased in a single group and no group is immune from pressures generated within its own membership and outside it stemming from alternate group loyalties and beliefs. Younger Catholics, influenced perhaps more by their peers than their Church, illustrate this fact, as do black Catholic congressmen with their conflicting identities and interests. If the institutional Church itself failed in projecting to Catholic politicians its vision of the antiabortion issue as only part of a liberal prolife agenda, it may be because that vision was partial and distorted as a result of an effort to accommodate both its socially activist and its conservative members. Also, the very slight, tentative movement against the rider approach to the abortion issue, seen only in a few votes in the Senate and the House, may indicate a belief on the part of some Catholic liberal politicians that the institutional rules of the Congress itself were being violated by the rider attachments and that perhaps the rules of the larger democratic society were also being violated: for example, such riders prevent abortion only for the poor. These problems and what they portend for Catholic political interest group strength and efforts will be explored in the concluding chapter.

6

Analysis and Reflections

FTER THE INSULARITY OF the immigrant Catholic ghetto was breached both by increasing mobility and, dramatically in the 1960s, by the diversity unleashed in the Church and among Catholics in general by Church reform and debate, a number of books appeared commenting upon the heterogeneity, even chaos, which their authors believed had overtaken the Catholic Church and the American Catholic world.[1] Most of these books appeared in the late 1960s and early 1970s and probably reflected the debates within the Church and among Catholics in general on liturgical changes, Catholic education, birth control, collegial leadership, and so on, all of which reached a peak in the late 1960s.

One can look at the Catholic world today and be impressed by its diversity. But I think one can be equally impressed by the extent and continuation of its unity, particularly in view of the enormous changes it has gone through during the postwar period.

The heterogeneity of American Catholicism has been demonstrated in a number of ways. Within the institutional Church conservatives argued that, to an extent, Catholicism was being swallowed up by liberalism. Some of those who had led the prophetic movement in the late 1960s and early 1970s certainly felt that the Church was too slow in responding to the Vietnam war and to social problems. By the mid-1970s, however, several elements tending toward cooperation and compromise appear, too. Some of the most noted of the prophets, the Berrigan brothers and James Groppi, for example, are actually no longer active in either the Church or politics in the catalyzing way they were previously. This means lessened conflict within the Church, although many of their ideas and followers have been and remain important in the institutional Church. The opening up of the leadership of the Church to include the hierarchy, the experts, and prophets means more conflict in decision making but a constructive rather than destructive heterogeneity. The ending of the war and the bishops' position on it and on amnesty, with which even the conservatives agreed in part, and general Catholic unity on abortion seem also to have done much to heal some of the breaches most pronounced ten years ago.[2]

Heterogeneity has been a characteristic of Catholic congressmen as well. Among them were different kinds of Catholics, responding to different facets of the Catholic experience—Jansenists and Council Catholics, ritualists, Christian Democrats. The older men, with memories of anti-Catholic discrimination, were more concerned with a strict separation of church and state, and of their religious and political lives. The younger men were more open to the new activism of the Church and more secure in their Catholicism as it affected them politically. Most of the congressmen showed the effects of countervailing influences, especially the norms of the Congress and of American political life generally. Still, for the most part they were Catholic, displaying the influences on their value systems of their Catholic upbringing and the Catholic group experiences of immigration and of the Council. They demonstrated ties to both the institutional Church and to their often largely Catholic constituents, most clearly in their abortion votes, but in other ways, too.

Some divergencies appear between Catholic leadership in the Church and Congress and the Catholic people. Neither Church nor political leaders seemed sensitive to the fear of crime felt by many of the Catholic people, as has been demonstrated dramatically in surveys. The leaders seemed more concerned about racial discrimination and racial problems than were the people, although Catholics were still at least as liberal on race as most other white Americans. Catholics in general displayed a continuing economic liberalism greater than that of white Protestants, as did the Church and Catholic congressmen, and they proved assertions by their leaders of Catholic upward mobility. Whether because of their resulting greater sense of security and self-confidence or of the liberalizing influence of the Council, they also showed themselves to be much more open to civil liberties and more questioning of the traditional Catholic support of American militarism and war. Certainly they demonstrated large accord with their Church on abortion.

In addition to some differences on issues and on the priorities to be assigned them, two other strains were demonstrated among American Catholics. The first was the obvious demographic and socioeconomic split between white Catholics of European descent and the growing Spanish-speaking sector of the Church. This division might not be overwhelming, given the Church and political leadership's concern for the Spanish-speaking and given the fact that, although they differed in socioeconomic status, there were still large similarities in religious, political, and social attitudes between Spanish-speaking and white Catholics. Certainly the similarities were greater between these two racially different Catholic groups than between black and white Protestants.

The second strain, potentially important, was the "slippage" evident among young Catholics, their lesser religious attendance and endogamous marriage rates and their lower levels of agreement with the general Catholic position on abortion. In many ways young Catholics were more like their Protestant age peers than older Catholics were like older Protestants. At the same time, young Catholics demonstrated strong ties to the Church and to the Catholic community, as measured by their still high religious attendance and by their attitudes on many issues.

Scholars of ethnicity maintain that a large group is necessarily a diffuse one. Certainly, as a quarter of our population, American Catholics form a large and diffuse group. Moreover, they are a group which has undergone what might be called a revolutionary experience in the past twenty years, tossed by large-scale Church reform at the same time that they (and their leadership) were feeling the effects of socioeconomic upward mobility. Whether influenced by the historical experience of immigration, poverty, and eventual mobility or by old and new values inculcated by their religion and its leadership, there still seemed to be a Catholic people and a Catholic leadership that were distinct from other Americans, at least in some ways. There seemed to be, too, at least rough parallels in values and in sociopolitical attitudes between the Catholic Church leadership, political leadership, and the Catholic people. If religion is defined as a group phenomenon, then I believe that, overall, on the basis of this study, American Catholics can be regarded as members of a particular religiously-based ethnic group with a well-developed system of values and strong institutional and communal structures.

That Catholics have tried to achieve group aims through political means and by way of political institutions was indicated again and again in my interviews. Catholics, therefore, must be reckoned a political interest group—at some times, on some issues.

For ethnically-based political interest groups, politics is understood as the attempt to achieve, through government, three main goals: to gain certain concrete benefits, especially economic benefits, for the group; to influence or replace general societal values with recognition of their own group values; and sometimes to gain or consolidate the achievement of these first two goals through influencing or even attempting to overturn the great institutions of society. As an ethnic political interest group, Catholics have given least attention to the last goal but have attempted and sometimes succeeded in attaining group benefits and recognition of group values.

Both grass-roots Catholic organizations and the institutional Church at the national level tried to gain benefits, especially economic benefits, for their group from political leaders. Lobbying efforts described by Catholic political leaders for the most part concerned this kind of issue. Catholics lobbied for aid to their schools, hospitals, and libraries. They wanted help to alleviate fuel costs to their institutions and social security changes for their employees and clergy. Political leaders indicated that aid to the institutions in their districts was sometimes obtained and that Catholic groups at least gained a sympathetic hearing from their political representatives for these requests. Many Church and political leaders were also convinced that the Church had successfully lobbied with the public and Congress on the general, national issue of federal aid to private schools and that only the Supreme Court decision of January 1973 prevented a favorable congressional vote. Although Church leaders persistently downplayed institutional issues, which were often economic, and stressed the importance to them of social justice issues, they apparently did lobby to a considerable extent on these institutional issues. Their political representatives, too, seemed willing to grant this kind of benefit when possible.

In three different ways Catholics also tried to achieve recognition of their own value systems. As community leader interviews demonstrated, a continuing goal of the Catholic working-class movement involves value recognition, the preservation of Catholic and specific national origin cultures. Many Catholic groups, for example, helped write and lobby for the Ethnic Heritage Studies bill that provides federal funding for research and teaching programs in what is being called "white ethnic"—German, Italian, Irish, Jewish, and so on—history, language, and culture as well as the black and Hispanic programs previously funded.

The most obvious attempt to achieve recognition of Catholic values was, of course, the strong effort launched both by the institutional Church at the national level and by grass-roots Catholic communal activity to abrogate the Supreme Court decision declaring restrictive abortion laws unconstitutional. Many Church leaders saw this decision as part of a vital conflict over value systems, even as a direct attack on the Catholic value system. Although attempts were made to depict the antiabortion movement as more than Catholic, as including people of other and of no faith, the movement was largely led by Catholics, and resources in numbers and money to a considerable extent also were apparently provided by the Church and by individual Catholics. Although no final decision has been made by the Congress or the states on a Constitutional amendment, in the preliminary votes strong Church and Catholic lobbying combined with their own internalized Catholic value systems have led most Catholic politicians to support the antiabortion movement.

Attempts to influence value systems, led largely by Church leaders, took place at another level, too. The insistence by Church leaders on the importance of greater Church effort to influence social justice issues can be read, I believe, as evidence of the second ethnic political goal of value influence and replacement. Social justice concerns are hardly a Catholic prerogative; many groups have struggled for liberal social change over the years. But Catholic concern for social change seems so tied to the teachings of the recent popes and the Vatican Council documents, as the great majority of Church leaders pointed out, that it must be understood as a manifestation of new or revivified Catholic values emphasizing the obligation of Christian concern for the world and especially for those suffering injustice. Council documents specifically stressed that Catholics should aid those suffering from poverty, discrimination, and degradation through inhumane imprisonment or political torture and should strive for peace and against "immoral" or "unjust" wars. The Catholic sector of the antiwar movement and the NCCB itself in its 1971 resolution condemning the war specifically alluded to these Church teachings. The statements of the Church leadership in regard to the Church's antipoverty program, the Campaign for Human Development, and the Chavez and Farah boycotts also alluded to them. Social justice as an essential Christian obligation and Church doctrine was a constant theme in interviews with Church leaders.

A concern for social justice had become an integral part of the Catholic value system, especially for Church leaders, by the middle and late 1960s. Church insistence on social justice must be viewed, then, as an attempt, made together with other groups, to influence the national value system. As such it was an important addition to or at least a new emphasis given the Catholic value system. It indicated that circumstances and experiences to which a particular group is subject can alter the group's value system in important ways.

It is difficult to judge how much of the Catholic world beyond the institutional Church leadership understood or agreed with these social justice goals and their basis in Church teachings or saw them as part of the Catholic value system. Certainly grassroots Catholic participation in the antiwar movement was widespread, especially in comparison with almost nonexistent Catholic opposition to earlier American wars. There was a certain degree of support and activity from grass-roots Catholics, besides the Spanish-speaking themselves, for the Chavez and Farah movements. Indeed, the Church in California was brought to support Chavez partly by the pressure exerted on it by hundreds of young lay and clerical Catholics working with Chavez in California and across the country in the boycott effort. Survey data also showed considerable agreement between the Catholic people as a whole and their Church leaders on a series of issues concerned with social justice. Church leaders insisted that continuing efforts were being made to educate the Catholic people as a whole on Christian obligations in social concerns.

The effect on Catholic political leaders of a change toward

concern for social justice issues is a mixed one. Few political leaders seemed to have been approached personally on these issues by Catholic lobbying groups or Church leaders, but they showed overwhelming awareness of this change in their Church, apparently from media reports and from observing changes in parishes and Catholic organizations in their own districts and states.

It is also difficult to gauge Catholic effectiveness in obtaining social justice goals. Church concerns here did have at least the generalized political effect of giving additional psychological and political support to those liberal Catholic politicians who concerned themselves with the same issues. Certain specific goals were also obtained. The war was finally ended, but the role Catholics played in the heterogeneity of groups pressuring for an end is impossible to determine. The Farah workers won the right to organize and choose their own union in secret ballot, but this was by court decision. The role played by the publicity given the issue by the boycotts—which involved more than Catholics—or the role played by the research provided strikers and the Court by Catholic organizations is also impossible to determine. Given their numbers, organization, and resources, though, Catholic participation in both these achievements was probably considerable. On many other issues, however, including issues listed by the USCC as those on which they have lobbied Congress, there has often been either no decision yet by government or a decision contrary to the Church's stand. In what may be true of other ethnic groups, Catholics seemed to be more successful in achieving or at least publicizing and gaining a hearing for goals involved with influencing values when these goals were perceived as being pursued at the grass-roots as well as the national, institutional level than when a specialized organization promoted them, even as highly organized and professional a group as the USCC.

The third goal included in the ethnic group political agenda—influencing or overturning the great institutional forces of our society—seemed rather undeveloped among Catholics. A reading of the rhetoric would lead to the conclusion that black groups, for example, have done more thinking, writing, and speaking in regard to institutional challenge than I found in my interviews and documentation on Catholics. Most challenge of this kind from within the Catholic group seemed to come from the prophetic element and perhaps from the working-class Catholic organizations in their efforts to gain "community control" over local institutions, health facilities, credit institutions, and so forth.[3] Since the essence of the prophetic stance is challenge to church and state, the prophetic role in institutional challenge is not surprising. Daniel Berrigan, for example, believed that simply ending the war was not enough to assure establishment of a peaceful and just society. To do that, he believed, required displacement of existing power that would mean the shaking of society's foundations. "It means the dismantling of the military as we know it; it means a new look at allocations of national resources, of wealth, brains and money; it means a new move in all directions."[4] The way to do this, he and much of the prophetic element believed, is not through violence but through the seeding effect of dynamic, Christian communities. Chavez has preached many of these same ideas, and Church interviewees associated with the prophetic movement also spoke of "standing outside of both church and state," and "building communities."

Most of the hierarchy and the experts interviewed, however, tended to see efforts at obtaining social justice in terms of working through the system. They spoke of working through political institutions, such as the Congress, and helping to establish unions and collective bargaining rights to negotiate with economic and industrial institutions. In addition to interviewees associated with the prophetic element, only two Church leaders discussed the necessity for institutional change. A bishop spoke of the necessity of changing "the institutional structures that keep people poor" and believed that movements and organizations like the antiwar movement and the Campaign for Human Development were beginning to awaken Catholics to the role present institutions played in maintaining societal ills.[5] A long-time Church social activist echoed this conviction in asserting that many people in the Church were coming to realize "the malfunctioning of the system, the welfare system, the education system, the economic system, the social system."[6]

Continued concern with social justice issues may lead Church leaders to the conviction that large-scale institutional change must be attempted, but for now at least this seems concentrated within the prophetic element. The experts and the hierarchy did not yet seem to have made the leap from working within traditional democratic, political processes for social justice goals to challenging society's institutions as the presumed causes of social injustice. This lack of interest in institutional change in a way was surprising, since the argument can well be made that the institution of the Church has been greatly challenged and changed by many Catholics over the past decade, including some of the Church experts and even some now in the hierarchy interviewed for this study.

An evaluation of the political agenda of the Catholic political interest group and the degree of success it has obtained indicates that, although different sectors of the Catholic world have been variously active in regard to the three major goals, there are fairly persistent patterns of activity and unity.

Catholic efforts thus far have been directed basically toward achieving concrete, especially economic, benefits for their own group and recognition of their particular value systems. In these areas there have been fairly widespread institutional Church and grass-roots efforts. Probably because the granting of economic benefits to racial, religious, and other groups has been widely and historically accepted in America, as long as there is a general feeling that these benefits are fairly equitably distributed, Catholic activity here seems to raise fewest problems and probably meets with most success. This may be true of ethnic political interest group activity in general. As Moynihan and Glazer pointed out, welfare states find it politically profitable to distribute benefits to ethnic groups.

The attempt to gain recognition for particular value systems raises much more conflict. The large-scale effort of Catholics to do this in the case of abortion immediately brought opposition groups into conflict with them. Attempts to influence societal values or replace them with a particular group's values entail emotional upheaval, for they strike at the psychological roots of all the people involved. The efforts of black groups to induce schools to consider black culture in giving and evaluating IQ tests or in teaching English and history showed the emotional intensity value struggles can arouse. Since this is so basic to any kind of ethnic political interest group, whether Catholic, black, or whatever, tension over political struggles based on value influence and recognition will surely be a part of our national political life if ethnic group politics continues to develop.

Thus far the goal of institutional change has not occupied

either the institutional Church or Catholics in general to any great extent. The working-class groups and the prophets have concerned themselves somewhat with institutional change and in a sense both are working toward community control, but theirs is hardly a united effort and the communities each envisions seem very different. Despite the "ghettoization" of the past and some expressions of alienation by antiabortion leaders, Catholics in general do not seem to feel locked out of the great institutions of our society or of its political process.[7] Their interest in social justice issues is often an interest "for others"—blacks, the Spanish-speaking and so forth—and not so much for themselves. Perhaps, then, they do not have the same kind of personal and emotional investment in these issues or view institutions as pernicious in quite the same way that, for example, many blacks do.[8] Only if Catholics begin on a large scale to feel locked out of the system, by the results of the research being conducted by working-class groups or by an increase in their perception of Supreme Court and other governmental decisions as anti-Catholic, might they be driven in the opposite direction, toward institutional challenge. This does not seem a likely development.[9]

To assess Catholics' general capabilities and problems in functioning as a political interest group, I return to the criteria Truman suggests for determining a group's likelihood of obtaining political influence.

Truman considers critical the degree of access the particular group attains. By this he means the ability of the group to generate popular and governmental support for its goals. In Truman's opinion, three criteria determine the effectiveness of a group's access to political influence and power. The first involves the group's strategic position in society; the second concerns internal characteristics of the group, especially its unity, leadership skills, and resources; the third is the operating structure of governmental institutions—the political parties and the branches of government that must be influenced by the political interest group.[10]

Much is involved in a determination of a group's strategic position in society: the group's status or prestige, which affects the deference and access it may expect from outside groups, including government; the usefulness, especially to governmental leaders, of the group's technical and political knowledge; the standing it and its activities have vis-à-vis the rules of the game—the generally accepted Constitutional and governmental traditions, rules, and procedures of the society.[11]

Catholics have certainly increased their strategic position in society. In twenty-five years they have greatly increased in educational and financial and partially in occupational status. This is important since previous studies of American politics show that in this country political interest, activity, and self-confidence correlate with higher economic and educational levels. Many Church and political leaders in their interviews emphasized growing Catholic self-confidence during the past few years in taking part in community, political, and civic affairs.

Further, Church and political leaders believed that both the reign of Pope John XXIII, a man widely admired by non-Catholics, and the Ecumenical Council, with its emphasis on opening up the Church to the problems of the world and to ecumenical efforts and its de-emphasis of "mysterious" ritual and rigid dogma, aided acceptance of Catholics by non-Catholics and encouraged Catholics to join with their non-Catholic fellow citizens in social, political, and cultural activities.

Political leaders, in particular, and Church leaders believed strongly that the election of John Kennedy set the seal on Catholic political acceptance and legitimacy in this country. All but one of the politicians I interviewed denied the existence of any serious anti-Catholic hostility in the country and only that person felt that his religion was a serious handicap to his political career. At least seven Catholics have been serious, open contenders for either the presidential or vice-presidential posts during the post-Kennedy period, with almost no negative public or media comment regarding their religious suitability.[12] Indeed, some commentators have suggested that since the late 1960s leaders in both parties have argued that political wisdom necessitates a Catholic in one of the two spots on the national ticket.[13]

In a sense Catholics seem to hold a strategic position superior to that of many other ethnic groups. This is in part because of their general upward mobility and of their increased presence in the Congress and in part because of their sheer numbers, an important political consideration. They make up, for example, twice the percentage of the total population that blacks do.

On the other hand, in what may be a warning to other ethnic groups, it seems clear that Catholic status may have been achieved to some extent at least by a denial of specialized group aims. A senator said, "John Kennedy put fear of Catholic political power to rest when he went to Dallas and talked to those ministers and said that a man's religious beliefs were his own and had no part in government." The same senator reported his chagrin at being asked by a prominent monsignor, one of his constituents, for an appointment with Kennedy. "I didn't dare tell him that John F. Kennedy didn't even want to be photographed with a priest because of what he was trying to put to rest."[14] Political commentators also make the point that it was not the election of John Kennedy which legitimized Catholic political office holding and political power so much as his conduct in office, including his failure to press specifically Catholic aims, such as permitting exclusion of funding for private schools from his federal aid to education bill.[15]

Status gained in part through downplaying group identity and aims would seem counterproductive to ethnic political interest group activity. Now that they have gained this status, some elements of the Catholic world seem ready to use it to pursue specifically Catholic economic and value goals. How forcefully they will or can do that and how such efforts will affect future Catholic status, even group unity, are still open questions.

A group's strategic position in society and thus its political access can also be affected, Truman maintains, by the usefulness of its technical and political knowledge, especially to governmental leaders. Catholics, especially institutional Church leaders, seem vulnerable here. Catholic representatives and senators seemed to show little appreciation for the technical and political knowledge of Church leaders but did indicate some respect for that of the Catholic constituency groups that lobby them. Catholic politicians who approved the Church's new direction toward social concern seemed to appreciate Church concern and activity because it provided them with additional political, propaganda, and emotional support rather than because Church leaders and organizations were providing them with useful information. There is recognition of this within the Church, especially from USCC officials concerned with increasing the expertise of their colleagues who testify and submit statements to congressional committees.

Then, too, although antiabortion leaders stressed the necessity of the educative process for both the public and Congress on abortion and its social implications, on the arguments for Constitutional guarantees of life, and on scientific investigations into how and when life begins, and so on, I found little of this indicated in congressional descriptions of and reactions to anti-abortion lobbying. Congressmen reflected instead the highly emotional and political quality of abortion lobbying. No representative or senator mentioned its educative aspect. In only one instance was the institutional Church at its national level recognized as a source of information. All three men who praised Church efforts to help the Spanish-speaking, especially the Chavez and Farah boycotts, emphasized the information regarding worker conditions provided by Church groups and people working with the strikers. Some of these were local groups, but even then much information was provided them through the field research done by the USCC's Monsignor George Higgins and others of its people.

In general, where congressmen did show recognition of Catholic political and technical information and its help to them, it was in regard to constituent lobbying. Several also expressed recognition, even astonishment, at the growth of political information among priests in their areas. A congressional leader's comment was typical: "Young clergymen know so much more now about social affairs, foreign affairs even . . . Young men in particular know far more."[16]

The impact of Catholic political and technical information on Catholic standing may come from constituency knowledge and not from bishops' statements or USCC pronouncements. There is some recognition of this by Church leaders. Two bishops pointed out the possible power that local Catholic groups could have on their political representatives. A lobbyist wanted a redirection of USCC activity so that it concentrated on educating the Catholic people on political issues. "If we did, there would be no need for us to go to the Hill. The Catholic people could go themselves."[17] The information local Catholic groups provide impresses congressmen. Official Church statements from the bishops or the USCC, on the other hand, seem to be largely regarded as spiritual homilies and not as information. They are gladly accepted as additional sources of support by politicians who agree with the Church position or viewed with irritation by those who disagree.

This problem may be only partially translatable to ethnic group politics as a whole. Probably only religiously based ethnic groups face the rather peculiar fact that pronouncements issued by them at the highest institutional levels will be regarded by politicians as lessons in morality and not as information valuable to them in analyzing and deciding issues.

A final factor affecting a group's strategic position in society is the standing of the group and its activities vis-a-vis the society's generally accepted rules of the game. The rules of the game seem to be the single greatest factor limiting successful Catholic ethnic political interest group activity. This seems true not just in regard to determining the group's position in society but in regard also to its effect on Catholic organizational strength and capabilities and the response its efforts evoke from governmental institutions. Because of this and because of the implications the Catholic experience may have for ethnically based political interest group activity in general, I shall discuss the effects of the rules of the game on Catholic political access in an overall way later in this chapter.

According to Truman, political interest group effectiveness can also be measured by a second criterion: the internal characteristics of the group, how well it is unified and organized to gain political influence. Important here are such factors as the degree and appropriateness of the group's organizations; the skills of the group's leadership; the group's resources in terms of members and money; its degree of cohesiveness in any given situation, especially in the face of competing group demands.[18]

Judged by internal characteristics, Catholics have both great strengths and great weaknesses when acting as a political interest group. One strength seems to be their quite remarkable unity and continuation as a group, even after undergoing drastic individual, communal, and institutional changes. Catholics identify as Catholics; they tend to perpetuate Catholic communities; they hold their Church leadership in respect; and they seem largely to have approved extreme changes in their Church.[19] The appropriateness and degree of their group organization to achieve specifically political influence, however, can be questioned.

One can argue that the 1960s saw the rise of many different kinds of Catholic organizations, some of them with conflicting goals and many with mixed Catholic/non-Catholic memberships. A wing of the antiwar movement was certainly Catholic-led and largely inspired by Catholic thought, stemming both from the Council and such earlier teachings as the just-war theory. Other Catholic groups, including many Catholics who had been involved with both the antiwar and antipoverty movements, formed around the Chavez movement. A rather loose alliance of people, generally referred to as the Catholic conservative movement, also arose in the late 1960s, originally to oppose not so much Council teaching as what they believed were radical, even heretical, extensions of those teachings. Although the conservative movement was primarily concerned with liturgical, ritualistic, and dogmatic conflicts, most members shared similar, and conservative, economic and political attitudes and were involved concurrently in such political activities as the New York State Conservative Party.[20] At the end of the 1960s and during the early 1970s the white Catholic working-class movement also developed with cultural and economic goals.[21] Some coordination was provided community groups through the efforts of the National Center for Urban Ethnic Affairs and EMPAC (Ethnic Millions Political Action Committee) and national voice was given Catholic working-class desires and grievances by such Catholic writers and intellectuals as Michael Novak and Andrew Greeley.

Except perhaps for some individuals on the extreme right and left fringes of this heterogeneity of groups, however, the institutional Church still provided a ring around which these groups formed. Much of the Church leadership I interviewed was involved with one or more of them. They all regarded themselves as Catholic and as part of the Church. Interviews with some of the conservative Catholic movement leaders showed acceptance, even, of some aspects of the institutional Church's antiwar pronouncements. Working-class leaders, although angry over what they saw as the Church's insufficient attention to their problems, still regarded preservation of Catholic culture as one of their main goals. Priests led much of the movement and the National Center for Urban Ethnic Affairs was originally organized at the behest of the National Conference of Catholic Bishops.

Thus, the ability of the Church to organize politically is an important element in determining Catholic interest group access to political power. A number of those I interviewed pointed out the facility of traditional Church organization for political education and activism. "We Catholics, you know," said one bishop, "have a marvelous organizational network, as ideal as any politician would want. We're organized down to the grass roots. First we have the parishes, then these are tied to the dioceses and the dioceses tied to the state Church organization and then to the regional organization and then nationally."[22]

When the Church does decide to organize politically, it seems to be able to do so with remarkable success. This has been particularly true in regard to antiabortion. Here parallel organizations emerged. Within its own institutional framework, the NCCB issued statements opposing abortion which were translated into a vast educational and organizational campaign at the diocesan and parish levels. At the same time antiabortion organizations stemming from both grass roots and the NCCB and USCC levels were set up. These had the value of being at least publicly and formally independent of the Church, although they were often largely Catholic-inspired, Catholic-led, and Catholic-funded, directly through the Church or through individual Catholic contributions. No one can predict reliably that these organizations will achieve their aims, but certainly the antiabortion movement does show formidable Church (and Catholic) organizational resources when it chooses to use them.

The ability of the Church to field such great organizational resources on this issue may have been due in part to its degree of cohesiveness in opposition to abortion. If a group's cohesiveness is a factor, as Truman says, in its ability to gain political access, then Catholics should be able to organize around other issues. The Catholic people seem to agree with their Church leaders on a number of issues and on generally liberal positions. They share new attitudes toward civil liberties, aid to the cities, improved health care, and other general welfare issues and substantially liberal attitudes toward blacks. They did develop organizations almost as strong as those on antiabortion to fight for aid to parochial schools. Church leaders were able also to join with their Spanish-speaking adherents in organizing boycotts of Farah goods in many dioceses around the country. My congressional interviews showed, too, that Catholic organization at district and state levels could be effective at least in gaining a political hearing and perhaps an eventual result.

Catholic leadership skills, another point deemed politically critical by Truman, probably have as their chief deficiency a lack of experience in practical politics. New people educated beyond the college level, often at professional schools or at secular universities in the country, and energized by the activist teachings of the Council, have assumed formal and informal Church leadership positions. A more open collegial leadership has emerged. This may not mean that there is now a more creative, more skillful Church leadership than that prevailing under the traditional, less professionally educated hierarchical leadership of an earlier day. It took great creativity and skill to keep immigrant poor people together, nurture them through an alien and often hostile society, and build the churches, schools, hospitals, and orphanages that helped give Catholics a community life and some kind of care before the emergence of the welfare state. Probably it does mean that the Church now has a more democratic leadership and one more suited to the present stage of development of American society, demanding more openness to that society and more professionalism.

Both Church and political leaders I interviewed, however, conceded political amateurishness in leadership skills. Many congressmen said the Church made statements but then did not organize properly, and sometimes not at all, for political follow-through. The antiabortion lobby was bitterly criticized by some political and Church leaders for its political amateurishness. ("Right to Life is the most obnoxious group ever to lobby Congress.")[23] Two of the bishops interviewed agreed that goals could be reached if the Church took the time to educate and organize its followers. The development of political skills and political organization is going on. In my interviews I found citations of such examples as the Sisters Network, a Washington-based organization of nuns who train their fellow nuns in lobbying techniques. The Jesuits run a similar organization and the diocesan-based political action groups discussed by one bishop have political skills and political leadership development as one of their aims.

Presumably such organizations would have resources in numbers and money. The Catholic percentage of the total population has become increasingly better educated and economically well off. On issues where the Church has organized and where there seems cohesion among Catholics, grass-roots participation has been strong. Antiabortion furnishes an example, as does the school aid issue. The numbers of young Catholics involved in antiwar protests, draft evasion, and desertion influenced Church leadership activity in their support and probably helped in influencing general public and congressional reaction against the war. Although the actual wealth of the Church as an institution is a hotly debated issue, Catholics have been able to raise large sums of money, at least for certain causes, from general Church funds and from individual Catholic contributions. One interviewee, remarking on the antiabortion movement in her state, called the display of power in financial and political pressure behind the movement "fantastic."[24] The Campaign for Human Development raised twenty million dollars during a three-year period from individual Catholic contributions for its antipoverty programs.[25]

Catholics, measured by the internal characteristics of their group, their organizational capabilities, cohesion, skills, and resources, probably should be in a position to gain political access to a greater extent than most ethnically based political interest groups. They seem to have summoned organizational ability, structure, and energy on four issues in the past decade: abortion, school aid, the Vietnam war, and help for the Spanish-speaking, especially for the Chavez and Farah movements. But except for purely local issues, these were also almost the only issues on which Catholic politicians seemed to recognize Church political organization and activity. Given the strong social justice emphasis of the Church leaders interviewed, with their wide range of issue interests, and given the Church's apparently strong organizational capability, it seems strange that thus far there has not been more organization on a wider range of issues.

From the interviews and from documentation I believe there is a hesitancy among Church leaders about attempts toward large-scale, public, political organization on many issues because of the effects of what Truman called overlapping membership and the rules of the game. Although cohesion on many political and social attitudes seems broad, Catholics are far from monolithic in their approach to political activity. The fear of arousing conflict and divisiveness among Catholics undoubtedly inhibits many Church leaders from politicizing issues and organizing around them. The Church has not publicized as widely as it might its conception of antiabortion as only part of a whole respect-for-life agenda and has allowed antiabortion organizations obviously under its control to pursue a narrowly construed antiabortion strategy possibly because it feared dividing antiabortion supporters. In California, too, the bishops hesitated for months to declare support for Chavez and his Mexican-American Catholic supporters partly because these Mexican-Americans were in contention with the heavily Italian-American Catholic grape growers. A bishop, in his interview, denounced some of his fellow bishops for backing down from the NCCB declaration opposing the war when conservative Catholic groups in their diocese criticized them for it.

Overlapping membership obviously is a problem in political interest group activity when this concerns a group as large and diverse as that represented by the American Catholic world. But Church leaders have organized skillfully around issues on which there was conflict, as shown in the foregoing examples. The Church has begun to press its wider agenda on respect for life, apparently even at the risk of antagonizing some members, while trying at the same time to educate them to both its social and political value. The Church in California finally did decide to support and aid Chavez.

There is a factor, it seems to me, more basic to the inhibition of Catholic political group activity than overlapping membership and that is the force of the rules of the game. When Church political activity was criticized in the Church and political interviews, often it is not the Church's actual position that is criticized so much as the fact of the Church taking a political position at all. Americans, including apparently many Catholic Americans, seem to have accepted the legitimacy under our system of two basic ideas that have enormous implications for Catholic political interest group activity. The first is the separation of church and state, and the second is the dubious morality or justice of pursuing particularized group aims, especially those based on ethnicity of race, religion, or national origin, that are sure to arouse intense intergroup conflict in our pluralistic society. Both of these ideas strongly inhibit Catholic political group activity, especially in regard to the bitterly contested goal of value recognition. If this activity is viewed as directed by the Church, the separation stricture appears to many to be violated. If it seems to come from the Catholic community, then dislike for particularized group aims is aroused. Since it is usually difficult to separate Church and community, both these strictures seem to censor much Catholic political interest group activity.

The force of the strictures, perhaps especially because they are endorsed by many American Catholics and many Catholic politicians, has caused hesitancy among Church leaders and Catholic leaders in general. Several of my institutional interviewees spoke of the reluctance of some bishops to make political pronouncements or engage in open political activity. Three also accented the fact that Church political activity had on occasion caused protests from the Catholic people, some of whom believed, in the words of one bishop, "that this kind of thing is out of place in the Church, in the pulpit."[26]

On the issues on which it has organized and fought, the Church seems to have tried to overcome criticism by taking one of two approaches. On the social justice issues of war and the plight of the Spanish-speaking, it has tended to couch its right to speak and act on these issues by emphasizing their moral overtones and the right of all churchmen to speak to moral issues, which in general has been long recognized in America.[27] On such institutional issues as antiabortion and private school aid, Church leaders and antiabortion and school aid leaders have tended to try to deemphasize the specifically Catholic nature of the lobbying effort and organization, to depict the organizations as nonsectarian, and to draw other groups into the struggle.

The problems posed for Catholic community and Church leaders by these rules of the game, accepted by many of their own people, are real, however. To varying degrees they probably affect all ethnic political group organization and operation. They mean that many Americans and many political leaders frown upon particularized group demands. Congressmen insisted that they did not think in these terms about their colleagues and tried to divorce lobbying appeals from this context. They mean also that the development of one ethnic group organization calls forth the development of others, partly in an attempt to counteract and equalize group power. Catholic leaders were in agreement, for example, that white Catholic ethnic, or Catholic working-class, organizations in the cities were sparked in part by the black pride and black power movements.[28] Catholics, seeing the renaissance of pride and interest in black culture and history, began to think in terms of Catholic culture, history, traditions, and values. Catholics, seeing black efforts to obtain economic and other benefits for their people, began to organize, not to counteract those efforts so much as to obtain benefits and goals of their own. The attempts to gain recognition for particularized cultures, values, and norms, to gain benefits for particular groups, and probably some degree of group conflict seem a growing factor in the future of American politics.

Conflict is probably also inevitable because the rules of the game, the strictures against Church and particularized group political activity, are being challenged by many different groups and certainly by Catholics. If these strictures inhibit Catholic political activity, there were also many signs in my interviews and documentation that Church leaders are challenging them and political leaders are at least questioning them. Activated by the Council's call for involvement in the world and for social justice, many Church leaders insisted upon the obligation as well as the right of the Church to speak and act politically. Many Church leaders were angry by what they saw as a Supreme Court determination to act against Catholics and thereby itself to violate the rules of the game, which, if they downplay particular group aims, historically have also protected the right of diversity. There was widespread feeling that the Catholic value system was being threatened, that Catholics were being told, in effect, that conformity to general societal values was the price of acceptance. Some leaders insisted that this had the effect of politicizing those bishops who had theretofore been reluctant to speak and act openly on issues.

The very rise of Catholics educationally and economically probably has also made them more active politically. Grass-roots Catholic activism helped spur Church organization and activity in regard to both the war and abortion. Greeley and Novak insist that there has been a rise in Catholic self-consciousness, and the development of white Catholic working-class groups seems to bear this out. This development would seem to lead to a challenge to the strictures against particularized group political activity. Almost surely there will be a see-saw period during which Constitutional and historical strictures against political activity will be in conflict with efforts to recognize the legitimacy of such activity. This is particularly likely since one of the main goals of ethnically based political interest groups, as Moynihan and Glazer point out, is the effort to combat the inequalities inherent in general societal values and to gain recognition also, or instead, of the value systems of religious, racial, and other ethnic minority groups in the society. This conflict is already discernible among my political interviews.

My political interviews form the basis for my attempts at a third measurement of Catholic political influence. According to Truman, the likelihood of a group's political access or influence is in part determined by the operating structure of governmental institutions — the makeup, functioning, and norms of the institutions of government which affect the success various groups will have in obtaining political influence.[29] Truman discusses in his book all of the branches of government: the judiciary, executive, and legislative and the party system. I have limited my analysis to the branch studied here, the Congress.

One important measure of the likelihood of a particular group's access to governmental institutions is the proportion of leaders in that institution who are themselves members of the particular group. Probably this is a source of strength for Catholic political interest group activity. Catholic membership is large and growing both within the House and Senate. Further, there is reason to believe that strong and continuing ties exist between Catholic politicians and the Catholic world from which they come. Most Catholic politicians come from states and districts with large Catholic populations, so that natural and emotional ties to fellow believers probably are strengthened by the politicians' ties to and regard for their constituents. A number of representatives and senators also showed that they had benefited from their Catholic connection because they attracted Catholic votes which normally would go to the other party, they had been supported by local priests and other Catholic leaders, Catholic meeting halls had been opened to them, and so on. They indicated also that they received Catholic lobbying groups, although they tried to discount these as having specific sectarian importance. Thus, most Catholic politicians demonstrated close, frequent communication and relations with other Catholics and with Church and Catholic communal organizations and groups. They were members, in this sense, of a Catholic interest group.

Truman makes the further point that a politician may represent the group to which he belongs, not as a result of any specific group lobbying but simply through a natural reflection in himself of the norms and goals of the group in which he grew up or developed business, professional, or other connections. Certainly, in the sense that they reflect American Catholic experience, history, and values, Catholic senators and representatives represent their religious ethnic group. In their own lives and careers, they reflected the postwar socioeconomic upward mobility of Catholics and their sense of increased community status and political security. In different ways a large number of Catholic politicians spoke of Catholic acceptance into the general society and especially into a role in political life. They also reflected the American Catholic memory of rather recent poverty and discrimination and, to a large degree, the post-Conciliar openness to non-Catholics and to the belief in a Christian obligation to be involved with the problems of the world. Although they were heavily lobbied by proponents of both sides of the abortion issue, it was apparent, also, that many of them, in their reactions to the issue, reflected the Catholic value system under which abortion is abhorrent. Indeed, some of the antiabortion leaders in the Congress insisted they had acted purely from their own sense of values, before lobbying had taken place.

Among Catholic senators and representatives, however, I found also the effects of both overlapping membership and the rules of the game. Perhaps these factors cause even more conflict for politicians than for other Catholics, simply because the politicians are in a public, decision-making role with its own strong norms.

The effects of overlapping membership showed strongly in many ways. Probably most clear-cut was the effect on black Catholic congressmen who apparently were subject to cross-pressures on the abortion issue from their Church, their black constituencies, and their own racial as well as religious backgrounds, and who, for the most part, seem to have responded to racial rather than religious ties. The ties to party and ideology also tended at times to strengthen, at times to weaken, religious ties. Conservative Republicans tended most often to disapprove of the direction of Church concern for political and social issues, with the possible exception of the abortion issue, while liberal Democrats tended most often to approve it.

The most important of the overlapping memberships for most Catholic politicians, however, is their membership in the Congress itself. There is a great deal of evidence that the norms and values of the Congress militate against some Catholic congressmen's ties to their religious group. Congressional and political values require that a politician not represent any group too completely, even one to which he belongs, and that, although he must have regard for constituency interest, he must also look beyond it to the public interest. These requirements might have influenced congressmen's tendencies to downplay recognition of religious differences and their effect among congressmen and to depict religious lobbying as ordinary constituency lobbying. Many political leaders even insisted on the nonsectarian nature of the abortion issue, pointing out antiabortion support from other than Catholic groups.

There is a further, subtler influence perhaps beginning to be exerted on Catholic politicians by the values and norms of their congressional membership. I found some slight evidence that some Catholic senators might be beginning to respond to pressures from within the Senate opposing antiabortion riders. Catholic senators who voted against the Helms rider may have been responding to charges that the riders violated Senate norms because of their legislative inefficiency and inappropriateness. The fact that the Catholic senators so voting were generally those oldest in age and most senior in membership lends credence to the interpretation.

Overlapping membership, as it applies to membership in the Congress, is inextricably tied with the problem of the rules of the game. Although the strictures of church-state separation and the prohibition against particularized group activity and goals affect Catholic politicians, in some ways, Catholic politicians reflect the tendency of the Catholic political interest group to oppose these strictures. I found some weakening among congressmen of the belief that churches should refrain strictly from any involvement in politics. Even the many politicians who downplayed the importance of religion in Congress and who described religious lobbying in constituent terms believed that the Church and Church-related groups had a right to speak out on political and social issues. Especially the younger men, more recently come to the Congress, wanted more Church involvement, sometimes not just in political and social issues but in electoral politics as well. Most of these men were liberal Democrats but there were Republicans, too, who took this position. This seems another example of how Catholic politicians reflect their religious group and its experiences. They display the new sense of status and right to participation by Catholics and the commitment to Christian social involvement of their Church.

Many people believe that the historical phase that emphasized assimilationist politics is over and that ethnic politics will become increasingly important. This examination of Catholics shows the strength of group identity even in this upwardly mobile and now overwhelmingly nonimmigrant group. Both media reports and scholarly studies seem to show continued, even intensified, feelings of group identity among many different racial, religious, and national-origin peoples in the country. Further, ethnic organizations are becoming increasingly politicized.

Ethnic interest group politics potentially poses the possibility of severe conflict. For example, conflict could potentially arise as a result of a division between groups with higher status who see the system as basically working for them and who would view any challenge as a threat to them and their interests, and groups of lower status who see the system as the source of their ills and want to challenge it. A second area of conflict might be value recognition and replacement, so vital politically to ethnic interest groups. Challenges over values affect every group and, although they need not be, often are regarded as situations which a group either wins or loses totally. The pro- and antiabortionists are engaged in a struggle both see as unsuitable to the pragmatic compromises of traditional American politics. Many other examples of this kind could be cited. Conflict will only be intensified if any group comes to believe it is being deprived of its right to express values and to voice demands.

To emphasize only the conflict, or potential for conflict, in ethnic politics would be a mistake, however. Proponents of ethnic politics believe that intensive, long-lasting conflict need not be the result of ethnic consciousness and organization. Instead, they believe it can result in a truly pluralistic, rather than a melting-pot, society marked by respect and appreciation of one another's differences and a more equitable, just, and creative national life. The Catholic experience may bear this out, although certainly this study shows that ethnic politics will mean a certain level of conflict and competition.

The current Catholic sense of self-confidence, participation, and political legitimacy is surely healthier than the feelings of a ghettoized people seemingly locked out of national politics. No matter how far apart opponents may be, their political participation in a democratic system seems to increase understanding and compromise. Although in many ways Catholics remain a distinct group, arguing in some cases for particularized goals, the Catholic of today is more like and better understands the Protestant or Jew than his grandfather was or did. A democratic society should benefit from the contributions in ideas, values, and action of all of its variegated citizenry. As one nun remarked in explaining the newly energized Catholic Church and people, "And then, you know, we have so much to give."

Bibliography

Books

Abramson, Harold J. *Ethnic Diversity in Catholic America*. New York: John Wiley and Sons, 1973.

Ahlstrom, Sidney. *A Religious History of the American People*. 2 vols. New Haven: Yale University Press, 1972.

Barone, Michael, Grant Ujifusa, and Douglas Matthews. *The Almanac of American Politics—1974*. Boston: Gambit, 1974.

Baroni, Geno. "Ethnicity and Public Policy." In *Pieces of a Dream*, ed. Michael Wenk, S. M. Tomasi, and Geno Baroni. New York: Center for Migration Studies, 1972.

Berrigan, Daniel, and Lee Lockwood. *Absurd Convictions, Modest Hopes*. New York: Random House, Vintage Books, 1972.

Billington, Ray Allen. *The Protestant Crusade*. Chicago: Quadrangle Books, 1964.

Dahl, Robert. *Who Rules? Democracy and Power in an American City*. New Haven: Yale University Press, 1961.

Demeroth, N.J. III, and Phillip E. Hammond. *Religion in Social Context*. New York: Random House, 1969.

Dexter, Lewis. *Elite and Specialized Interviewing*. Evanston: Northwestern University Press, 1970.

————. *The Sociology and Politics of Congress*. Chicago: Rand McNally, 1969.

Dohen, Dorothy. *Nationalism and American Catholicism*. New York: Oxford University Press, 1968.

Duff, Edward J. "The Burden of the Berrigans." In *The Berrigans*, ed. William V. Casey. New York: Praeger, 1971.

Ebersole, Luke. *Church Lobbying in the Nation's Capital*. New York: Macmillan, 1951.

Ellis, John Tracy. *American Catholicism*. Chicago: University of Chicago Press, 1956.

Fenton, John. *The Catholic Vote*. New Orleans: Hauser Press, 1960.

Finn, James. "American Catholics and Social Movements." In *Contemporary Catholicism in the United States*, ed. Philip Gleason. Notre Dame: University of Notre Dame Press, 1969.

Fogarty, Michael. *Christian Democracy in Western Europe*. Notre Dame: University of Notre Dame Press, 1957.

Forest, Jim. "Philip Berrigan: Disturber of Sleep." In *The Berrigans*, ed. William V. Casey. New York: Praeger, 1971.

Glazer, Nathan, and Daniel Moynihan. *Beyond the Melting Pot*. Cambridge: M.I.T. Press, 1963.

Glazer, Nathan, and Daniel Moynihan, eds. *Ethnicity: Theory and Experience*. Cambridge: Harvard University Press, 1975.

Glock, Rodney, and Charles Stark. *Religion and Society in Tension*. Chicago: Rand McNally, 1965.

Greeley, Andrew. *The American Catholic*. New York: Basic Books, 1977.

———. *Ethnicity in the United States: A Preliminary Reconnaissance*. New York: John Wiley and Sons, 1974.

———. *Why Can't They Be Like Us?* New York: E.P. Dutton, 1971.

Greeley, Andrew, William C. McCready, and Kathleen McCourt. *Catholic Schools in a Declining Church*. Kansas City: Sheed and Ward, subsidiary of Universal Press Syndicate, 1976.

Herberg, Will. *Protestant—Catholic—Jew*, rev. ed. Garden City: Doubleday, Anchor Books, 1960.

Hitchcock, James. *Decline and Fall of Radical Catholicism*. New York: Herder and Herder, 1971.

Krickus, Robert. *Pursuing the American Dream*. Garden City: Doubleday, Anchor Books, 1976.

Lane, Robert. *Political Ideology: Why the American Common Man Believes What He Does*. New York: Free Press of Glencoe, 1962.

Lasswell, Harold. *Politics: Who Gets What, When, How*. New York: McGraw-Hill, 1936.

Lenski, Gerhard. *The Religious Factor*, rev. ed. Garden City: Doubleday, Anchor Books, 1963.

Matthiessen, Peter. *Sal Si Puedes*. New York: Dell, 1969.

Nie, Norman, Sidney Verba, and James Petrocik. *The Changing American Voter*. Cambridge: Harvard University Press, 1976.

Novak, Michael. *The Rise of the Unmeltable Ethnic*. New York: Macmillan, 1971.

O'Brien, David. *American Catholicism and Social Reform: The New Deal Years*. New York: Oxford University Press, 1968.

———. *Renewal of American Catholicism*. New York: Oxford University Press, 1972.

Parenti, Michael. "Political Values and Religious Cultures." In *American Mosaic: Social Patterns of Religion in the United States*, ed. Philip E. Hammond and Benton Johnson. New York: Random House, 1970.

Rieselbach, Leroy. *Congressional Politics*. New York: McGraw-Hill, 1973.

Stouffer, Samuel. *Communism, Conformity and Civil Liberties*. Gloucester: Peter Smith, 1963.

Strout, Cushing. *The New Heavens and the New Earth*. New York: Harper and Row, 1974.

Thompson, Hunter. *Fear and Loathing on the Campaign Trail*. San Francisco: Straight Arrow Books, 1973.

Tocqueville, Alexis de. *Democracy in America*, ed. Phillips Bradley. 2 vols. New York: Alfred A. Knopf, 1945.

Truman, David. *Governmental Process*, 2nd ed. New York: Alfred A. Knopf, 1971.

Weed, Perry. *The White Ethnic Movement and Ethnic Politics.* New York: Praeger, 1973.

Whalen, Richard. *Catch the Falling Flag.* Boston: Houghton Mifflin, 1972.

White, Richard. "Toward a Theory of Religious Influence." In *American Mosaic: Social Patterns of Religion in the United States*, ed. Phillip Hammond and Benton Johnson. New York: Random House, 1970.

Wills, Garry. *Bare, Ruined Choirs: Doubt, Prophecy and Radical Religion.* Garden City: Doubleday, 1972.

Periodicals

"Abortion under Attack." *Newsweek*, 5 June 1978, pp. 36-47.

"Ages, Occupations, Sex, Religion." *Congressional Quarterly Almanac*, 19 (1963): 33-37.

"Ages, Occupations, Religions, Sex." *Congressional Quarterly Almanac*, 21 (1965): 33-37.

Axelrod, Robert. "Where the Votes Come From: An Analysis of Electoral Coalitions, 1952-1968." *American Political Science Review*, 66 (June 1972): 11-20.

"Bishop Rausch Sees Hope in Carter Funding Remarks." *National Right to Life News*, September 1977, p. 4.

Burnham, Walter Dean. "Revitalization and Decay: Looking toward the Third Century of American Electoral Politics." *Journal of Politics*, 38 (August 1976): 142-172.

"Catholics and Abortion." *Commonweal*, 31 May 1974, pp. 299-300.

Chamberlain, Henry. "The Abortion Debate Is Revealing Our Values." *New Catholic World*, September/October 1972, pp. 206-208.

"Characteristics of Members of the 90th Congress." *Congressional Quarterly Almanac*, 23 (1967): 33-41.

"Characteristics of Members of the 91st Congress." *Congressional Quarterly Almanac*, 25 (1969): 38-45.

"Characteristics of Members of the 92nd Congress." *Congressional Quarterly Weekly Report*, 15 January 1971, pp. 126-133.

Converse, Philip, Warren Miller, Jerold Rush, and Arthur Wolfe. "Continuity and Change in American Politics." *American Political Science Review*, 63 (1969): 1,083-1,105.

Converse, Philip, Angus Campbell, Warren Miller, and Donald Stokes. "Stability and Change in 1960: A Reinstating Election." *American Political Science Review*, 55 (June 1961): 269-280.

"Demonstrators Strike Connecticut Clinic." *National Right to Life News*, December 1977, p. 9.

Fleming, Thomas. "Divided Shepherds of a Restive Flock." *New York Times Magazine*, 16 January 1977, p. 39.

Forest, Jim. "The Roots of Catholic Resistance." *Catholic World*, November 1971, pp. 61-65.

Glazer, Nathan, and Daniel Moynihan. "Why Ethnicity?" *Commentary*, October 1974, pp. 33-39.

Golden, Edward. "Evolution of Right to Life as a National Movement." *National Right to Life News*, February 1974, p. 12.

Grant, Janet. "House Members Explain 'No' Votes on Amendment." *National Right to Life News*, September 1974, p.12.

——. "In Defense of 'One-Issue' Groups." *National Right to Life News*, November 1973, p. 8.

——. "RTL Members Discover Real Goal of Syracuse 'Death' Groups." *National Right to Life News*, January 1975, p. 13.

——. "State Rallies Show Pro-Life Strength." *National Right to Life News*, February 1974, p. 2.

——. "What You Should Know about the Priests' Abortion Attitudes Study." *National Right to Life News*, December 1974, p. 7.

Greeley, Andrew. "The Political Attitudes of American Ethnics." *Public Opinion Quarterly*, 36 (Summer 1972): 213-220.

Hartle, Alice. "Human Life Amendment Authors All Have Same Objectives." *National Right to Life News*, November 1973, pp. 1, 14.

——. "Massive Rallies Mark Decision Anniversary." *National Right to Life News*, February 1974, pp. 1, 4, 5.

——. "Washington Watch Bird." *National Right to Life News*, November 1973, p. 9.

Herous, George. "Let's Kill Off Uncle Charlie." *National Right to Life News*, December 1974, p. 13.

"House Votes on Pro-Life Issues in the 93rd Congress." *National Right to Life News*, October 1974, p. 6.

Ladd, Everett Carll, Jr. "Liberalism Upside Down." *Political Science Quarterly*, 91 (Winter 1976-77): 577-600.

Marx, Paul. "The Mercy Killers." *National Right to Life News*, February 1974, p. 15.

"Members' Religious Affiliations." *Congressional Quarterly Weekly Report*, 8 January 1960, p. 61.

Miller, Arthur, et al. "A Majority Party in Disarray: Policy Polarization in the 1972 Election." *American Political Science Review*, 70 (September 1976): 753-805.

"NRLC, Inc. Puts It All Together." *National Right to Life News*, November 1973, pp. 1, 16.

"The New Congress: Its Members and Its Mood." *Congressional Quarterly Weekly Report*, 6 January 1973, p. 13.

Novak, Michael. "The Communal Catholic." *Commonweal*, 17 January 1975, pp. 321, 342.

Pomper, Gerald. "From Confusion to Clarity: Issues and American Voters, 1956-1968." *American Political Science Review*, 66 (June 1972): 415-428.

"Questions on NRLC Amendment Answered by New York Lawyer." *National Right to Life News*, February 1975, p. 13.

"Religious Affiliations of Members of the 87th Congress." *Congressional Quarterly Almanac*, 16 (1960): 36-38.

"Senate Votes on the Pro-Life Issues in the 93rd Congress." *National Right to Life News,* October 1974, p. 7.

Shaw, Russell. "The Alienation of American Catholics." *America,* September 1973, pp. 138-140.

"Thunder on the Catholic Right." *Newsweek,* 6 August 1973, pp. 50-51.

"Voting Study." *Congressional Quarterly Weekly Report,* 30 March 1974, pp. 814-817.

"Washington March." *National Right to Life News,* March 1975, pp. 5, 11.

Reports

National Conference of Catholic Bishops. *Resolution on the Imperatives of Peace.* Washington, D.C.: United States Catholic Conference Publications Office, 1972.

————. *Resolution on South East Asia.* Washington, D.C.: United States Catholic Conference Publications Office, 1971.

National Conference of Catholic Bishops/United States Catholic Conference. *Collegiality and Service.* Washington, D.C.: United States Catholic Conference Publications Office, n.d.

————. *Documentation on the Right to Life and Abortion.* Washington, D.C.: United States Catholic Conference Publications Office, 1974.

————. *In Support of the United Farm Workers.* Washington, D.C.: United States Catholic Conference Publications Office, 1973.

United States Catholic Conference. *Campaign for Human Development: Annual Report, 1973-1974.* Washington, D.C.: United States Catholic Conference Publications Office, 1973.

Vickers, Carmen, ed. *Toward a Renewed Catholic Charities Movement: A Study of the National Conference of Catholic Charities. Final Report.* Washington, D.C.: National Conference of Catholic Charities, 1972.

Newspaper Articles

"Abortion Decision." *New York Times,* 23 January 1973, p. 1.

"American Bishops Showing a New Readiness to Take Issue with the Vatican." *New York Times,* 19 November 1973, p. 26.

"Demonstrations Mark Anniversary Abortion Decision." *New York Times,* 23 January 1974, p. 38.

"Anti-Abortion Forces Demonstrate a Growing Influence on State Legislatures across the Country." *New York Times,* 28 June 1972, p. 21.

Briggs, Kenneth. "Southern Baptists Call for Arms Limit." *New York Times,* 15 June 1978, p. 22.

"Catholic Abortion Survey." *New York Times,* 29 December 1974, p. 12.

Hyer, Marjorie. "Abortion, Congress, Churches, Convictions." *Washington Post,* 22 January 1974, pp. B1, B3.

"Senate Passes Bill Barring Fetus Research." *New York Times,* 12 September 1973, p. 25.

"Senate Passes Bill Protecting Human Subjects." *New York Times,* 17 September 1973, p. 34.

Notes

1. Introduction

1. The studies that have been done will be discussed in the course of this book. Suffice it now to say that in recent times two periods saw the emergence of significant studies of religion and politics. What many considered the revival of interest in religion and religious practice in the United States in the 1950s spurred publication of a small number of books including Gerhard Lenski's study of religion and its effect on the family and on political, social, and economic activities, a pioneer effort in its use of survey research: Gerhard Lenski, *The Religious Factor*, rev. ed. (Garden City: Doubleday, Anchor Books, 1963). Then the growing interest in ethnic studies and ethnic politics in America in the late 1960s and 1970s led to a number of studies of American ethnicity, including the study of racial, religious, and national-origin groups. The most important of these were the following: Nathan Glazer and Daniel Moynihan, *Beyond the Melting Pot* (Cambridge: M.I.T. Press, 1963); Andrew Greeley, *Ethnicity in the United States: A Preliminary Reconnaissance* (New York: John Wiley and Sons, 1974); and Cushing Strout, *The New Heavens and the New Earth* (New York: Harper and Row, 1974).

2. Alexis de Tocqueville, *Democracy in America*, ed. Phillips Bradley (New York: Alfred A. Knopf, 1945), vol. I, p. 308.

3. General Social Survey, National Opinion Research Center of the University of Chicago, 1973.

4. Will Herberg, *Protestant—Catholic—Jew*, rev. ed. (Garden City: Doubleday, Anchor Books, 1960). See particularly the concluding chapter.

5. See Michael Parenti, "Political Values and Religious Cultures," in *American Mosaic: Social Patterns of Religion in the United States*, ed. Phillip E. Hammond and Benton Johnson (New York: Random House, 1970), p. 229; Strout, *New Heavens*, p. 297.

6. Richard White, "Toward a Theory of Religious Influence," in *American Mosaic*, ed. Hammond and Johnson, p. 17.

7. Michael Novak, "The Communal Catholic," *Commonweal*, 17 January 1975, pp. 321, 342.

8. Nathan Glazer and Daniel Moynihan, "Why Ethnicity?" *Commentary*, October 1974, p. 39.

9. Ibid., pp. 34-35.

10. David Truman, *Governmental Process*, 2nd ed. (New York: Alfred A. Knopf, 1971), chap. 16.

11. Geno Baroni, "Ethnicity and Public Policy," in *Pieces of a Dream*, ed. Michael Wenk, S. M. Tomasi, and Geno Baroni (New York: Center for Migration Studies, 1972), p. 8.

12. David O'Brien, *Renewal of American Catholicism* (New York: Oxford University Press, 1972), pp. xii-xiii.

13. Institutional interview no. 10.

14. "The New Congress: Its Members and Its Mood," *Congressional Quarterly Weekly Report*, 6 January 1973, p. 13.

15. In addition to works already cited, see, for example, the following: Nathan Glazer and Daniel Moynihan, eds., *Ethnicity: Theory and Experience* (Cambridge: Harvard University Press, 1975); Andrew Greeley, *Why Can't They Be like Us?* (New York: E.P. Dutton, 1971); Michael Novak, *The Rise of the Unmeltable Ethnic* (New York: Macmillan, 1971).

16. N. J. Demeroth III and Phillip E. Hammond, *Religion in Social Context* (New York: Random House, 1969), p. 132.

17. James Hitchcock, *Decline and Fall of Radical Catholicism* (New York: Herder and Herder, 1971), p. 221.

18. Herberg, *Protestant—Catholic—Jew*, p. 4.

19. Lenski, *Religious Factor*, pp. 18-19.

20. White, "Toward a Theory of Religious Influence," p. 19.

21. See, for example, how politics is defined by O'Brien, *Renewal of American Catholicism*, pp. 231-232, and by Glazer and Moynihan, "Why Ethnicity?" pp. 34-35.

22. Harold Lasswell, *Politics: Who Gets What, When, How* (New York: McGraw-Hill, 1936); Robert Dahl, *Who Rules? Democracy and Power in an American City* (New Haven: Yale University Press, 1961).

23. Scholars interested in group studies have more and more adopted this technique of combining similar surveys to provide statistically significant samples of even relatively small ethnic, class, and regional groups. See, for example, Greeley, *Ethnicity in the United States*, chap. 2; Norman Nie, Sidney Verba, and James Petrocik, *The Changing American Voter* (Cambridge: Harvard University Press, 1976), chaps. 13 and 14.

24. Lewis Dexter, *Elite and Specialized Interviewing* (Evanston: Northwestern University Press, 1970).

25. Robert Lane, *Political Ideology: Why the American Common Man Believes What He Does* (New York: Free Press of Glencoe, 1962).

26. O'Brien, *Renewal of American Catholicism*, chap. 1; Strout, *New Heavens*, chaps. 16, 18, and 20.

2. The Leadership of the Catholic Church

1. Institutional interview no. 5.

2. Reverend Silvano Tomasi, Director, Center for Migration Studies, Staten Island, New York, private interview held in New York, 15 May 1973.

3. The National Council of the Catholic Laity, organized in 1970, amalgamated, at the national level, the National Council of Catholic Men and the Na-

tional Council of Catholic Women, two long-time Catholic lay associations. Organized originally only on a diocesan basis, Catholic Charities in its history provided child care, family relief, and protective care. In 1910 a National Conference of Catholic Charities was organized in Washington, D.C., to provide direction, consultation, and liaison services for local groups throughout the country and to promote research and training of Catholic social workers.

4. See, for example, "Thunder on the Catholic Right," *Newsweek*, 6 August 1973, pp. 50-51.

5. David O'Brien, *American Catholicism and Social Reform: The New Deal Years* (New York: Oxford University Press, 1968), p. 225.

6. Dorothy Dohen, *Nationalism and American Catholicism* (New York: Oxford University Press, 1968), pp. 52-53.

7. Institutional interview no. 14.

8. Institutional interview no. 13.

9. The Jesuit Office for the Social Ministry is an organization devoted to educating the public and public officials on social justice issues. Catholics Concerned for the Urban Ministry is a group of lay and clerical Catholics, writers, teachers, social workers, and so on, who exchange ideas and programs to promote more effective Church work in urban ghetto areas. Baroni's organization is the National Center for Urban Ethnic Affairs, begun by Msgr. Geno Baroni. It works to help especially white urban working-class people to form community action organizations and to forge liaisons between these and similar black and Hispanic organizations. The National Council of American Nuns, the National Federation of Priests' Councils, and the Conference of Major Superiors of Men are examples of the coalitions of religious mentioned earlier.

10. Institutional interview no. 20.

11. Carmen Vickers, ed., *Toward a Renewed Catholic Charities Movement: A Study of the National Conference of Catholic Charities. Final Report* (Washington, D.C.: National Conference of Catholic Charities, 1972), p. xi.

12. Institutional interview no. 12.

13. Institutional interview no. 15.

14. The Synod Document of 1971 was a report published by the World Synod of Bishops, *Justice in the World*. Meeting in Rome, the Catholic bishops of the world called for aid to the developing world and the elimination of discrimination, poverty, and injustice everywhere. They also called for Church expansion of the concept of sin to include the structural injustices perpetrated by major social institutions.

15. Institutional interview no. 13.

16. Institutional interview nos. 17 and 8.

17. Institutional interview no. 17. *Humanae Vitae* (On Human Life) is an encyclical issued by Pope Paul VI in July 1968. It reaffirmed the Church's traditional teachings on artificial birth control and urged economic and social solutions to the problems of poverty and over-population.

18. Institutional interview no. 8.

19. Institutional interview no. 11.

20. Institutional interview no. 20.

21. Ibid.

22. Institutional interview no. 16.

23. Institutional interview no. 13.

24. From the text of the interviews it is apparent that by "Vatican Council" they intended not just the Council itself but also factors they see connected with the Council—the general teachings and openness of the reigns of John XXIII and Paul VI and various bishops' attempts to extend Council reforms and attitudes.

25. Institutional interview no. 8.

26. Institutional interview no. 14.

27. Institutional interview no. 15.

28. Institutional interview no. 10.

29. Institutional interview no. 20.

30. Institutional interview no. 12.

31. Institutional interview no. 13. *Quadragessimo Anno* (Fortieth Year) was an encyclical issued by Pope Pius XI in 1931. It was so called because it was issued on the fortieth anniversary of publication of Pope Leo XIII's great social encyclical, *Rerum Novarum* (On New Things), and confirmed the Church's concern for such social issues as the rights of labor. The Eightieth Year Letter (*Octogesima Adveniens*) was an apostolic letter issued by Pope Paul VI in April 1971 on the eightieth anniversary of Leo's encyclical and was a confirmation and updating of both *Rerum Novarum's* and *Quadragessimo Anno's* social justice teachings in the light of Vatican Council and later papal statements on social justice and the new problems of today's world. *Populorum Progressio* (On the Development of Peoples) was an encyclical of Pope Paul VI issued in March 1967. It concerned such social justice issues as, for example, the economic, social, and spiritual development of Third World nations.

32. Institutional interview no. 15.

33. Institutional interview no. 21.

34. Institutional interview no. 7.

35. Institutional interview no. 10.

36. Institutional interview no. 18.

37. Institutional interview no. 8. This view of Cardinal Cooke is widespread among the Catholic leadership. Some merely remarked that "he is more of a pastor" (than a politically-oriented man). Others were not as charitable.

38. Institutional interview no. 18.

39. Institutional interview no. 1. While denying that politicians listen to the Church, this same individual, asked specifically about two congressmen representing districts in his diocese, answered, "Oh, yes, they listen to the Church, but they're still old-style Irish politicians, the Curleys. The diocese is constantly in communication with them and they listen. But not the young politicians like Kennedy." This interview took place, of course while President Nixon was still in office—in 1973.

40. Institutional interview no. 5.

41. Institutional interview no. 20.

42. Institutional interview no. 13.

43. Institutional interview no. 12.

44. An interview with a member of the government affairs office of the

USCC (officially, the Government Liaison Office) indicated agreement with this assessment. "I'd like to see more success," he admitted. "Sometimes it's frustrating—the lack of success . . . When I see certain things where Congress should respond and it doesn't, I feel so frustrated." The sense of pessimism and frustration felt by these experienced men, both primarily interested not in institutional but in social welfare issues, can be understood when one realizes how few of the issues lobbied for by the USCC have been resolved by the Congress in the liberal terms the USCC advocated.

45. Institutional interview no. 15.

46. Institutional interview no. 16.

47. NCCB/USCC, *Collegiality and Service* (Washington, D.C.: USCC Publications Office, n.d.), p. 4. Internal evidence shows that the publication must have been printed after 1966.

48. O'Brien, *American Catholicism and Social Reform*, p. 121.

49. Luke Ebersole, *Church Lobbying in the Nation's Capital* (New York: Macmillan, 1951), chap. 3.

50. Ibid., pp. 52-54.

51. Evidence shows that a residue of the "armed camp" mentality still persists among some Church leaders in regard to the abortion issue but even on this issue it was strongly displayed by only a minority of Church leaders.

52. NCCB/USCC, *Collegiality*, pp. 31-45, passim.

53. Ibid., pp. 29-45, passim.

54. It should be noted, however, that certain issues included by Ebersole under these "citizenry benefit" interests, such as health insurance and federal aid to education, would seem to be of benefit not just to citizens in general but certainly as well to such Church institutions as the large Catholic hospital and school systems.

55. Institutional interview no. 20.

56. Ebersole, *Church Lobbying*, p. 48.

57. Dohen, *Nationalism*, pp. 52-53. *Corpus Christi mysticum* (the mystical body of Christ) is the union of all Catholics on earth, in heaven, and in purgatory which forms the Body of Christ, or the Church.

58. See the First Letter from Paul to Timothy: "A presiding elder . . . must have an impeccable character. He must not have been married more than once, and he must be temperate, discreet and courteous, hospitable and a good teacher; not a heavy drinker, nor hot-tempered, but kind and peaceable." See also Letter from Paul to Titus: "An elder . . . must be irreproachable, never an arrogant or hot-tempered man, nor a heavy drinker or violent, nor out to make money; but a man who is hospitable and a friend to all that is good; sensible, moral, devout and self-controlled." Citations are taken from the *Jerusalem Bible* (Garden City: Doubleday, 1966). This version was chosen because it has become virtually the official version used by the American postconciliar Church.

59. Institutional interview no. 5.

60. Institutional interview no. 13.

61. Institutional interview no. 14.

62. NCCB/USCC, *Collegiality*, p. 3.

63. Institutional interview no. 11.

64. Institutional interview no. 15.

65. Institutional interview no. 20.

66. Hitchcock, *Decline and Fall*, p. 47.

67. Among writers and scholars drawing this conclusion are many already cited, including Will Herberg, Dorothy Dohen, and David O'Brien. The priest and historian, John Tracy Ellis, made the same point, indeed seemed to rejoice in it, in his book, *American Catholicism* (Chicago: University of Chicago Press, 1956).

68. For a strong statement of this position, see the letter written by Philip Berrigan and quoted by Jim Forest, "Philip Berrigan: Disturber of Sleep," in *The Berrigans*, ed. William V. Casey (New York: Praeger, 1971), pp. 174-176. See also Garry Wills, *Bare, Ruined Choirs: Doubt, Prophecy and Radical Religion* (Garden City: Doubleday, 1972), especially part V.

69. Jim Forest, "The Roots of Catholic Resistance," *Catholic World*, November 1971, p. 62.

70. Hitchcock, *Decline and Fall*, pp. 142, 175.

71. Institutional interview no. 4.

72. Institutional interview no. 5.

73. Anyone familiar with the history of the Catholic Church in America must find ironic the depiction of the Church as a monolith. Internal conflict was rife in the Church in the nineteenth century, for example, as American Catholicism and its bishops struggled with a host of problems: the reconciliation of Catholicism with the principle of church-state separation; the continuous waves of Catholic immigrants from many different countries and cultures; nativist hatred and fear; the difficulty of reconciling the demands of Rome and the necessity of trying to exist and grow in a democratic, pluralistic, officially secular society and nation. See Dohen, *Nationalism*; Ellis, *American Catholicism*; Greeley, *The American Catholic* (New York: Basic Books, 1977).

74. Thomas Fleming also views the abortion issue as important in bringing about compromise and increased unity in the American Catholic Church. See Thomas Fleming, "Divided Shepherds of a Restive Flock," *New York Times Magazine*, 16 January 1977.

75. Chapter 5 will show the same process in effect in regard to the abortion issue.

76. Institutional interview no. 4.

77. Institutional interview no. 13.

78. Peter Matthiessen, *Sal Si Puedes* (New York: Dell, 1969), esp. chap. 4.

79. NCCB/USCC, *In Support of the United Farm Workers* (Washington, D.C.: USCC Publications Office, November 1973).

80. Advertisement: "From the Bishop of El Paso to the Catholic Bishops of the United States," *New York Times*, 14 February 1973, p. 47.

81. "American Bishops Showing a New Readiness to Take Issue with the Vatican," *New York Times*, 19 November 1973, p. 26.

82. Dohen, *Nationalism*, chap. 3, passim.

83. Ibid., pp. 182, 185.

84. Ibid., p. 154.

85. Ibid., p. 1.

86. Forest, "Roots of Resistance," p. 65. The roots behind the emergence of the Berrigan brothers as adopters of the prophetic stance and resisters to the war probably reach back to their early lives. These were not sudden decisions. The influence of their labor organizer father, the deep and active piety of their mother, Phil's experiences in a black ghetto and Dan's with the worker-priest movement in France, all probably played a part. See, for example, Daniel Berrigan and Lee Lockwood, *Absurd Convictions, Modest Hopes* (New York: Random House, Vintage Books, 1972).

81. James Finn, "American Catholics and Social Movements," in *Contemporary Catholicism in the United States*, ed. Philip Gleason (Notre Dame: University of Notre Dame Press, 1969), p. 144.

88. Ibid., pp. 141-142.

89. NCCB, *Resolution on South East Asia* (Washington, D.C.: USCC Publications Office, November 1971). Also, institutional interview no. 13.

90. Institutional interview no. 13.

91. Andrew Greeley quoted NORC survey responses to show that as of February 1970, forty percent of northern Protestant respondents favored immediate withdrawal from Vietnam, whereas 45.6 percent of northern Catholic respondents favored withdrawal. See Andrew Greeley, "The Political Attitudes of American Ethnics," *Public Opinion Quarterly*, 36 (Summer 1972): 213-220.

92. NCCB, *Resolution on South East Asia.*

93. Dohen, *Nationalism*, pp. 140, 146-147.

94. NCCB, *Resolution on the Imperatives of Peace* (Washington, D.C.: USCC Publications Office, November 1972).

95. Institutional interview no. 17.

96. Institutional interview no. 14.

97. Institutional interview no. 13.

98. Institutional interview no. 15.

99. Edward J. Duff, "The Burden of the Berrigans," in *The Berrigans*, ed. William V. Casey, p. 27.

3. The Catholics in Congress

1. "Members' Religious Affiliations," *Congressional Quarterly Weekly Report*, 8 January 1960, p. 61.

2. John Fenton, *The Catholic Vote* (New Orleans: Hauser Press, 1960), p. 87.

3. All figures are based on statistics published by the *Congressional Quarterly Almanac* or the *Congressional Quarterly Weekly Report*. See the following: "Religious Affiliations of Members of the 87th Congress," *Congressional Quarterly Almanac*, 16 (1960): 36-38; "Ages, Occupations, Sex, Religion," *Congressional Quarterly Almanac*, 19 (1963): 33-37; "Ages, Occupations, Religions, Sex," *Congressional Quarterly Almanac*, 21 (1965): 33-37; "Characteristics of Members of the 90th Congress," *Congressional Quarterly Almanac*, 23 (1967): 33-41; "Characteristics of Members of the 91st Congress," *Congressional Quarterly Almanac*, 25 (1969): 38-45; "Characteristics of Members of the 92nd Congress," *Congressional Quarterly Weekly Report*, 15 January 1971, pp. 126-133.

4. Although this chapter concerns mainly the Ninety-third Congress (1973-1974), it should be noted that Catholic membership in the Congress continued to rise in subsequent Congresses. The Ninety-fourth Congress (1975-1976) contained 124 Catholic senators and representatives. The Ninety-fifth Congress (1977-1978) contained 132 Catholic senators and representatives. Thus, between the Ninety-third and Ninety-fifth Congresses Catholic representation rose by almost a third.

5. "The New Congress," *Congressional Quarterly Weekly Report*, 6 January 1973, pp. 16-20.

6. Information on the educations of senators and representatives was derived from biographical sketches published in the following: Michael Barone, Grant Ujifusa, and Douglas Matthews, *The Almanac of American Politics—1974* (Boston: Gambit, 1974).

7. Half of these Ivy League congressional graduates went to Harvard (forty-three), as did slightly more than half of the Catholic Ivy League graduates (five out of nine).

8. Barone, Ujifusa, and Matthews, *Almanac*.

9. "Voting Study," *Congressional Quarterly Weekly Report*, 30 March 1974, pp. 814-817.

10. Leroy Rieselbach, *Congressional Politics* (New York: McGraw-Hill, 1973), pp. 146-149, passim.

11. Political interview no. 20.

12. Political interview no. 26.

13. Ibid.

14. Political interview no. 11.

15. Political interview no. 12.

16. Political interview no. 13.

17. Political interview no. 4.

18. Since James Hanley (D.-N.Y.) has never achieved national renown, the fact that he was one of the very few congressmen identified as Catholic by a colleague may seem odd. Probably the mention came because he was a leader in organizing the congressional (and Catholic) First Friday group, discussed later in this chapter.

19. Political interview no. 21.

20. Political interview no. 14.

21. Political interview no. 7.

22. Political interview no. 17.

23. Political interview no. 16.

24. Political interview no. 15.

25. Political interview no. 18.

26. Political interview no. 17.

27. Political interview no. 19.

28. Political interview no. 9.

29. Political interview no. 25.

30. Political interview no. 14.

31. Background interview no. 3.

32. Truman, *Governmental Process*, pp. 348-349.

33. Political interview no. 5.

34. Political interview no. 6.

35. Political interview no. 9.

36. Political interview no. 13.

37. Political interview no. 4.

38. Political interview no. 15. Local priests may not have wanted to get involved with this man's campaign because he was a Republican running in a heavily Catholic and Democratic state against a Catholic, Democratic opponent.

39. Political interview no. 18.

40. Political interview no. 14.

41. Political interview no. 17.

42. Political interview no. 8.

43. Political interview nos. 3, 22.

44. Political interview no. 18.

45. Political interview no. 22. For a historian's version of this same story see Ray Allen Billington, *The Protestant Crusade* (Chicago: Quadrangle Books, 1964), pp. 313-314. The congressman's account, however, is more colorful and reasonably accurate.

46. Political interview no. 1.

47. Political interview no. 14.

48. Background interview no. 2.

49. Three did mention church-state separation, one remarking mildly, " 'Render unto Caesar,' you know," but this was definitely a secondary theme.

50. Politicial interview no. 9.

51. Political interview no. 24.

52. Political interview no. 5.

53. Political interview no. 16.

54. Political interview no. 6.

55. Political interview no. 11.

56. Political interview no. 5.

57. Political interview no. 8.

58. Political interview no. 1.

59. Political interview no. 5. To say that there was no Catholic vote before the John Kennedy election may seem incredible. This congressman, however, was probably only reflecting the general feeling I found on the part of many Catholic politicians that the Kennedy election was a milestone, conferring the seal of legitimacy on Catholic office holding. A group of scholars from the Michigan Survey Research Center insisted that the Kennedy candidacy actually spurred a greater percentage of normally Democratic or nonvoting Protestants to vote against him than of normally Republican or nonvoting Catholics to vote for him. See Philip Converse, et al., "Stability and Change in 1960: A Reinstating Election," *American Political Science Review*, 55 (June 1961): 275-279.

60. Political interview no. 4.

61. Political interview no. 23.

62. The average age of the men in the first group was fifty-six years; their average tenure in their political office was fourteen years. In the second group,

the average age of the men was thirty-six years; their average tenure in office was four years.

63. Political interview no. 22.

64. Political interview no. 15.

65. Political interview no. 20.

66. This respondent was referring to then House Majority Leader now Speaker Thomas P. O'Neill and Massachusetts Congressman James Burke, both older men, long-time members of the House, and in this respondent's opinion representative of an older generation of Catholic.

67. Political interview no. 26.

68. For other statements of the Ecumenical Council, Vatican II, on abortion and the pastoral letters of the American bishops on the same subject see NCCB/USCC, *Documentation on the Right to Life and Abortion* (Washington D.C.: USCC Publications Office, 1974).

69. Institutional interview nos. 3, 20.

70. Political interview no. 19.

71. Political interview no. 1. Diocesan officials in this congressman's district volunteered that they were in frequent touch with his office.

72. Political interview no. 3.

73. Political interview no. 2.

74. The tax credits bill, of great interest to the Church, was a bill sponsored by Congressman James Burke of Massachusetts. It would have given a tax credit to parents of non-public-school pupils, reimbursing them, in effect, for the tuition they paid to private schools for their children's education. Work toward passage of the bill was halted as a result of a January 1973 Supreme Court decision declaring similar state laws unconstitutional.

75. Political interview no. 4. The reference is to the late William Cardinal Cody, Archbishop of Chicago.

76. Political interview no. 17.

77. Political interview no. 13.

78. Background interview no. 4.

79. Lewis Dexter, *The Sociology and Politics of Congress* (Chicago: Rand McNally, 1969), esp. pp. 131-150, passim.

80. Political interview no. 12. The congressman may have been referring to a Catholic organization called Save Our Schools.

81. Political interview no. 7.

82. Ibid.

83. Political interview no. 5. Later conversation indicated that he actually had been approached in Washington, too, at least on the abortion issue.

84. Political interview no. 14.

85. Political interview no. 13.

86. Political interview no. 16.

87. Political interview no. 11.

88. Ibid.

89. Political interview no. 1.

90. Political interview no. 25.

91. Political interview no. 5.

92. Political interview no. 6.

93. Ibid.

94. Political interview no. 15.

95. Political interview no. 19.

96. Political interview no. 12.

97. Political interview no. 11.

98. Political interview no. 19.

99. Political interview no. 4.

100. Political interview no. 8.

101. Political interview no. 7. This same senator, however, later talked of Catholicism as giving one a set of standards, a measure for one's performance. He is the man quoted later on values and senatorial performance.

102. Political interview no. 4.

103. Political interview no. 17.

104. Political interview no. 16.

105. Political interview no. 17.

106. Political interview no. 4.

107. Political interview no. 17.

108. Political interview no. 13.

109. Political interview no. 18.

110. A number of Catholic interviewees who believed that Catholic membership did have an influence on Congress gave examples in more than one category.

111. Political interview no. 17.

112. Background interview no. 3.

113. Political interview no. 3.

114. Institutional interview no. 15.

115. Political interview no. 14.

116. Political interview no. 6.

117. Political interview no. 25.

118. Political interview no. 2.

119. Political interview no. 18.

120. Political interview no. 7.

121. Political interview no. 1.

122. Political interview no. 12.

123. Political interview no. 11.

124. Background interview no. 2. The interviewee is referring here to Fathers Daniel and Philip Berrigan, Terence Cardinal Cooke, Archbishop of New York, and Pope Paul VI.

125. O'Brien, *Renewal of American Catholicism*, p. 178.

126. Eugene McCarthy, private interview, New York City, October 4, 1973.

127. Political interview no. 21.

128. Political interview no. 6.

129. The Christian Family Movement began in 1947. Its goals were to strengthen family life but also to involve couples in their communities and in social concerns generally. The *Cursillo* movement began in Spain and spread to this country after World War II. It is essentially a retreat movement but of a

much more emotional type than has been generally prevalent in American Catholicism.

130. Political interview no. 10.

131. Political interview no. 24.

132. Several scholars who have written extensively on the sociology of religion, as applied to American Protestantism in particular, insist that people of the same formal denomination will relate to different aspects of religion. Glock and Stark, for example, on the basis of extensive survey research, have insisted that the essence of religion is different for different people, and they believe that what that essence is determines the function religion will fulfill in a person's life. They isolated five different dimensions they believe religious essence can take: (1) the intellectual, the degree to which a person is informed and knowledgable about the basic tenets of his religion; (2) the ideological, the degree to which religious beliefs are held with conviction; (3) the ritualistic, with such common indicators as church attendance, practice of worship, and so on; (4) the experiential, a continuum reflecting emotional contact with or knowledge of the supernatural; (5) the consequential, in which religious tenets show consequences in one's life, motivate one to be charitable, or courageous, or to act in the community interest, and so on.

When I examined the forms religiosity took among Catholic politicians in this sample, what was for these various men the essence of religion, I found a pattern closely approximating that of Glock and Stark. Here my intellectual category resembles their description of the intellectual dimension of religiosity; my Jansenist equates with their ideological; the ritualistic dimensions are nearly identical; what I am calling the personalistic seems much like their experiential; and their consequential probably approximates what I have called the Council Catholic, the person, in Catholic context, spurred by Council teachings to become committed, involved with the world and its problems as a Christian act. I believe I have isolated two additional dimensions, the nationality and the transitional, which may well be peculiar to Catholicism and result from its immigrant history and its recent turbulent history of Church reforms. For a fuller explanation of the Glock and Stark analysis, see Rodney Glock and Charles Stark, *Religion and Society in Tension* (Chicago: Rand McNally, 1965), chap. 4.

133. Political interview no. 26.

134. Political interview no. 21.

135. Political interview no. 1.

136. It should be noted, however, that some of the thirteen politicians of Irish-American descent, the largest single group in the interview sample, are to be found among many of the kinds of Catholic I describe. Two of the men making up the group showing no religious influence of any kind in their lives were Irish-Americans, as were two of the three Council Catholics, and all three of the politicians representing the intellectual Catholic. I did not find Irish-Americans among those in whom religion took the form of a search for personal salvation — the personalistic Catholic — or among the transitional Catholics.

137. Political interview no. 19.

138. Political interview no. 25.

139. Political interview no. 4.

140. Political interview no. 18.

141. Political interview no. 5.

142. Political interview no. 13.

143. See, for example, Michael Fogarty, *Christian Democracy in Western Europe* (Notre Dame: University of Notre Dame Press, 1957).

144. I am presently engaged in a comparative study of the political interest group behavior of white Catholics, Jews, blacks, and Hispanics. Early analysis of congressional voting seems to indicate that for each of these ethnic groups there are trigger issues which call forth bloc voting by the congressional representatives sharing that particular ethnic identity.

145. Institutional interview no. 15.

4. The Catholic People

1. As noted in chapter 1, a small number of interviews (nine) were conducted with community leaders, that is, leaders of what has been called the white Catholic working-class, or Catholic "ethnic" movement (ethnic in the sense of national origin as well as religion). Seven men and two women were interviewed. Four of these served at the national level in two organizations involved in providing liaison and other services for local groups, the National Center for Urban Ethnic Affairs and Ethnic Millions Political Action Committee; five led local groups in cities in the northeastern and north central United States. All but one were college graduates who had maintained their ties with their Italian-, Slavic-, or Irish-American communities and had helped organize community associations, usually with both cultural and economic aims. In the climate of increased ethnic consciousness of all kinds of the late 1960s and early 1970s, these community associations sought to develop and legitimize Catholic and national-origin (Irish, Italian, Polish) differences. Mainly composed of working-class people, they also sought such economic goals as a share in anti-poverty and community development funds, better housing and health facilities, and neighborhood credit unions.

2. Community interview no. 1.

3. The data for this chapter were derived from national surveys (the General Social Surveys) undertaken in 1972, 1973, 1974, and 1975 by the National Opinion Research Center of the University of Chicago. The composite sample derived from combining the four NORC surveys included the following: 1,349 white Catholics of European descent; 123 Spanish-speaking Catholics; 42 black Catholics; 1,974 nonsouthern white Protestants; 1,197 southern white Protestants; 663 black Protestants; 163 Jews. Four hundred and sixty-three respondents professed either another or no religion. The rest (117) were Orientals or American Indians, or non-Catholic Spanish-speaking, groups not examined in this book. The total of all respondents included in the combined sample surveys was 6,091.

The NORC national surveys and those of the Survey Research Center of the University of Michigan are considered by scholars to be the best designed and most reliable of all academic national surveys. Both centers have more than twenty-five years of experience in sampling ansd surveying techniques. Indeed, they have been major technical innovators. However, readers should be aware of one instance in which the NORC surveys used in this chapter and chapter five almost surely include an under-sampling. New census data seem to indicate that the percentage of Spanish-speaking Catholic respondents in the NORC 1972-1975 surveys is lower than their actual percentage in the population during those years. In these surveys Spanish-speaking Catholics form only a little more than 2 percent of the entire sample and 8 percent of the Catholic sample. Government data indicate that by early 1976 the Spanish-speaking formed 5.3 percent of our population. About 85 percent of the Spanish-speaking were and are Catholic. Of all Spanish-speaking respondents in the NORC surveys, 41.5 percent are young adults, eighteen to twenty-nine years old. This is a much higher percentage of young adults than is found in any other racial or religious group, but it seems accurate, for all data indicate that the Spanish-speaking are an extraordinarily youthful population. NORC should probably not be faulted for the under-sampling of the Spanish-speaking, since more and more evidence is emerging that both government and Church organizations severely undercounted this population throughout the early 1970s.

4. Two works which do analyze Catholics by racial and national origin background are Andrew Greeley, *Ethnicity in the United States*, and Harold Abramson, *Ethnic Diversity in Catholic America* (New York: John Wiley and Sons, 1973).

5. Exact percentages are difficult to determine because the Spanish-speaking were apparently seriously undercounted in the 1970 United States census and because the 1970s seems to have been a period of great growth in this sector of the population. When I began this study in 1973, government and Church figures indicated that the Spanish-speaking Catholics probably made up 8 to 10 percent of the American Catholic population. Greeley, using NORC sampling data from the General Social Survey of 1972, estimated the Spanish-speaking as 7.4 percent of the Catholic population (Greeley, *Ethnicity in the United States*, p. 39). However, United States census estimates in 1978 assessed the numbers of the Spanish-speaking (including Mexican-Americans, Puerto Ricans, Cuban-Americans, other peoples from Central and South America) as 12,000,000. Illegal aliens from these countries may raise that figure to as high as 19,000,000, about 9 percent of the American population. No other sector of the population increased at such a rate during this decade. Analysts have estimated that the Spanish-speaking population increased by 14.3 percent in only five years, 1973 to 1978.

Mexican-Americans make up more than half of all Spanish-speaking Americans, followed in size by the Puerto Ricans and the Cubans. Estimates vary, but probably about 85 percent of the Spanish-speaking are Catholics. Based on this and on 1978 census estimates, I believe that there are now about 10,200,000 Spanish-speaking Catholics, that is, that they compose 20.8 percent of the total American Catholic population of about 49,000,000. Estimates of illegal aliens, if correct, would raise these figures to about 16,150,000 Spanish-speaking Catholics, or 32.9 percent of American Catholics. It is nearly impossible to determine how accurate the estimates of illegal aliens are or to assess the position of these people: Do they remain in the country and in the American Church or go back and forth across borders? Are they integrated into or really isolated from the Catholic Church and community?

6. In terms of theoretical justification for treating white Catholics as a whole, this is a study of religion and its possible effects on politics, not of national origin. To divide Catholics into their various national origins and then to analyze each of these separate groups, comparing them then to Protestants and to Jews, also divided into various nationality groups, would result in both an extremely cumbersome study and a very different one from the religious study intended. Those interested in the national origin differences among white Catholics of European descent may refer to the Greeley and Abramson books cited in note 4, above.

7. For comparison, I will occasionally note data on Jews, who in general have a much higher socioeconomic status and are much more liberal on social and political issues than either Catholics or Protestants.

8. Greeley, *American Catholic*, p. 38.

9. Unless otherwise noted, all surveys and statistical references used in this chapter pertain to the combined sample derived from the General Social Surveys of 1972-1975 conducted by NORC.

10. Abramson, *Ethnic Diversity*, p. 106.

11. See, for example, Samuel Stouffer, *Communism, Conformity and Civil Liberties* (Gloucester: Peter Smith, 1963), p. 142; Herberg, *Protestant-Catholic-Jew*, pp. 219-220.

12. Abramson, *Ethnic Diversity*, p. 107.

13. Andrew Greeley, William C. McCready, and Kathleen McCourt, *Catholic Schools in a Declining Church* (Kansas City: Sheed and Ward, Subsidiary of Universal Press Syndicate, 1976), p. 30.

14. Community interview no. 8.

15. Greeley, McCready, and McCourt, *Catholic Schools*, chap. 5.

16. The 1950s data cited here and throughout this chapter come from two national surveys undertaken in 1954 by the American Institute of Public Opinion and the National Opinion Research Center. Principal investigator was Samuel Stouffer. The results of the surveys were published in his book, *Communism, Conformity and Civil Liberties*. Although the surveys were undertaken to examine reactions of Americans to the danger of internal and external Communism and the effect such reaction might have on attitudes toward civil liberties, they also provide much information on the religiosity and occupational and educational status of Americans. Material was gathered and coded so as to permit me to divide respondents according to the major racial, religious, and national origin groupings I am utilizing in the NORC combined sample. I can thus make many useful comparisons between the circumstances and attitudes of Catholics, Protestants, and Jews over a twenty-year period. The Stouffer surveys reached 4,933 respondents. They included 1,989 white northern Protestants, 1,150 white southern Protestants, 1,032 white Catholics of European descent, 152 Jews, and 388 blacks.

17. Among Jews it is the least educated who are the most faithful religious service attenders. Percentages attending religious services at least monthly among Jews by educational level are: college graduates, 21.4%; some college, 15.9%; high school graduates, 16.2%; less than high school, 23.8%.

18. Fleming, "Divided Shepherds," p. 39.

19. Greeley, McCready and McCourt, *Catholic Schools*, pp. 28-30.

20. Abramson, *Ethnic Diversity*, p. 39.

21. Income figures are based on a single year of the NORC surveys, 1974, rather than on the combined sample, 1972-1975, to avoid possible distortions by inflation. The year 1974 was selected because it was the midpoint in the surveys used in this chapter.

22. Community interview no. 5.

23. See, for example, Gerald Pomper, "From Confusion to Clarity: Issues and American Voters, 1956-1968," *American Political Science Review*, 66 (June 1972): 415-428; also Arthur Miller et al., "A Majority Party in Disarray: Policy Polarization in the 1972 Election," *American Political Science Review*, 70 (September 1976): 753-805.

24. See especially Walter Dean Burnham, "Revitalization and Decay: Looking toward the Third Century of American Electoral Politics," *Journal of Politics*, 38 (August 1976): 142-172.

25. Nie, Verba, and Petrocik, *Changing American Voter*, p. 234.

26. Robert Axelrod, "Where the Votes Come From: An Analysis of Electoral Coalitions, 1952-1968," *American Political Science Review*, 66 (June 1972): 16.

27. Robert Krickus, *Pursuing the American Dream* (Garden City: Doubleday, Anchor Books, 1976), pp. 259-260.

28. Jews are twice as likely as either Christian group to call themselves liberals. The percentages for Jews are: liberal, 52.2 percent; middle-of-the-road, 34.3 percent; conservative, 10.5 percent.

29. For a discussion of the earlier period, see Lenski, *Religious Factor*, p. 361. In regard to discussions of recent Catholic conservative trends, see Krickus, *Pursuing the American Dream*, especially introduction.

30. Political interview no. 14.

31. Community interview no. 7.

32. Jews, in every case except spending on defense, are more supportive of government spending than white Catholics, but white Catholics are generally more supportive than white Protestants, north or south.

33. Lenski, *Religious Factor*, pp. 159-163.

34. Stouffer, *Communism*, p. 142.

35. Institutional interview no. 16.

36. Political interview no. 6.

37. Political interview no. 1.

38. Protestant responses may be somewhat weighted by their larger rural residency and its possible conservative effects. However, with type of residential place controlled, Catholics are still generally more liberal than white northern Protestants in regard to civil liberties.

39. Stouffer, *Communism*, p. 142.

40. See, for example, Greeley, *American Catholic*, chap. 6.

41. Nie, Verba, and Petrocik, *Changing American Voter*, p. 259.

42. NORC surveys asked several additional questions on racial attitudes which were eliminated from this analysis. For example, respondents were asked if they would agree to sending their own children to schools with student bodies

which were one-quarter, one-half, or three-quarters black. I analyzed only the question querying willingness to send children to schools which were one-half black, regarding this as the question most revealing of respondent attitudes toward racial intergration. Surveys also asked a small number of questions regarding the extent to which respondents were willing to have social relations with blacks, for example, would you have a black visit your home? These were rejected for analysis since they did not involve public policy questions and since more significant measures of willingness to relate to blacks seemed inherent in questions two, three, and four.

43. Racial attitudes seem to vary less by type of residential place than do attitudes on civil liberties. The large percentage of Protestant farm residents are no less liberal on race than Protestants in general, so the Protestant rural factor does not depress the group's liberal rating on race as it does on other questions. Refer to table 4.1.

44. Political interview no. 15.

45. Political interview no. 7.

46. Community interview no. 5.

47. Community interview no. 2.

48. Glazer and Moynihan, for example, in discussing Italian-American neighborhoods, cite the issue of value conflicts: "The tight little Italian neighborhood can accommodate a special group that really doesn't participate in its life, just as an Italian village can live comfortably with tourists; but it rigidly resists invasions of new immigrant groups, who have their own form of community existence. In New York, of course, these new groups are Puerto Rican and Negro." Glazer and Moynihan, *Beyond the Melting Pot*, p. 190. Ladd in a recent article discussed the ways in which the lower middle class and working class, which includes many white Catholics, have become the financial contributors to new social policies uniquely benefiting minorities and the resultant anger this has caused. "In contrast to the 1930s when policy innovation often involved efforts by the working class to strengthen its position vis-a-vis the business strata, some of the most tension-laden areas where equalitarian change has been sought over the past decade have found the white working class (or lower middle class) and the black underclass confronting each other." Everett Carll Ladd, Jr., "Liberalism Upside Down," *Political Science Quarterly*, 91 (Winter 1976-1977), p. 590.

49. Sidney Ahlstrom, *A Religious History of the American People*, 2 vols. (New Haven: Yale University Press, 1972).

50. NORC respondents were asked if they had a "great deal," "only some," or "hardly any" confidence in thirteen public and private institutions: the three branches of the federal government, the executive branch, the Congress and the Supreme Court, the military, education, medicine, the scientific community, organized religion, the television industry, the press, organized labor, major companies, banks and financial institutions. On an overall basis, a "great deal" of confidence is expressed in these institutions by 33.2 percent of the Spanish-speaking Catholics, 32.9 percent of white Catholics of European descent, 32.9 percent of white southern Protestants, 31.8 percent of white northern Protes-

tants, 28.5 percent of black Protestants, and 26.4 percent of Jews.

51. Almost a third of the Spanish-speaking, 32.8 percent, call themselves liberals as opposed to 27.6 percent of white Catholics of European descent.

5. A "Catholic" Issue—Abortion

1. Institutional interview no. 3.

2. Janet Grant, "What You Should Know about the Priests' Abortion Attitudes Study," *National Right to Life News*, December 1974, p. 7.

3. "Abortion Decision," *New York Times*, 23 January 1973, p. 1.

4. Grant, "Priests' Abortion Attitudes Study," p. 7.

5. Institutional interview no. 17. The interviewee was referring to William F. Buckley, founder of the weekly journal of conservative opinion, the *National Review*, host of the television program, "Firing Line," and, of course, a prominent Catholic.

6. Lawrence Hogan, private interview, Washington, D.C., 3 October 1974.

7. Institutional interview no. 21.

8. Ibid.

9. NCCB/USCC, *Documentation on Right to Life*, pp. 69-70.

10. "Anti-abortion Forces Demonstrate a Growing Influence on State Legislatures across the Country," *New York Times*, 28 June 1972, p. 21.

11. Msgr. James McHugh, Director, USCC Division on Family Life, private interview, Washington, D.C., 4 June 1974.

12. Institutional interview no. 21.

13. Robert Lynch, President, National Committee for a Human Life Amendment, Inc., private interview, Washington, D.C., 4 June 1974.

14. See, for example, Janet Grant, "State Rallies Show Pro-Life Strength," *National Right to Life News*, February 1974, pp. 2, 10, 11, 16; also, "Abortion under Attack," *Newsweek*, 5 June 1978, p. 39.

15. "Anti-abortion Forces Demonstrate Growing Influence," *New York Times*, 28 June 1972, p. 21; Edward Golden, "Evolution of Right to Life as a National Movement," *National Right to Life News*, February 1974, p. 12; "NRLC, Inc. Puts It All Together," *National Right to Life News*, November 1973, pp. 1, 16.

16. Janet Grant, "In Defense of 'One-Issue' Groups," *National Right to Life News*, November 1973, p. 8.

17. "NRLC, Inc.," *National Right to Life News*, November 1973, p. 8.

18. "Anti-abortion Forces Demonstrate Growing Influence," *New York Times*, 28 June 1972, p. 1.

19. "Abortion under Attack," *Newsweek*, 5 June 1978, p. 39.

20. Institutional interview no. 15.

21. NCCB/USCC, *Documentation on Right to Life*, pp. 71-72.

22. "Evening News," WSYR-TV, Syracuse, N. Y., 1 May 1973.

23. Henry Chamberlain, "The Abortion Debate Is Revealing Our Values," *New Catholic World*, September/October 1972, p. 207.

24. Institutional interview no. 6.

25. Institutional interview no. 16.

26. Institutional interview no. 13.

27. Institutional inverview no. 21. The NCCB did put out a position paper opposing capital punishment late in 1974.

28. Institutional interview no. 14.

29. Paul Marx, "The Mercy Killers," *National Right to Life News*, February 1974, p. 15; George Herous, "Let's Kill Off Uncle Charlie," *National Right to Life News*, December 1974, p. 13; Janet Grant, "RTL Members Discover Real Goal of Syracuse 'Death' Groups," *National Right to Life News*, January 1975, p. 13. During 1975 some antiabortion organizations also began to be involved with the world hunger problem and in 1978 some individuals connected with the antiabortion movement became active in the disarmament issue.

30. See, for example, the following: "Anti-abortion Forces Demonstrate Growing Influence," *New York Times*, 28 June 1972, p. 21; "Demonstrations Mark Anniversary Abortion Decision," *New York Times*, 23 January 1974, p. 38; Marjorie Hyer, "Abortion, Congress, Churches, Convictions," *Washington Post*, 22 January 1974, pp. B1, B3; or, more recently, "Abortion under Attack," *Newsweek*, 5 June 1978, pp. 36-47.

31. Institutional interview no. 19.

32. Institutional interview no. 22.

33. Russell Shaw, "The Alienation of American Catholics," *America*, September 1973, p. 139.

34. Russell Shaw, private interview, Washington, D.C., 15 November 1973.

35. Institutional interview no. 14.

36. Institutional interview no. 18.

37. Institutional interview no. 14.

38. Institutional interview no. 12.

39. Institutional interview no. 19.

40. Institutional interview no. 20.

41. Institutional interview no. 21. This interview was conducted in 1974 before major acts of civil disobedience had taken place. By 1977-1978 antiabortion groups, some related directly to the Church and some to Right to Life and other antiabortion organizations, were involved in a number of acts of civil disobedience. In addition to marches and demonstrations on the streets and sometimes in state and local government offices, and the picketing of speeches by proabortion politicians and political candidates, abortion clinics were picketed, sit-ins held in some, and entrances to operating rooms blocked. The rationale for these actions was in general "the common law principle of plausible necessity where a person may justifiably violate the law of trespass if he has reason to believe that human life is at stake" ("Demonstrators Strike Connecticut Clinic," *National Right to Life News*, December 1977, p. 9). In a few cases in 1978 abortion clinics were fire-bombed and ransacked. These outbreaks of violence were strongly denounced by the Church, National Right to Life, and local right-to-life groups in the cities where they took place, and the Church and right-to-life organizations vehemently denied any kind of participation. No evidence linked either the Church or the right-to-life groups to such violence.

42. Institutional interview no. 17.

43. Institutional interview no. 13.

44. Institutional interview no. 22.

45. Institutional interview no. 8.

46. Institutional interview no. 17.

47. Msgr. James McHugh, private interview, 4 June 1974.

48. Robert Lynch, private interview, 4 June 1974. The state conferences referred to are state counterparts of the United States Catholic Conference.

49. See, for example, Hyèr, "Abortion, Congress," *Washington Post*, 22 January 1974, pp. B1, B3; Alice Hartle, "Massive Rallies Mark Decision Anniversary," *National Right to Life News*, February 1974, pp. 1, 4, 5. The Washington march is actually coordinated by a special organization, March for Life, headed by Nellie Grey, but *National Right to Life News* publicizes it and thousands of Right to Life members participate in the state and local as well as Washington marches.

50. As noted, it has also begun to take an interest in the euthanasia issue, which it sees as closely linked to abortion.

51. Many of these amendments have been reintroduced and several new ones offered in subsequent Congresses.

52. In testimony submitted to the Sub-Committee on Constitutional Amendments of the Senate Committee on the Judiciary by the USCC on 7 March 1974, the USCC wrote, "The so-called 'states' rights' approach to the amendment is unacceptable . . . by its actions the United States Supreme Court has removed the unborn child from protection under the U.S. Constitution, and thereby the Court has raised the abortion issue to the level of a federal question." See NCCB/USCC, *Documentation on Right to Life*. An official of the National Right to Life Committee also said in an interview with me: "There are so many questions. The whole question, for example, of states' rights versus federal power. I don't know how the states can get around the [Supreme Court] decision."

53. Alice Hartle, "Human Life Amendment Authors All Have Same Objectives," *National Right to Life News*, November 1973, pp. 1, 14.

54. Ibid.

55. "Questions on NRLC Amendment Answered by New York Lawyer," *National Right to Life News*, February 1975, p. 13.

56. A NQRC national survey of Catholics only, made in 1974, did ask women respondents if, regardless of their attitudes on the removal of legal restrictions on abortion, they themselves would obtain an abortion. Eighty percent of these Catholic women said they could envision no circumstances in which they would do so. See "Catholic Abortion Survey," *New York Times*, 29 December 1974, p. 12.

57. "Catholics and Abortion," *Commonweal*, 31 May 1974, pp. 299-300.

58. See, for example, the comments of then House Majority Leader, now Speaker, Thomas O'Neill in Janet Grant, "House Members Explain 'No' Votes on Amendment," *National Right to Life News*, September 1974, p. 12. In 1977 the House and Senate passed legislation permitting federal funding for abortions when the mother's life was endangered or the pregnancy caused by rape or incest. Although many Catholic congressmen supported the bill with these restrictions, many others wanted even more restrictive legislation, permitting funding only when the mother's life was endangered.

59. Abortion of a defective fetus is regarded as a particularly evil form of euthanasia because even a defective human being is considered to have a soul and because this kind of abortion epitomizes, in the Church's view, what it regards as the extreme materialism, individualism, and pragmatism integral to the proabortion movement as a whole.

60. Dexter, *Sociology and Politics of Congress*, p. 133.

61. Political interview no. 2.

62. Political interview no. 18.

63. Political interview no. 21.

64. Political interview no. 26.

65. Lawrence Hogan, private interview, 3 October 1974.

66. Political interview no. 9.

67. Political interview no. 5.

68. Political interview no. 24. The interviewee here was referring to Peter Rodino, congressman from New Jersey and chairman of the House Judiciary Committee which has jurisdiction over the human life Constitutional amendment.

69. Political interview no. 15.

70. Political interview no. 14.

71. Political interview no. 5. The effect of the pro- and antiabortion lobbying groups on congressional elections has become a hotly debated issue. During the 1974 elections, for example, local groups on both sides of the issue tried to get commitments of support from candidates, campaigned for candidates seeming to support their positions, and opposed those who did not. Both sides also claimed victory after the election. Representative Bella Abzug noted that three men who had been prime movers of antiabortion legislation in the House had not been returned: Harold Froehlich, R.-Wis. (actually replaced by a strongly antiabortion priest, Robert Cornell), Angelo Roncallo, R.-N.Y., and Lawrence Hogan, R.-Md. Carol Burris, head of Women's Lobby, Inc., declared that the importance of abortion as an issue in the Congress may have been reduced by the election results since forty-one House members consistently supporting antiabortion legislation were either defeated or retired. National Right to Life, on the other hand, claimed slight gains for their stance from the election. The Senate races, in their view, saw the election or reelection of eight antiabortion senators, eight proabortion senators, and four termed undeclared but "educable" (Birch Bayh, D.-Ind., Dale Bumpers, D.-Ark, Patrick Leahy, D.-Vt., and Robert Morgan, D.-N.C.). In the House, they asserted the victory of "at least thirty-six new good 'pro-life' votes," while conceding the loss of thirty-two supporters through retirement or defeat. That the election did not mean the reduction of the importance of abortion as an issue in Congress is demonstrated by the fact that within the first few months of the Ninety-fourth Congress human life amendments similar to those introduced by the previous Congress were all reintroduced and an amendment bearing the language suggested by National Right to Life had by June 1975 gathered more House co-sponsors than any of the amendments offered in the Ninety-third sessions. There is no doubt, however, that neither the pro- nor the antiabortion forces were able to make the issue as central and determining a factor in the 1974 campaigns as they had hoped. Watergate and the economy both overshadowed it. The effect of the abortion

issue on the 1976 elections was equally disputed, although certainly the meetings between a group of Catholic bishops and presidential candidates Gerald Ford and Jimmy Carter over the issue helped focus much attention on it. In 1977 a special organization was formed, Life Amendment Political Action Committee, headed by Catholic Sean Morton Downey, Jr., to work for the election of an antiabortion Congress in 1978.

72. Political interview no. 6.

73. Political interview no. 23.

74. Political interview no. 22.

75. Political interview no. 14.

76. This may be beginning to change as somewhat greater publicity is being given to the Church's broader concept of "right to life." At the January 1975 rally in Washington by antiabortion forces on the anniversary of the Supreme Court's decision, Bishop James Rausch strongly stated the wider concept and Congresswoman Lindy Boggs made a speech similarly linking opposition to abortion with "social programs" and the "dream of life, liberty and the pursuit of happiness." See "Washington March," *National Right to Life News*, March 1975, pp. 5, 11. Bishop Rausch also affirmed that at the preelection meeting between Catholic prelates and then presidential candidate Jimmy Carter, "the bishops managed to get the message to Carter that they believed in human rights in other matters besides abortion." Bishop Rausch said such a message had not been communicated to Carter by the general press. See "Bishop Rausch Sees Hope in Carter Funding Remarks," *National Right to Life News*, September 1977, p. 4.

77. Political interview no. 1.

78. Political interview no. 4.

79. Political interview no. 7.

80. Political interview no. 15.

81. Political interview no. 24.

82. They often spoke emotionally on the subject but the emotion was catalyzed by the intense pressure they felt under on the issue and not by its moral implications.

83. Political interview no. 18. The interviewee was referring to Senator Birch Bayh, Democrat from Indiana, Protestant, and chairman of the Senate Subcommittee on Constitutional Amendments.

84. Political interview no. 20.

85. Political interview no. 19.

86. Political interview no. 7.

87. Political interview no. 9.

88. Political interview no. 1.

89. Political interview no. 18.

90. Background interview no. 1.

91. Political interview no. 22. The congressman's argument obviously contains more heat than light. It is difficult to know of which states he is thinking. None approaches an 85 percent Catholic population, let alone a 100 percent one. Rhode Island is generally believed to be the most highly Catholic state in the nation and Catholics make up about two-thirds of its population. See Barone, Ujifusa, and Matthews, *Almanac of American Politics*, p. 903.

92. Political interview no. 1.

93. Political interview no. 10.

94. Lawrence Hogan, private interview, 3 October 1974.

95. In this chapter detailed analysis is carried out on abortion-related votes taken during the Ninety-third Congress (rather than on more recent votes) because my congressional interviews were conducted during that Congress. This permits correlation and discussion of votes and material gained from the interviews. Activity in regard to the abortion issue certainly did not abate in subsequent congressional sessions. Human life Constitutional amendments were reintroduced in the Ninety-fourth and Ninety-fifth Congresses. In 1977 and 1978 the abortion issue became even more important politically in view of another Supreme Court decision. In 1977 the Court ruled that, although states must allow abortions, the use of government funding for abortions may be decided by the legislatures. This precipitated a major battle in the Congress as the Senate and House deadlocked for six months in 1977 over conditions under which the federal government would pay for abortions; the battle was renewed in 1978.

96. Lawrence Hogan, private interview, 3 October 1974.

97. Background interview no. 2.

98. Political interview no. 9.

99. The discharge rule provides that after a bill has been in committee for more than thirty days without having been reported, it can be removed and brought to the floor upon the petition of a majority (218) of House members. If 218 signatures are collected, the committee in question is discharged of the bill, which then goes on a discharge calendar from whence it can be called up for consideration. Between 1937 and 1960 only twenty-two discharge petitions obtained the required number of signatures.

100. Political interview no. 5.

101. He lost to priest Robert Cornell, an antiabortionist, in the November 1974 congressional elections.

102. Riders are nongermane amendments attached to bills. Legislators use the device to force executive compliance on an unpopular measure by attaching it to vital leglislation which must be signed, or to gauge legislative sentiment on a divisive issue otherwise blocked by rules or procedures from coming to a vote, or, as I have suggested, to attempt to assuage powerful lobbying or constituent sentiment without necessarily enacting that sentiment finally into law.

103. The antiabortion movement and antiabortion senators consider this amendment important to the abortion issue because they maintain that it put the Senate on record as recognizing mother and child as legally separate individuals.

104. "Senate Votes on the Pro-Life Issues in the 93rd Congress," *National Right to Life News*, October 1974, p. 7.

105. "Senate Passes Bill Barring Fetus Research," *New York Times*, 12 September 1973, p. 25; "Senate Passes Bill Protecting Human Subjects," *New York Times*, 17 September 1973, p. 34.

106. Alice Hartle, "Washington Watch Bird," *National Right to Life News*, November 1973, p. 9.

107. Only Catholic senators Edward Kennedy and Philip Hart voted not to restrict. Catholic senators John Tunney and Marlow Cook did not vote. The ten

other Catholic senators, Republicans and Democrats, old and young—from seventy-year-old Senator Mike Mansfield to thirty-one-year-old Joseph Biden—voted to restrict funding for abortion.

108. The exception was Senator Thomas Eagleton who had an ADA rating of ninety and voted to restrict.

109. Catholic senators in subsequent Congresses continued to vote much more heavily than non-Catholics for antiabortion measures. During the long battle in 1977, for example, over the conditions under which the federal government should pay for abortions, Catholic senators consistently voted much more heavily than senators as a whole for the more restrictive language favored by the House. A series of five votes taken from August to November 1977 illustrate this clearly. On the first of two separate votes taken August 14, 34 percent of the whole Senate but 64.3 percent of Catholic senators voted what *National Right to Life News* called "the pro-life way"; on the second vote 33 percent of the whole Senate but 71.4 percent of Catholic senators voted "pro-life." On a vote taken 28 October, 33 percent of the whole Senate, but 64.2 percent of Catholics voted "pro-life." On 2 November, in a first vote, 29 percent of all senators and 57.1 percent of Catholics voted "pro-life" and, in a second, 27 percent of the whole Senate but 50 percent of Catholics voted "pro-life."

110. "House Votes on Pro-Life Issues in the 93rd Congress," *National Right to Life News*, October 1974, p. 6.

111. Percentages do not add up to 100 because of the congressmen who did not vote at all on this measure.

112. "House Votes," *National Right to Life News*, October 1974, p. 6.

113. *National Right to Life News* does not report how many congressmen did respond to the inquiry.

114. Grant, "House Members Explain 'No' Votes," p. 12.

115. Ibid.

116. Ibid.

117. Several members gave more than one reason for their negative vote.

118. Like Catholic senators, Catholic representatives in subsequent Congresses continued to vote more heavily than their non-Catholic colleagues for antiabortion measures. During the long battle in 1977 over the conditions under which the federal government would fund abortions, Catholic representatives consistently voted more heavily than their non-Catholic colleagues for severely restrictive conditions and against compromise with the more lenient Senate bill. The House as a whole adopted a strongly antiabortion stance during this debate but Catholic members were even more strongly antiabortion than other members. Three votes taken in September, October, and November 1977 in efforts to compromise with the more lenient abortion funding language of the Senate bill demonstrate this. On 22 September 58.1 percent of the whole House and 74.3 percent of Catholic members voted not to moderate the severely restrictive conditions for abortion funding of the House bill, that is, they cast antiabortion votes. On 13 October 53.9 percent of the whole House but 70.9 percent of Catholics cast antiabortion votes. On 2 November 47.2 percent of the whole House and 69.2 percent of Catholic members cast antiabortion votes.

119. Six cases in which seats were not held continuously by the same member

throughout the Ninety-third Congress were eliminated.

120. Rieselbach, *Congressional Politics*, p. 213.

121. Dexter, *Sociology*, chap. 8.

122. Political interview no. 22.

123. Political interview no. 14.

124. Political interview no. 5.

125. Political interview no. 13.

126. Barone, Ujifusa, and Matthews, *Almanac of American Politics*, pp. 445, 449-459.

127. Abramson, *Ethnic Diversity*, p. 29.

6. Analysis and Reflections

1. See, for example, O'Brien, *Renewal of American Catholicism*; Hitchcock, *Decline and Fall*; Wills, *Bare, Ruined Choirs*.

2. See Fleming, "Divided Shepherds." Also, the Church's wider understanding of what "respect for life" encompasses seems to have helped this trend toward unification. Church radicals and Catholic antiabortion leaders recently have both become involved with the disarmament movement, for example. In reporting on the participation in the movement of Catholic radicals Daniel Berrigan and Dorothy Day, the *New York Times* added, "An impetus among Catholics has been the extension of the 'right-to-life' movement to such areas as arms control. Joseph Fahey, a founder of Pax Christi, a Catholic group that focuses on disarmament, said the group had grown from 20 to 1,500 in three years, partly as the result of this expansion of interest." See Kenneth Briggs, "Southern Baptists Call for Arms Limit," *New York Times*, 15 June 1978, p. 22.

3. Major goals of the working-class Catholic movement are opposition to institutional decision making affecting their lives without their consultation and consent and the development of a kind of participatory democracy in the form of community organizations with the power of decision in their neighborhoods. This has taken such concrete forms as the attempt by Chicago branches of the movement to denounce the power that banks exercise over their neighborhoods through the practice of "red-lining" working-class areas (excluding them from mortgage money), and to set up community credit unions (financed in part through foundation money) to supplant them.

4. Berrigan and Lockwood, *Absurd Convictions, Modest Hopes*, p. 200.

5. Institutional interview no. 13.

6. Institutional interview no. 18.

7. Some white Catholic working-class organizations are conducting research to document and publicize the small percentage of Catholics in the highest ranks of the banking and corporate worlds. Groups in Chicago and Buffalo have done this. Research of this kind may lead Catholics in the future to believe they have been excluded from some institutions but there seems no evidence that they feel this now.

8. Research I have been conducting over the past two years comparing white Catholics, Jews, blacks, and the Spanish-speaking seems to support these differences in feeling. The sense of being "locked out" of our political and social systems and institutions, and of race as a permanent barrier to participation

and change, has been greatly intensified among many black leaders by what they perceive as a "roll-back" in the 1970s of gains made and hopes held out in the 1960s.

9. Even in regard to the abortion debate, non-Catholics have begun to support the Church's right to organize politically and publicize its point of view. Protestant theologian Martin Marty was recently quoted as saying that when the Catholic Church backed civil rights in the 1960s many politicians were grateful. "Now the bishops are supporting a cause many people don't like, but I don't think we can change the rules of the game. Whoever says 'You can use your moral power for my cause and not yours' is in trouble." Harvard Constitutional law professor, Alan Dershowitz argued a similar point of view. See "Abortion under Attack," *Newsweek*, p. 40.

10. Truman, *Governmental Process*, part 3.

11. Ibid., pp. 506-507.

12. Eugene McCarthy, Robert Kennedy, Edward Kennedy, Thomas Eagleton, Edmund Muskie, Sargent Shriver, and Edmund Brown, Jr.

13. See, for example, Hunter Thompson, *Fear and Loathing on the Campaign Trail* (San Francisco: Straight Arrow Books, 1973), pp. 321-322; Richard Whalen, *Catch the Falling Flag* (Boston: Houghton Mifflin, 1972), p. 199. In 1976 there were reports that the desirability of having a Catholic on the ticket was also urged on Jimmy Carter.

14. Political interview no. 18.

15. See, for example, Strout, *New Heavens*, pp. 298-300; O'Brien, *Renewal of American Catholicism*, pp. 165-168.

16. Political interview no. 22.

17. Institutional interview no. 20.

18. Truman, *Governmental Process*, p. 507.

19. I did not quote survey responses to questions on confidence in institutions to any great extent, but NORC surveys showed that Catholics, both white and Spanish-speaking, expressed a greater degree of confidence in the leaders of organized religion than Jews or Protestants, black or white.

20. Institutional interview no. 17.

21. For the best description published thus far of this movement, see Perry Weed, *The White Ethnic Movement and Ethnic Politics* (New York: Praeger, 1973).

22. Institutional interview no. 13.

23. Political interview no. 15.

24. Institutional interview no. 6.

25. USCC, *Campaign for Human Development: Annual Report, 1973-1974* (Washington, D.C.: USCC Publications Office, 1973), opening page (unnumbered).

26. Institutional interview no. 14.

27. Such an approach, however, probably increases the tendencies of politicians to regard the political opinions of Church leaders as spiritual homilies rather than as sources of political or technical motivation.

28. Weed, *White Ethnic Movement*, chap. 1.

29. Truman, *Governmental Process*, pp. 506-507.

Index